CALLED FOR TRAVELING

MY NOMADIC LIFE PLAYING PRO BASKETBALL
AROUND THE WORLD

TYLER SMITH

SPORTS
PUBLISHING

Sports Publishing books may be purchased in bulk at special discounts for sales promotion, corporate gifts, fund-raising, or educational purposes. Special editions can also be created to specifications. For details, contact the Special Sales Department, Sports Publishing, 307 West 36th Street, 11th Floor, New York, NY 10018 or sportspubbooks@skyhorsepublishing.com.

Sports Publishing® is a registered trademark of Skyhorse Publishing, Inc.®, a Delaware corporation.

Visit our website at www.sportspubbooks.com.

10 9 8 7 6 5 4 3 2 1

Library of Congress Cataloging-in-Publication Data is available on file.

Cover design by Tom Lau

Cover photograph courtesy of the Hitachi SunRockers
All photos in insert from the author's collection, unless otherwise noted.

ISBN: 978-1-68358-076-8

Ebook ISBN: 978-1-68358-077-5

Printed in the United States of America

Dedication

This book is dedicated to my beautiful and amazing wife, Cara. You braved many adventures with me and I can't thank you enough for your love and support along the way. The journey is SO much better with you. All my love!

And to my three amazing daughters, Hannah, Lexi, and Tori. I love being your Daddy! I love you all so much and am thankful to be able to have shared this journey with you cuties. You sure made it WAY more interesting. Enjoy a peek into a time that you may not remember so easily by yourself. Big hugs and kisses!

"I had the pleasure of coaching Tyler Smith in the minor leagues of basketball and found him to be a very intelligent young man with a unique ability to write engaging letters. He has now taken that skill and written a book that I find to be extremely entertaining. I am confident that this will be the first of many successful books in his writing career."

—Hall of Fame forward Rick Barry

CONTENTS

Chapter 1

DELIVERING GATORADE: MY FIRST CONTRACT OFFER

There are some things you remember clear as day. And this is a picture that's firmly printed in my brain.

My first pro basketball offer.

I was riding in the back of an unmarked white van around the Penn State University campus (I know, sounds creepy, keep reading), delivering Gatorade to more than eighty sports camps throughout the summer of 2002. I had just graduated with a major in Telecommunications and was making six bucks an hour before taxes. Good thing I got that degree.

There were other perks, though, like unlimited Gatorade and working alongside my girlfriend (who would later become my wife), whose great legs made for a much happier all-around work environment. Life wasn't bad. But I was hoping for a phone call. And it finally came from Sue, the Penn State basketball office staff assistant.

"Tyler, you need to call this guy back right away," Sue's voice shook over the phone. I could feel her excitement. "He has a contract for you that's worth $230,000!"

Sue was the first line of defense when anyone called or entered the office. And apparently she already knew the details of my first pro contract.

"He said it's extremely urgent, and you need to call him back right away, and he's only in the US for two days," she gasped. Sue almost sounded angry that I wasn't on the phone with him already.

"He just called here, and I told him I couldn't give out your phone number," she continued. "But you need to call him back right now!"

"OK, thanks, Sue," I said. "I'll call him."

Man, this was incredible! I had been waiting anxiously for a couple of months to hear any news at all about continuing my basketball career with a pro deal overseas.

Other former Penn State players had told me about their experiences and some of their salaries early in their overseas careers. One player said he signed a three-year, $500,000 contract. And he said that signing it was a mistake! My mistakes had ended up with a visit from campus police. Looking back, he felt he should have signed a one-year deal, and then he would have had major leverage for a much bigger contract the following year. What? I'd take the half-million right now, even if it meant tattooing the team's name on my face and rocking the 1970s short shorts.

Another former PSU player was making six figures right off the bat in Italy.

I asked a younger German teammate at Penn State, who had played with one of the top German clubs, ALBA Berlin, before coming to the States, how much he thought I could make in my first year.

"Probably about $90,000 or so," he said.

Yeah. I'd be cool with ninety. That sounded about right to me. In my mind, the equation looked like this: If those guys were All-Big Ten players and made around $150,000 in their rookie years, then I should make about $100,000, seeing as I wasn't All-Big Ten but was the captain of our team, put up decent numbers with 12 points and five rebounds per game, and had pretty good size at 6-foot-8, 235 pounds. And those guys didn't bring the added bonus of taking charges or fronting the post like I did. I didn't want to get my hopes up too high, but I felt pretty good about my future earnings. The NBA never even entered my mind because I didn't think I was good enough.

No matter, I was ready for croissants, techno music, and cash—piles of cash.

So when the deal arrived for two years at $230,000, I was ready. I was also shocked. But I thought, This is it.

Lord, please let this be the big break I've been praying for.

I called the team's general manager, Terry Donahue, back at his hotel. He was staying in Atlantic City.

"Hey, Tyler," he said as he got right down to business. "Man, I'm really glad we are getting a chance to talk. Listen, I want to sign you to a two-year deal for $230,000. Our team, the Kings Cross Admirals, is based out of London, England, and we have some really big-time owners who want good players and good people. We want to sign you and one other guy. Do you know Ryan Hogan from University of Iowa?"

This was crazy. Know him? He only crushed my dreams in high school when he torched us for 30 points and prevented us from playing at the Illinois Class AA super-sectional at Northwestern University and possibly advancing downstate. Ryan Hogan was a legend around Chicago. He could score anytime, anywhere. After high school, Ryan signed to play for Rick Pitino at Kentucky and even won a national championship his freshman year there. He later transferred to Iowa and still managed to cause nightmares for every Big Ten team with his deadly shot, despite battling knee injuries.

"Yes, I know Ryan," I said. *Tell me more!*

"Well," he continued, "I think you and Ryan would be two great Americans for our team. Do you have his number where I could call him?"

"No," I said, "I don't have his number. But you could just call the Iowa basketball office and I'm sure you'll be able to reach him."

It seemed odd that he could track me down so easily and not be able to reach Ryan. But who cared? I was still trying to bring my blood pressure under control. Let's talk British pounds. Lots of 'em.

"OK sure," he said. "Now here's the thing about the contract. I can make you this offer, but I need to know right away whether you can take it or not. We can't be waiting around for players to sign. My owners want to move things along and I'll need to know your answer. There are a lot of players out there, and if you say no, we need to make moves before other quality players get signed by other teams and we miss out."

It made perfect sense to me. The market was moving.

"How long do I have to decide?" I asked.

"I need to know by tomorrow," he said. "I'm staying at this hotel here in New Jersey, but I'll be leaving really soon and won't be in the country long."

We talked for two hours. Actually, *he* talked for two hours. I listened to Mr. Chatterbox and took notes. He talked about the team, the ownership, his failed marriage, God, and mostly about the urgency of getting my deal done. One thing I did notice was that he never mentioned anything about my style of play. You'd think it would come up at some point in a discussion about playing for a pro team.

"Just say the word and I can have $10,000 wired to you tomorrow," he said.

This was insane. My heart was pounding and I wanted more than anything to scream out, "YES! Send the money! SEND THE MONEY!" Inside, I was doing slow 6-foot-8 cartwheels and dancing like Mark Madsen after he won the 2001 NBA title with the Lakers. (Look it up if you don't remember or have blocked it out.) But I acted as if I received these offers all the time.

"OK," I said. "Just give me a little time to think about it." Time to think about what? If he said I needed to wear a yellow tutu during warmups, I'd have done it. But I draw the line at the tiara. Apparently my idiotic impulse reaction felt the need to weigh my options and compare this deal to all of the other non-offers I currently had. "Let's talk tomorrow."

I hung up the phone and tried to put everything in perspective. England. Two years. Two-hundred-thirty thousand! That's a lot of tea and crumpets.

But something was holding me back. My dad's voice popped into my head with one of his many teachings: "If it's too good to be true, it probably is."

I'd heard of guys playing professionally in England. But I'd never heard of them making that kind of money. Why was this guy in such a hurry to seal the deal? It was only June. How come he didn't seem to know anything about my game? I needed to do some homework.

I called his hotel.

"Atlantic City Best Western, how may I help you?" the hotel staffer said.

"Is there a Terry Donahue staying at your hotel?" I asked.

"Yes, would you like me to connect you to his room?"

"No thanks. How much are your rooms? Like the one Terry is staying in?"

"Around $69 per night, sir."

If this guy is rolling in dough, why in the world is he staying at a hotel that's $69 per night?

My next call was to an agent, Rick Smith, who was well-connected in Europe.

"Rick, have you ever heard of a guy named Terry Donahue?" I asked.

"No, not that I can think of," Rick said.

"He called me and offered me a deal for $230,000 for two years in England," I continued. "Does that sound legit?"

"That sounds like way too much money for England. Nobody makes that kind of salary over there."

"I see. I'm just trying to figure out if this is real, or what."

"Let me see what I can find out and I'll get back to you," Rick said.

Could this be a scam? I had never been scammed before, other than by my "long-lost African prince cousin" who tracked me down via email to share his "$5 million inheritance" with me out of the goodness of his heart. I'd also never been offered a pro contract, so I had no idea what to expect. I was stuck in the awkward middle of desperately wanting it to be true and being cautious enough not to do anything stupid.

Rick called the next day.

"Hey Tyler," Rick began. "This guy is a con artist. He pretends to represent pro teams over in Europe and calls players who don't know any better and offers them a contract. Then he will try and get them to pay for some paperwork or a work visa up front and promises he will reimburse them later."

"But he never asked me for any money," I replied.

"He would have," Rick continued. "And once he has your money, he's gone. Good job checking up on it. More players than you think get fooled by this guy and others like him. Stay away from him."

Man, was I pissed. I was mad that the contract wasn't real. I was furious that this guy tried to take advantage of me. And I really hated the idea that he was going to keep on doing it to other players.

I called Terry back at his hotel.

"Hi Terry," I said.

"Hi Tyler," he said. "So where do we stand? Are you ready to sign?"

"Terry–" I started. I didn't know exactly what to say, but I wanted to say something so that it would be over. *Do I tell him what a freakin' jerk he is, call him a liar and a thief and cuss him out?* Tempting. But who knew who this guy really was? Who knew what he might do if I pissed him off too much? He already was able to hunt me down easily at Penn State.

"Terry, I don't think I'm ready to sign right now," I said.

"You're not gonna sign?" he said.

"No, I'm just not ready."

"OK, bye," and he hung up immediately.

Wow. Not even an attempt to negotiate the offer or persuade me to think about it. It only confirmed the obvious—it was all a scam.

I called an FBI agent I knew in town and asked if there was anything we could do. Maybe set up some sort of a sting operation. After all, I'd seen *Point Break* with Keanu Reeves and was pretty sure I could infiltrate his operation undercover as long as I didn't have to go skydiving. The FBI agent said it wasn't worth it and to just move on. Move on to what? The next gallon of Gatorade?

My first pro contract wasn't even real. Thankfully, I held back just enough and didn't get bamboozled. I was *this close* to giving him my bank account information (not that there was much in it) and who knows what else. Despite avoiding being duped and giving a con artist access to what little funds I had, I was anything but relieved; I still had as many overseas job offers as my grandmother did.

Chapter 2

AS LONG AS THE SHOES AREN'T WOODEN: IT'S HOLLAND

During my freshman year at Penn State, I was playing out of position and wasn't very good. I played and worked extremely hard and I was pretty fundamentally sound. The problem was I needed to loosen up and adjust to the speed and size of the college game. I was a power forward trying to play the small forward spot, but ended up getting abused by studs such as Michigan State's Morris Peterson and Ohio State's Michael Redd.

My sophomore year was better, and I managed to start about a third of our games. But I still played much too tight. We had a nice run to finish the season and made it to the NIT Final Four in Madison Square Garden, where we finished third, knocking off North Carolina State in our final game of the season.

By my junior year, things started to click for me. I shot the ball pretty well from three-point range and played my role, which was play defense, get boards, set screens, and get the ball to Joe Crispin, or any of our other players for that matter —Titus Ivory, Gyasi Cline-Heard, and Joe's younger brother, Jon. We beat Kentucky on the road in the second game of the season, their home opener, and we went 9–1 in our non-conference slate. Then we were up and down throughout the Big Ten season but knocked off Michigan and No. 3-ranked Michigan

State in the Big Ten Tournament. It was enough to earn a trip to the 2001 NCAA tournament.

As a seventh seed, we faced tenth-seeded Providence, where I was dunked on harder than I had ever been dunked on before. Thankfully, YouTube hadn't been invented yet. A Providence player sprinted toward the basket and took off just inside the free throw line. He put his knee in my chest, went higher, and threw down a thunderous dunk right on my head. Fortunately the ref came to my rescue and called a charge, saving me from complete and utter embarrassment. I never did get a chance to thank him.

We went on to beat Providence and then met second-seeded North Carolina, who had been ranked No. 1 in the country for a couple of weeks earlier that season. Joe Forte (NBA first-round pick), Brendan Haywood (NBA first-round pick), and Julius Peppers (future NFL sack leader) led the way for the Tar Heels and were the obvious favorite.

By the first media timeout, we were down by about nine already and 7-foot, 270-pound Haywood was destroying me inside. Our point guard, Joe Crispin, walked into our huddle and declared with assurance, "We got this! We're going to win this game!"

He was right. We had nothing to lose and could be very dangerous with our outside shooting from Ivory and the Crispin brothers. We beat the UNC basketball powerhouse and the Penn State Nittany Lions advanced to the Sweet 16 for the first time since 1954.

Unfortunately, our season ended the next game versus Temple. Nevertheless, it was a memorable run for us at Penn State and was the program's best season in almost fifty years.

* * *

Then we went from winning 21 games my junior year to losing 21 games my senior year. Key players graduated, one transferred, and one was kicked off the team, leaving us with a young and inexperienced roster. I was playing my best basketball and had finally loosened up, but we struggled and finished last in the Big Ten.

Despite the poor finish, I cherished my time at Penn State. I played against the top teams in the country and earned my degree in Telecommunications—not to be confused with telemarketing. It's an interesting field, and I enjoyed the TV and radio production aspect of it the best.

At PSU, I grew a ton in my faith as a Christian, too. I arrived my freshman year with thankfulness in my heart—thankful that I could finally sleep in on Sundays and didn't have to go to church anymore if I didn't want to. I had grown up going to church because that's what our family did, but I found it boring most of the time. I was much more interested in playing sports or hanging out with my friends. So the freedom and new independence I had at college was awesome.

Like most eighteen-year-olds, I was trying to find my way as a young man. College offered so many opportunities to choose from, especially at a large university like Penn State with 40,000 undergrads. There were countless majors. A new club or organization to join every day if I felt like it. New teammates who listened to different music. A crazy roommate from the west coast of Africa. What parties should I go to? Where do I draw the line when I'm there? It was a lot to take in.

I played hard on the court and worked hard in the classroom. But looking back, deep down I didn't know what I wanted to do or who I wanted to be.

As a sophomore, I started having some conversations about faith and God with my teammate Joe Crispin, a tough as nails All-Big Ten guard who would go on to play in the NBA and overseas for 11 years. We shared similar backgrounds growing up—middle-class family, obsessed with sports, and we both had gone to a Protestant church more out of tradition than out of any real religious desire. Frankly, it just wasn't that interesting.

But the more we talked and asked questions, the more interesting it became. We visited with his relatives, Mitch and Rebie Smith, who lived near campus, and we would have great discussions about religion and the Bible with them. Mitch was the pastor of a local church, Christ Community Church, and very easy to talk to. Rebie was the sweetest woman you'd ever meet and just happened to make the best brownies we'd ever tasted.

The more I explored the Bible and my understanding of God, the more it impacted my life. I began to see that there was more to life than just basketball and getting good grades. A deeper understanding of Jesus and his teachings had begun, and it took my faith to a whole new level. That bulky book now seemed so full of wisdom and common sense and compassion. What had seemed like silly Sunday School stuff when I was a kid now made sense: meet the world with kindness, understanding, and forgiveness. When life got tough, I felt that I had something to stand on that was bigger than basketball or anything else. Lord knows I would need it with the journey ahead.

* * *

Even though my senior season was disappointing, I knew one thing for sure: I didn't want basketball to be over.

I had no desire for a job in the real world. Why begin now if I could keep playing basketball and actually make a living playing a game? I had all my life to work. And it's not like you can just switch careers to pro athlete in your mid-thirties if you didn't like your office job. It was a no-brainer. Continue doing what I had done since I was eight years old and now get paid to do it, who needed a backup plan?

I spoke with several basketball agents after my senior year and tried to make a smart decision on who should represent me. It was important to find someone who would work hard to find me a job in a good situation and not just see me as a number at the bottom of his list. If I had a problem with a team, I wanted to know that he would be accessible and willing to help me solve it.

I called one agent who had a big name, with connections all over the top European leagues and the NBA. We chatted for less than five minutes on the phone as I could tell he was busy.

He said, "I'll send you a contract and get it back to me." A few days later a contract arrived in the mail stating that I was committed to him exclusively for a few years. I didn't sign it. We hadn't even really talked about my level of play or a game plan for where he could see me playing. I wasn't very interested in committing to one guy after a brief phone conversation, no matter who he represented. I had the feeling that I'd be just another player to him. It wasn't that I wanted to feel special. Rather, I had just enough sense to know it might take some work to place a slow, 6-foot-8 white guy who just came off a 7–21 senior season. Despite my stellar ability to box out and set hard screens, being captain of a team that finished dead last in the conference is not a big-time selling point.

One of the advantages to playing internationally is that players typically do not have to pay their agents. The teams will pay agents a 10 percent commission on each contract a player signs. Even though an agent may work for a player and find him a job, the team actually covers the fee. As a result, players will often have multiple agents working for them at the same time. Whichever agent can find the best job for the player will receive the commission. I would later find out the hard way that you can run into some serious problems with this approach. Some agents will ask a player to sign an exclusive contract so that no other agent can sneak in and lure him away with another job offer. However, many players and agents simply have verbal agreements to work together.

That was the approach I used and hoped it would pay off. Rather than lock into one agent and sign a contract with just one person, I had two or three different agents scanning the globe for possible jobs. I needed all the help I could get.

* * *

A few weeks after the scam, I received a call from a legitimate American agent, Patrick King, who lived in Germany. Patrick was recommended by a friend of mine, who summed up Patrick with, "This guy knows his s---." I respected that because I did not need someone to tell me how pretty my hair was. I wanted someone who could find me a job, preferably a high-paying one. After all, the guys I knew who had played before me at Penn State were doing extremely well for themselves.

"Tyler, I just got an offer for you from a team in Holland," he said.

Holland, I thought. *Not the biggest basketball country in the world, but it could be decent.*

"The coach there is a really good person who knows the game," he continued. "They are looking for a player exactly like you who can play inside and outside. The season is nine months long and I think it's a really good opportunity for you to get started."

"How much is the contract for?" I asked.

"They offered $2,250 per month," he said.

I didn't think I heard him right.

"Two-thousand, two-hundred, fifty dollars per month?" I asked.

"Yeah. They don't have a big budget and they have to pay three Americans. I'm going to ask for $2,500 because you're a big guy, plus a meal every day for you, which will help," he said.

Help? Yeah, help like here's a free stick of gum and some coupons for an oil change, help. I wanted my $230,000 scam back.

How much was $2,250 per month anyway? C'mon brain—quick math. That's barely $20,000 for the whole season! I was new to the workforce, but I figured I could make at least that much working at Walmart or the library. *Are you serious?*

"Tyler, I know it's not big money. But it's a place to get a good start in a good country and situation," Patrick said. "Holland is a pro-American country and pretty easy to adapt to as an American. Their TV is even in English."

Unless the TV spits out hundred-dollar bills, I wasn't that impressed.

He continued. "You'll have a chance to really play a lot, and if you do well you can move up from there. I know the salary isn't incredible, but you'll save a lot of it, as they will pay for your apartment and insurance and give you a car. You don't even have to pay taxes on the money because they do that for you as well."

"Thanks," I said.

I wasn't doing backflips at the proposal. I was happy to get my first official offer by a pro team to play basketball. A real one this time. But I thought for sure that it would have been for at least twice that amount.

I called the friend who recommended this agent to me. I told him about the offer from that hotbed of basketball, Holland.

"What do you think?" I asked.

"Well, it's obviously not a huge contract," he said. "But look at it like this. You are an a--hole if you don't save $10,000 from that. Seriously, you are an a--hole. That's not bad for your first year out of school. How many guys save that amount, especially at your age? I am a Division I assistant college basketball coach, and I don't save $10,000 per year. You get to play pro ball in Europe, and they'll pay your taxes and everything along with it. All you have to do is not be stupid with your money and you'll be fine."

He had a point. Maybe I wouldn't be buying a yacht in the Bahamas after the season, but I *would* be fine. It could be a good start. I tried to convince myself that English-speaking TV and two other Americans on the team would be a bonus.

In addition to the monumental salary, the contract did include additional perks that some first jobs didn't offer. The team would provide $1,000 for plane tickets to be used at my discretion. Three pairs of shoes were included. I hadn't paid for shoes the last four years in college and didn't want to begin now. As long as the shoes weren't wooden, I was okay with that. The $250 playoff bonus—did I mention that?—was not impressive, but it was something. And there was that one meal per day. I was hoping it wasn't breakfast, because I'm a big eater and wanted to get my money's worth. Bring on the steak dinners.

Chapter 3

COLD GYM, HARD TIME: HERMAN'S HOLLAND

On the Fourth of July in 2002 I signed my first professional basketball contract. I celebrated my country's day of independence by committing to play in a foreign country and increase its GDP—meager as my salary was to be.

What did I know about Holland? Funny wooden shoes, something about a "red-light district" filled with prostitution and marijuana, and a monstrous NBA player, Rik Smits, who spelled his last name wrong. Maybe I should have paid more attention in social studies.

Coincidentally, my parents had moved from the United States to Holland just six months prior to my signing. My dad received a job opportunity from his company, John Deere, to head up a manufacturing plant based in a town called Enschede (EN-shka-day). That's a mouthful. The city is best known among the Dutch for an infamous accidental explosion several years ago at a fireworks factory downtown that leveled a few city blocks while putting on quite a show.

Needless to say, my parents were thrilled that I would be so close. Amazingly enough, the team I was going to play for was in fact the closest professional basketball team to my parents' new house. What were the chances of that?

My dad enlightened me about some strange Dutch norms before my arrival.

"Tyler, everybody here rides bikes," he said during a phone call within the first few months of his own arrival.

"You mean like on the weekends?" I asked.

"No. I mean to work," he said. "They ride bikes to their jobs or the store or school or anywhere they need to go. Almost half of the people who work here at John Deere ride their bikes to work. Rain or shine."

"That's crazy. Who rides bikes in the rain?" I asked.

"The Dutch," my dad said.

In Holland, there are literally more bikes than people as it is the most bike-friendly country in Europe. In some cities like Amsterdam and The Hague, up to 70 percent of all journeys are made by bike. They even have stoplights and parking garages designed just for bikers.

This I had to see for myself. I hadn't ridden my bike in years. What did a bike stoplight even look like? This was only one of many cultural differences in Holland. My wild ride was just beginning.

* * *

I said a very tearful goodbye to my girlfriend, Cara, who had accepted a job teaching kindergarten in Pennsylvania that year. I shamelessly packed my luggage well over the weight limit and managed to shoulder five carry-ons, including a guitar. Fortunately, due to my watery eyes and the pretty young woman on my arm, the airline employees looked the other way and didn't charge me any extra baggage fees. I boarded my flight to Amsterdam knowing that the hardest part of the next nine months would be the separation from the girl I loved.

When I landed, a young-looking man in his thirties who was of medium build approached me with a smile on his face. He had dark hair and just a hint of gray above his ears.

"Hello, Tyler. I'm Coach," he said as he held out his hand.

Herman van den Belt would be my coach for the next nine months. He had a great heart, and I immediately got the impression that he cared deeply not only for the game of basketball but for his players.

We sat down at a cafe in the airport while we waited for our other American player to arrive on a later flight. We each ordered a drink, and Herman chatted about his philosophy on basketball and what he expected from the team.

"Tyler, I believe that deep down in every player's heart, he wants to be a part of a team," Herman said with a Dutch accent. "Basketball is like a ..." He stopped suddenly mid-sentence. He blinked hard three or four times. The next words wouldn't come out. I waited for him to finish.

"D-d-dance," he stammered. "And when people move together and work in harmony ... ahhhh." He paused again. But this time it was not from stuttering. His face lit up as if he had just discovered something unique. He looked at me closer with his eyes opened a little wider and his eyebrows raised. "It's a beautiful thing."

Herman stuttered now and then. It wasn't extreme, and I didn't know if it happened much, if at all, when he spoke Dutch. He was open about it, though, and it didn't seem to bother him.

He went on to tell about the success of the previous year's team. The league awarded him Coach of the Year. When I asked him about it, he suggested modestly that it was because he had so many faithful fans who voted multiple times online for him. He also talked about the expectations of Americans in the league and on his team. He made it clear that I would have a very large responsibility as an example to the younger Dutch players. I could tell that he held a special place in his heart for the young guys he was trying to develop.

We waited in the airport about an hour for Scott Ungerer to arrive. Scott was a 6-foot-7 American point guard who could play any position on the floor. Herman loved watching Scott's college game film from the University of Richmond so much that he decided to learn Scott's team's system and teach it to us. The offense was very team-oriented and required all five players to "dance together," just as Herman preached. John Beilein, Scott's head coach at Richmond (now at Michigan) and the author of this offense, was having a profound effect on Dutch basketball without setting one foot inside the country.

When Scott's plane landed, we crammed all our luggage into a small van and drove the hour and fifteen minutes northeast to our new home, Zwolle (ZWO-la).

* * *

Our first stop: the car dealership. They didn't waste any time arranging our own transportation. I was impressed. We were getting our cars before we even learned how to say "Hello" in Dutch. I hopped in my new ride, which felt about half the size of a Volkswagen Beetle. My very own Ford Ka. To this day, I do not know what Ka stands for, possibly "Not for tall people." Or maybe "Ka" had been translated by a Bostonian. *"Hey, check out my new Ka!"*

This two-door mini-me presented more problems than miniatureness. For one, it was a stick shift. I was as adept at operating a stick as flying a WWII bomber. I had received one crash course in a barren parking lot six years earlier, maybe a week after getting my driver's license. I tore my poor family friend's transmission up so badly that I'm not sure it was ever the same.

The last problem was a big one: the weather and new traffic rules were about to make things very interesting. Little did I know at the time, but bikes actually have the right of way on the streets, especially when it comes to roundabouts, which act as a substitute for a straight-ahead four-way stop. The Dutch weather and unfamiliar traffic rules were about to make things very interesting.

Rather than admitting I could use some serious help, I grabbed the keys and fired it up. *I got this.* Whoom! The car lurched forward and stalled instantly. *Oh yeah, that clutch thingy.* Maybe I needed an American flag bumper sticker to notify the locals. Better yet, where could I pick up one of those "Student Driver" signs to attach to the hood? With some flashing lights. I was trying to exude a "can-do" attitude and was excited to have my own European car, no matter how miniscule it might be. Instead, I looked like a moron.

Despite the grinding of gears, I was lucky. Actually, the bikers were the lucky ones. No casualties were reported. No transmissions were left behind in the street. At one point I did manage to stop at a red light, watch it turn green, then yellow, then red, without moving a single meter. First gear sucked.

* * *

We went to the two-story house where I would be staying with two other teammates. It was fairly nice, with three bedrooms, a living room, kitchen, and a tiny bathroom. It was only partially furnished but remarkably clean. I later discovered that Herman personally cleaned the entire house with one other friend, because everyone else in the organization was on vacation—he felt so strongly that the foreign players should feel welcomed. I was very impressed by his humility and kindness. As hard as I tried, I couldn't conjure up the image of my college coach, Jerry Dunn, scrubbing my dorm room floor prior to my arrival on campus at Penn State.

The "facilities" were by far the most interesting. The "bathroom" was the size of a small hallway closet with room only for a toilet. The sink was upstairs on the second floor with the shower. The shower had no barrier to keep the water contained. So water sprayed all over the small room, which also housed our washing machine. There was no TV, telephone, or Internet yet. And no telling when those lifelines back to the States would be ready.

* * *

The next day I went to the gym and saw my first Dutch basketball stadium. The word "stadium" is generous, as only one side of the court had bleachers, seven rows. The other side was an old brick wall. Its official name was the Stilohal (STEE-lo-hall). But we called it the Stilodome to amuse ourselves, even though the roof was flat. When your home-court advantage consists of *maybe* 800 fans at maximum capacity, the outside of the building is covered in graffiti, and it's across the street from a dozen sheep wandering about within a small fenced pasture, a sense of humor is required. Temporary stands were set up during games along with what seemed like a thousand advertisements lining the court. The ads were necessary because the team paid for much of its expenses through sponsors.

The playing floor, surprisingly, was pretty good quality. It was a wooden surface that was used for every sport imaginable. In fact, within the basketball court were eight different colors and patterns of lines marking everything from handball to indoor soccer. Some were curved. Others had dash marks every 12 inches. You really had to focus to find which boundary line belonged to your particular sport.

The main reason for the gym floor being so well kept was the building supervisor. He had extremely strict rules about which shoes were worn. If you wore your outside shoes into the gym, he would freak out. This was his gym. Occasionally, if Herman didn't bring a pair of gym floor–appropriate shoes to practice, the building Nazi made him conduct practice in his socks. I thought of Jerry Dunn coaching in his stocking feet. No way.

The upside to the gym being used by so many different leagues, schools, and community events was that there was a strict time limit to any practice or game. We never had a practice run a single minute past the two-hour mark: someone was always waiting to use the gym. This seemed like vacation after three- and four-hour practices in college.

Every day we would set up our own baskets for practice, rolling the giant catapults out from the corner of the gym and locking them down into the floor. They were heavy, awkward, and a huge pain to set up, always needing two or three players. Herman had the system down, though. I saw him single-handedly drive that beast to its precise spot on the baseline and have it click in perfectly. After practice we would have shooting competitions to see who would put the baskets away.

I was coming from Penn State where student-managers arranged for towels, Gatorade, and even four flavors of gum for every practice. In our spacious college locker room, each player had his own individual wooden locker. Here, we had a wooden bench attached to a brick wall. There were no full-size Pepsi refrigerators, large video screens that descended from the ceiling, or leather couches. My days of being spoiled were officially over. Bring your own towel. Bring your own ball. If you were smart, bring your own toilet paper rather than submit to the recycled-brown-paper-bag version on location.

There was no training room or full-time trainer for that matter. Fortunately, our Dutch point guard was in the early stages of studying to be an athletic trainer, so he taped our ankles. Close enough.

* * *

After Scott Ungerer and me, the team signed our third American about a week later. He was a guard named Todd Manuel. We thought he might be Spanish before he arrived. Instead, he had reddish hair and was just a regular slow white guy like us—with one exception. Todd was a shooter. Check that. Todd was a *maker*. I had only seen one other guy shoot as deep and as accurately as Todd in all my life. Joe Crispin, my point guard from college, could shoot the lights out. From *deeeeep*. I never beat him in H-O-R-S-E, and the same was about to be said of Todd.

Todd once scored 52 points in a college game—about twice my career high. One of Herman's favorite drills was called "seven-minute shooting." During the drill, a decent shooter would hit 60 to 70 shots out of roughly 100 attempts. Todd would *routinely* make between 90 and 100 with only a handful of misses. One day he needed a challenge, so he started moving around the three-point line with each shot. He knocked down 113 out of 124 threes. Todd only missed 11 shots in seven minutes. The guy was a freak.

He was also strong. What he lacked in foot speed he made up for in strength. He did 200 push-ups per day and had a chiseled upper body. He didn't lower the ball a single inch when he received a pass, which made for a quick release on his shot. Teams thought twice about playing zone against us because we had Manuel the Mexican sniper. Well, not really Mexican, but he liked tacos.

* * *

Since we didn't have Internet access when we first arrived, Scott, Todd, and I would stop by Thijs' (TICE's) apartment after almost every evening practice. Thijs was one of the junior team coaches, and he and his girlfriend, Chantal (shan-TALL), were a godsend. They were such friendly people, spoke perfect English, and helped make the transition to living in a foreign country much smoother for us.

We learned a lot about the Dutch culture from them. On Sundays, just about everything was closed. Owning (and actually riding) a bike with a basket on the handlebars wasn't uncool, but rather the norm. Food, drink portion sizes, and parking places were often half of what they were in America. Holland is one of the flattest countries in the world (fully a third of it is below sea level), and it took ingenious engineering to make sure that the country didn't flood every time it rained, which was often. The Dutch were famous for their cheese (*kaas*), black licorice (*drop*), and beer (*beer*). I'm sure we overstayed our welcome time and again late into the night, but they never complained, even when we devoured their mini-snacks and drinks.

* * *

Practice was scheduled in the evenings from 7 to 9 p.m. because some of our guys had full-time jobs. A couple others were full-time students. After four years of classes and earning my degree, I was thrilled to just be able to relax and watch movies in my downtime during the day. Two of my teammates, Rein (RINE) and Wim (VIM), were twins and worked 9-to-5 during the day, grabbed a quick dinner, and then came to practice.

These guys were an identical 6-foot-7 and 175 pounds of ligament and bone. Wim was a righty. Rein was a lefty. They weren't very strong. But they could run all day. No conditioning drill could exhaust them. And boy, they could jump. They would fly out on the break and throw down dunks with ease. I swear their wiry frames made them more aerodynamic, and I was without my "white men can't jump" excuse watching these guys. They were best friends and would finish each other's sentences. Both had a great sense of humor, making fun of themselves and teasing teammates constantly. You'd have sworn they were doping the way they'd bounce into practice after a full day's work. Like kangaroos on Red Bull, they hit top speed even before they stretched. Bartender, I'll have what they're having.

* * *

I walked into Herman's office during the preseason one day and noticed a Mike Krzyzewski book on his desk. When I glanced up, I saw a whole library of basketball books neatly arranged on shelves behind him. He must have had 500 books or more.

"Coach, that's a ton of books! Have you read all these?" I asked.

"Yeah, most every one," he said. "If you want to borrow one just let me know. I really like learning from some of the great coaches, studying how they lead their teams, and what makes them successful."

"Which one is your favorite?" I asked.

"I just finished one about Bobby Knight," he said with his eyes lighting up. "Ho ho, boy, he is really tough and can really coach."

Great. Just what we needed—a coach who idolized Bobby Knight. I was already having a mini-panic attack imagining five-hour practices full of lane slides, sprints, and charge drills. Basketballs optional.

It looked like Herman was going for his PhD in coaching. He loved learning the nuances of the game, and it was reflected in how he coached. He adopted principles from John Wooden's "Pyramid of Success," Coach K's leadership philosophies, and, of course, Bobby Knight's hard-nosed style. He wanted his teams to be tough, but he wanted them to be very smart and, perhaps most importantly, to play together. To Herman, basketball was much more than a job and more than winning or losing. It was about working together and being in sync with your teammates so that we could play as one body instead of five different parts.

Before one preseason game, our team crammed onto the two wooden benches in our brick-walled locker room of champions, waiting for Herman's pregame speech. He brought out a huge easel and a blank pad of paper.

"OK, fellas," he started. "What makes us a good team?"

What? We have a game in thirty minutes, Herman. How about some strategy. A scouting report. Something.

Herman waited with his marker ready.

"Why are we good?" he repeated. "Who are we?"

"We play together," Rein said.

"Yes," Herman agreed. He wrote it down.

"We play good defense," I added.

"Right," Herman said.

He got more excited with each answer. Instead of a blood-pumping pregame speech, Herman delivered more of a lecture, jotting down ideas on paper. He was more Professor van den Belt than General Patton.

Halftimes could be a very different story. When we failed to perform as instructed, his inner Bobby Knight emerged spewing expletives, and you did not want to be the guy who missed an assignment or wasn't playing hard enough.

* * *

At the end of the first month, it was finally payday. I'd been playing basketball all of my life for nothing but the fun of it and the sheer desire to win. I'd never been offered a dime to make a shot or set a screen. So when it came time to get paid, I was ecstatic. It was a strange feeling, as I hadn't done anything different during the last thirty days than I had done for the previous fifteen years. Was the team aware of my history of playing for free? Did I really deserve $2,500 for wearing shorts a couple hours a day? People got paid for working, not playing. Some days we didn't even practice. I just sat around and watched *The A-Team* reruns. I was stealing money. We hadn't even played any league games yet—just a bunch of practices in a funny gym. But now on applications under occupation I could write, "Professional basketball player."

I called my bank in Pennsylvania to see if I was any wealthier. I'd been down to the last $100 to my name, and I prayed that the salary transfer had gone through.

"Hi, was there a deposit made recently to my account?" I asked while trying to contain my enthusiasm.

"Let me check on that for you," the teller said. I hoped they didn't reject it or something. I had never made a deposit for more than maybe a couple of hundred bucks. And that was in person. This wire was coming from some obscure overseas account.

Great, they think I'm some sort of drug lord and I'm red-flagged. I'll never see the money. The IRS is probably auditing me as we speak.

"Oh, yes," she said. "Here it is."

Hallelujah!

"A deposit was made for $1,250," she said.

I'm rich! Think of all the stroopwaffles and cheese. I'd never had a paycheck anywhere near that. But why was it only half?

It turned out that the team wanted to pay half of the salary to my personal account and the other half to a different account to take advantage of some Dutch tax loopholes. I didn't care if they paid me in two-dollar bills as long as I received what was in my contract.

* * *

Our first game of the season was away against Groningen. They were just over an hour up the road from Zwolle, and they played in the biggest gym in the league, which held 3,500. It was a far cry from the 15,000 seat arenas of the Big Ten. But it was a home-court advantage for them nonetheless. Their fans were the rowdiest in Holland. You'd think that with strong fan support, a solid basketball history, and a marquee place to play, they'd have a nice court. It was anything but. The floor was made of some sort of multipurpose material better suited for beginning ice skaters. It was a cross between Styrofoam and cardboard with the slickness of a bowling alley. It was impossible to make a sharp cut. Players were slipping all over the floor the entire game.

Our three Americans may have set a new unofficial record for traveling violations in a game. The international rules called traveling much tighter as the ball handler had to put the ball on the floor before his back foot left the ground. Scott, Todd, and I had to consciously re-train our brains and feet to adjust to the new rules.

Tweet!

"How's that a travel??"

Tweet! Tweet!

"You've got to be kidding me."

Tweeeeeeeeeet!!!

"I'm not traveling! This is unbelievable."

Every American kid is taught to push the ball out in front on the first dribble from the time they can hold a basketball. Now, we were turnover machines. The traveling violation was the hardest rule for Americans to adjust to overseas.

A few other differences included players not being able to call time-out. Only coaches could do that during a dead ball. The three-point line was midway between the college and NBA distance. And goaltending was allowed also in that a defensive player could tap the ball off the rim. Given my stellar athleticism, it wasn't a rule I was overly concerned with.

Somehow we pulled out a win, and I scored 15 points in my first pro basketball game—and probably tallied just as many traveling calls.

* * *

We started the season off well, going 3–1. Then we went the opposite direction, losing games left and right. I can't explain exactly why, but we just couldn't seem to put a streak together. We'd win one, then lose two or three. We struggled to get back to .500. It was frustrating, but maybe not too surprising given that we played a brand-new system that both the players and coaches were still getting acclimated to. Additionally, our team was young—I felt like the old man of the group at twenty-two.

Holland's pro league allowed for three foreign players per team, which were typically comprised of players from the US. Americans were the best players on every team in the league. A few teams had Americans who'd played at least five years in Holland and had "earned" Dutch citizenship. So they played as Dutch players, which allowed teams to have an additional American on the court. These dual-passport players didn't speak any Dutch or have any family heritage from Holland, but on paper they were as Dutch as a windmill.

There were nine teams in the league, and each had a couple of very good Dutch players. The top two or three teams in Holland could be competitive in the Big Ten, but the overall athleticism and talent in the Big Ten were much stronger than the FEB— Federation Eredivisie of Basketball (or "Floors Exceptionally Brutal").

* * *

Back in college, when I made a post move, I was always taught to "Take it strong to the basket!", "Draw contact", and "Get to the free throw line." This was all fine and dandy for guys who were really athletic. They could hang in the air, eat some chicken wings and pizza, and then find a way to get the shot off. I couldn't outjump a turtle. And I couldn't out-quick a tree. So that "go up strong" mentality often resulted in my shot getting smackety-dacked by a bigger defender. No foul would be called, and I ended up looking like one big crappy basketball player.

So once my senior season at Penn State was complete and I was no longer under my college coaches' dominion, I began working on a fadeaway jumper in the post. I had to be creative since Dr. J was not planning a comeback through a spiritual takeover of my body anytime soon. But I had a nice shooting touch and the fadeaway allowed me to score inside more effectively, no matter how big or high-flying my defender was. It really freed me up to play with more confidence with my back to the basket.

By the time I arrived in Holland, it had become a regular part of my post game. But I was nervous to see if my new coaches would be as accepting of my new move as I was. We were working on post moves one day in practice with our Dutch assistant coach, Mark. He was a 6-foot-7 lefty and in charge of the big guys. Mark was thirty-three years old and had been a very good Dutch pro player. He also had a great sense of humor, and everybody loved being around him and playing for him. During the drill, I made a move toward the basket and then spun and shot my new bread-and-butter fadeaway. It swished through.

"Yeah, Tyler," Mark said. "That's a good shot for you. That's your shot."

If you only knew, Mark. I buried my laughter and smile deep within. Mark had no way of knowing that the fade dawg wasn't in my repertoire at all just a few months earlier. I probably would have been benched for even attempting that shot in college. But we were in Holland now. No one knew me. No one knew my game. I could be whoever I wanted to be. As long as the shot went in, hey, it was a good shot. *Ever see a sky hook from the free throw line, guys? Sha-bam!* And that was my game.

* * *

When we won our first home game, the announcer called Todd out to the middle of the floor to recognize him as the MVP of the game, known there as "Man of the Match," a phrase borrowed from soccer. I thought matches were reserved for tennis and starting fires. Someone walked up to Todd with a massive bag overflowing with groceries. Inside was coffee, cereal, mayonnaise, cookies—you name it. The bag was reusable and practically indestructible. It needed to be in order to hold half of the store packed inside. One of our sponsors was a grocery chain named "C1000," and one lucky player would win that bag every home game. My eyes lit up. Being Todd's roommate just got a little sweeter. Not only did his brother send us movies from the States, but Todd surely couldn't eat all that mayonnaise and chocolate on his own. I decided that our new goal was for someone in our house to bring home that grocery bag of love after each game. Between Ivan, Todd, and me, I figured we could keep our cupboards well-stocked with Dutch delicacies like stroopwaffles, a caramel waffle-type cookie that quickly became my favorite.

Ivan, a brick wall of a man from Belgrade, Serbia, was the biggest guy in the house, but because he arrived last, he got the smallest room. Legally you could call it a bedroom because there was a window and a door. But practically you would call it a mistake. I give him lots of credit for not losing his mind living in that room.

When I first arrived in Holland they had given me a nice house to live in. But it apparently belonged to a volleyball team. So one week later, they moved me into another house which was far less modern. I went from 2002 to the 1970s.

The furniture was old and may have been discarded by a homeless person. We were still without Internet and the ability to watch movies. To me, these were as important—if not more so—than the fridge or clean air.

Upstairs were the three bedrooms and our shower/laundry room. The third bedroom was where we'd hang up our wet clothes. There was no dryer, and I immediately became homesick for soft cotton socks. All of my socks turned to cardboard and could walk down the stairs on their own.

We actually had a decent-sized backyard filled with potential. I peeked over the fence to our neighbor's yard, which was beautiful. Their grass was practically a putting green, and it's gorgeous flowers and plants were strategically placed. But potential was as far as ours would ever get. We had no lawnmower, zero gardening tools, and even less motivation to do anything about the situation. Every month that went by, our grass grew higher, the bushes grew scarier, and the weeds grew meaner. Who knew what creatures lurked beneath the foliage? We nicknamed it "The Jungle."

A team manager actually showed up unannounced one day with a lawn mower. The three of us opened the curtains to witness "Man vs. Nature." He was able to start the engine, but the walk-behind mower was no match for the grasses of the savannah. He should have brought a machete or a tractor. After going about three feet, the mower started smoking. He fought to maneuver it forward and back, but it was useless. Then the engine died. No grass was cut. We laughed behind the window. And the shrubbery just laughed in his face.

Nature 1, Man 0.

* * *

Every week, Herman would volunteer our time and his for basketball clinics in different schools and clubs around Zwolle. He felt strongly that we should all share in the responsibility of coaching young players and exposing them to the game of basketball. One added bonus was that we could tell them about the mighty Landstede (LAHND-sted-uh) Hammers and maybe they'd come see a game and boost our attendance by ten or twenty. Since basketball was at best the fourth most popular sport in Holland behind soccer (a.k.a "football" in Europe), volleyball, and handball (I know, weird), he wanted to give Dutch kids the opportunity to learn the game. Children in the Netherlands wouldn't play basketball in the average gym class, which was curious to me. Every gym class across America played basketball—dodgeball, kickball, and every other game was just borrowing the basketball floor. Basketball was what gyms were created for. How in the world could these Dutch kids not know anything about basketball?

Most of them were terrible. It was as if they had never picked up a basketball before. Which, to be fair, many hadn't. But the kids always had a great time because that was one of the requirements. Herman had these clinics down to a science. He was firm with the kids and could organize them into a drill in a flash, but he always made sure that they had fun. He kept the games simple and entertaining, so that even if they had never seen a basketball before, they were guaranteed to have a good time.

When I went with him to my first clinic I noticed something strange on every one of the junior basketballs we brought.

"Herman, what's up with all the smiley faces?" I asked. They were hand-drawn on every single ball in black permanent marker.

"I put them on there to remind the kids that basketball is a game, and it should be fun," he said. "Even I need that reminder sometimes."

* * *

Partway through the season, Scott, Todd, and I met at Herman's office before heading out to a clinic.

"How far away is this one, Coach?" I asked.

"Not too far, maybe fifteen, twenty minutes," Herman said.

"Another school?" I asked.

Herman smiled. "You'll see," he said.

We pulled up to a gated facility with barbed wire covering the fences surrounding a group of buildings.

Are you serious? Is this what I think it is?

"Uh, Herman," I said. "This looks a lot like a prison."

"Exactly," he grinned.

"We're going to coach the inmates?" Todd asked.

"Yes," Herman said. "They get some recreation time each week, so I thought it would be a good idea to bring basketball to them. I mean, they are people, too."

Point taken, Herman. But I can think of a lot less dangerous people we could coach.

We were slightly out of our comfort zone. I'd been inside as many prisons as I had space shuttles. We were about to instruct, correct, and teach these model citizens who weren't real big on following rules in the first place. *Herman, have you not seen* Shawshank Redemption?

My mind was racing. *I'm a big guy, but how am I going to defend myself against a lifer with a shiv and nothing to lose? What if I get the prisoner who got cut from his sixth-grade team by a coach who just happened to look like me and his repressed raging memories come roaring back?*

How hands-on was this clinic going to be? I wasn't so sure the smiley faces were going to have the intended effect here.

I could already imagine the phone call home from the hospital.

Hi, Mom. So we did a basketball clinic at this prison ...

And yet it was exciting. I hadn't done any clinics where I questioned whether I'd be alive or maybe just maimed at the end.

We walked through the metal detectors in our basketball shoes and handed an officer our wallets and cell phones through a caged window.

It reminded me of a time when I played in high school against a team in our conference, North Chicago. It was a rough town and we walked through metal detectors to enter the school. My dad spoke to the security guard as we entered the first time and said, "I bet you have some stories about these metal detectors."

The security guard smiled. "On the first day we put them in, one kid froze and stared at it. He said 'What's that?' I said, 'It's a metal detector'. He said, 'Oh, does it detect drugs?' 'Nope.' He said, 'Oh, okay' and started to walk through. Well, it didn't detect brains either and he didn't get very far after that."

Prison ball. Here goes nothin'.

The gym was small and indoors, unlike most prison-yard basketball in the movies. The court was not nearly regulation length, but it had a basketball hoop at either end bolted to the walls. I couldn't remember the specific instructions from the guards, but all I knew was that I wasn't making anybody run sprints or do push-ups today. It was going to be all positive. The last thing I wanted was to push the buttons of someone who had one week until parole.

The gym door opened, and in they came. No orange jumpsuits. No ankle chains. No *Silence of the Lambs* masks. Ving Rhames was nowhere to be found. Most of them were very average-sized, normal-looking people. I relaxed a little. Not completely, but enough to let go of some of some of the uneasiness that had clouded my brain earlier. We jumped right in to ball handling and shooting games, which everyone enjoyed.

But these guys didn't want to just do drills. They wanted to play. With us. Game on.

We split up into teams and it was go time. These guys were flying all over the place. I made sure to do much more passing than shooting. It was definitely not about me. There really was only one guy that made me nervous. He seemed to have as much energy as ten of the other guys combined. He'd laugh and jump around, throwing up crazy shots that bounced off the back wall and flinging passes to everyone in the gym, even if they weren't on his team. I couldn't help but wonder if there wasn't a little something extra running through his veins. Maybe he just really loved basketball. I'm not sure, I'm just sayin'.

I looked around cautiously to determine how protected we really were, and the guards seemed very relaxed as they took it all in. There may have only been three or four guards watching from the doorways. The non-prisoners in the gym were highly outnumbered, but we never really felt threatened.

After the final game, we shook hands and high-fived our new teammates. They were all sweating and most had a smile on their faces. It seemed a nice escape for them to have a chance to play a game with freedom and for pure fun.

Basketball is an amazing game. You can get lost in it and forget where you are or what is happening in your life. It sounds hokey, but it was a special feeling to experience that with this group of people, who had so little freedom in their current season of reality. During games, I often play an entire forty minutes when my mind and body are so focused on playing that I don't hear or recognize any other thing happening around me. At some Dutch games, loud, obnoxious music would play and drums would beat nonstop for four quarters—and I didn't have a clue that it was going on until watching the game video the next day. *Was that awful techno beat blaring all game?* I might as well have been wearing earplugs in a different building altogether.

We had no doubt that the guys who went back to their cells had a great time. But the ones who really got the most out of it were smiling and laughing even harder during their car ride home.

* * *

Because we could only practice when the rest of the Holland wasn't using our gym, Herman scheduled 7 a.m. and 7 p.m. practices. Delightful. Waking up at 6 a.m. and eating dinner at 11 p.m. was not the glorious pro lifestyle I'd imagined. I had my fill of pre-dawn wake-up calls in college.

One particularly snowy mid-December morning, we pulled into an icy Stilodome parking lot at 6:45 a.m. The sun hadn't come up yet, and the building's heating system was broken. After a quick change in the meat freezer of a locker room, we walked into the gym with our practice jerseys on.

We shouldn't have even taken our winter coats off. Herman didn't. But it's hard to shoot in a parka, so we had no choice. I looked over, and a side door was wide open. Snow was blowing in hard along with the winter's fierce chill. *Can someone please close the freakin' door to the North Pole?*

The crazy building warlord was going in and out of the door doing who knows what. Herman told him to shut the door, but the manager had got up on the wrong side of the dike and snapped back at him. The door remained open for the next ten minutes or so.

It was nearly impossible to feel our fingers, and seeing our breath mist in front of our faces didn't add hope to the situation. To say that I was annoyed that I'd gotten up at six to freeze my tail off while it snowed inside the gym would be the understatement of the season. But this was Herman's world and there was a side to him that relished a challenge and an opportunity to make his players tougher. I prepared myself to suffer through it.

All of a sudden, the prayers of some righteous people somewhere were answered.

"That's it, fellas," Herman announced. "We're done."

I had thought for sure he was going to make us work out in the icebox. Thankfully, he had a change of heart. It wouldn't be the last time Herman surprised us with his response to a difficult situation.

* * *

The new offensive system Herman had us running wasn't exactly dis-mantling opponents like we'd hoped. We had a good team in terms of talent, though not the best. We worked as hard as or harder than the other teams in the league. There were no easy practices. We ran sprints at the end of practice, and if we missed free throws, we ran more sprints. We were young and needed to out-hustle other teams and really coalesce in order to be effective. For example, at the end of games when we were winning and other teams would foul to try to keep the game close and get the ball back, we'd run the length of the court to the free throw line and huddle up. It was a small thing, but Herman knew the psychology of those little things.

"Make them feel it," he said. "Show them that, 'Hey, I'm here to play, too. We're not tired and we won't let you beat us.'"

The offensive style that Herman wanted from us was much differ-ent from his team the previous season. His three Americans that year had outstanding seasons. Two of them averaged 22 points per game each, and they played a faster-paced game with lots of drives and break-ing down of defenses with individual talent. From the moment we arrived in Holland, all we heard about was J. J. Miller, Steve Marshall, and Travis Young.

Those three were clearly the heroes, and now they were gone. It was a lot for Scott, Todd, and me to live up to. They'd had a very successful year and surprised a lot of people. The organization and the fans got a taste of cheering for an exciting team that won often. I could feel the pressure of people's expectations with every comment made by teammates, fans, and team management.

"They were so fast."

We weren't fast.

"They beat all the top teams."

We were trying to get above .500.

"They were such good scorers and shooters."

Well, we could put the ball in the basket, too, you know.

But this year's team was almost the opposite in American personnel and style of play. Our system called for lots of reads, quick cuts, and sharp passing. Guys had to play together to be effective because we didn't rely on one or two guys to penetrate and do the bulk of the scoring.

The one guy who seemed to be able to do it all, though, was Scott Ungerer. He was an unbelievable passer. He saw two or three steps ahead of everyone, the opponent and us too. He would put the ball exactly where it needed to be, and it was up to the rest of us to finish the play. He was leading the league in assists at over eight per game. And it's not like we had Kobe and Shaq on our team to put the ball in the basket. Scott was not just a captain but also the conductor of our offense. He even ran practice some days when we would focus on specific parts of our offense. He was one of the smartest players I've ever played with, and he rarely came out of the game.

* * *

We were fighting to climb back to .500 heading into Christmas break, and we were all thankful for some time off. One of my teammates, Nitzan, was from Groningen, the city north of us where we played our first game, and we decided to celebrate New Year's at his place. Todd, Scott, Ivan, and I borrowed the eight-passenger team van with LANDSTEDE HAMMERS plastered all over the side and drove the hour and fifteen minutes to Nitzan's apartment. Todd's and Scott's girlfriends were visiting from the United States, so they joined us as well. Cara had come to Holland over Christmas but had flown back to the States a couple days before, as she had to return to work. I missed her like crazy. So ringing in the New Year without her was bittersweet.

The party was fun, and we all enjoyed ourselves without breaking any major laws. I was the designated driver and started to get sleepy around 2 a.m. Naturally, no one else was ready to leave. An hour later, we were finally able to round up everyone from our crew and pile back in the van for the drive home.

Within ten minutes the entire van was asleep. No one else was on the road, and I drove us in silence back towards Zwolle. As we chugged along, I fought the urge to nap and blinked hard to keep myself awake and alert.

There were radar detectors on the highways and local roads all over Holland that tried to keep drivers honest. They were very sensitive, and if the speed limit was 80 kilometers per hour and you were going 82—FLASH! Congratulations, you just won an expensive award that would show up in your mailbox in three to six weeks. "The Dutch government wishes to thank you for your support. You may want to re-think how 'in a hurry' you really are next time."

It was a sickly feeling to see that light bulb go off in your rearview mirror as a picture was taken of your license plate. Sometimes I thought the pictures were for me, but another car would fly past me, ending my brief cardiac arrest.

Some cameras even caught you before you passed them and would take a picture of the entire front of the car with the faces of driver and passenger in full view, so there was no dispute as to who violated the speed limit. Apparently the pictures of the passenger's face became an issue with the citizens of Holland. People would receive their speeding ticket and glamour shot in the mail along with an unintended consequence. Husbands and wives caught their spouses having affairs via the photos, and enough complaints were made that the government started to blur or black out the faces of the person in the passenger seat. Even so, if a cheating driver's spouse opened the mail that particular day, there might be some serious repercussions.

I glanced down and noticed our fuel gauge's red light was on. We had at least another forty-five minutes to go before we landed in Zwolle. *No problem, I'll just stop at the next gas station and everyone will probably sleep right through it anyway.*

A sign appeared. Two kilometers to the next gas station. *I can make that.* But as I approached the exit, I looked ahead and the entire gas station was pitch black. *Are you serious? I know it's the middle of the night, and it is New Year's, but c'mon.* It was another untimely reminder that I was a long way from home.

I started to get nervous. It was about 3:30 a.m., and I was ready to be in bed two hours ago. But we still had a ways to go.

I kept driving, and the red gas light on the dash continued mocking me. *"You stupid American. I might stay on for ten more minutes or you might stall in thirty seconds. You'll never know. You're welcome to feel like a fool in the meantime. Good luck when your passengers wake up in the back, stranded on the side of some cold, random Dutch highway with no one to call for help."*

Two more gas stations passed by in complete darkness, crushing what hope I had. Any minute now we were going to run out of gas and start to freeze our buns off in the subzero (Celsius) night.

Scott woke up in the passenger seat next to me.

"How's it going?" he asked, rubbing his eyes.

"Well, that's a good question," I said, trying to sound positive yet not lie or completely freak out.

"Dude, the red light is on," he said.

"Yes, it is," I replied.

"How long has it been on?" he asked.

"Too long," I said.

"Why didn't you stop for gas?" he asked as if I was quite possibly the dumbest person on the face of the earth.

"Everything is closed," I said.

"What do you mean? Gas stations don't close at night," he said.

"That's what I thought! But apparently they do in Holland. Even the gas pumps need to sleep," I said.

"Why didn't you stop before we left? There were places open in Groningen," he said, very annoyed.

"I didn't notice we were low," I said.

It was my fault. I was the driver. I hadn't even been drinking, and I missed a crucial detail. One that was about to cause a very big inconvenience and make my soon-to-be-awake friends quite unhappy.

Happy New Year everyone! We are out of gas, far from home, and all gas stations are closed until probably next week. The good news is that there's plenty of space to pee alongside the highway. Thank you for allowing me the privilege of serving you as your trusty designated driver.

"How far do we have left?" he asked.

"At least thirty minutes," I said.

"We're not gonna make it," he said.

"I know," I said.

One more exit sign appeared with the gas logo. One kilometer. *Lord, please let it be open.*

Then I felt the slight jolt. The speedometer started dropping even though my foot hadn't moved from the gas pedal. We were out of gas. *Crap!*

I looked ahead.

"I think I see lights," I said. I was nervously giddy. I wanted to believe, but I had been let down too many times before by approaching gas stations.

"I do, too," Scott said.

"You think it's open?" I hoped aloud.

"Maybe," he said. "It's our last chance."

I put the van in neutral. We kept slowing down. 50. 40. 30.

"It's open!" I said.

The bright lights of glory welcomed us. We glided in to the station without a drop of fuel in the tank. I'd never been so happy to squeeze that pump and see those numbers skyrocket away. I didn't care if I paid 300 euros for that tank of gas. What were the chances that this station would be the only one open on our ride home and not one kilometer further than we needed it to be? We'd be able to sleep in our own beds after all. But the best news was that four players wouldn't have to wake up their head coach to wish him a "Happy 2003" from the side of a highway somewhere between his house and Groningen. *And, oh by the way, can you bring a few liters of gas and some blankets?*

* * *

I was enjoying most everything about my first year overseas. I really liked the guys I was playing with and I had adjusted to basketball, the different foods, and customs of a new country. But one thing continued to bother me more and more—my salary situation.

This was getting a little ridiculous. Every month I'd receive a bank transfer for half of my salary. The other half was nowhere to be found. The team accountant assured me that it was being sent to my uncle's bank account. I assured the accountant that it never arrived. Neither one of us believed the other. Then I found out that other players were having money issues as well.

I called my agent, Patrick King, and informed him of the problem. This had been going on for over half of the season. Fortunately, my expenses were pretty low, so the snafu didn't send me into debt. But it was a pain to have to fight this battle that shouldn't even have been an issue.

The agreement was simple. I play. The team pays. It's awkward to complain about money. Some people don't have it, and I didn't want to appear ungrateful. This was my first pro job, so I didn't know exactly how much to push on the issue. But I knew I had to press the team on it some because I certainly didn't want the season to end and be stuck with having played for $11,000 instead of $22,000. If I did my job and gave 100 percent, they should do theirs and pay me 100 percent of what they owe.

* * *

I was excited to meet Patrick in person. We had only spoken on the phone and via email up until that time. My recruitment out of college wasn't like *Jerry Maguire*, with agents flying into State College, Pennsylvania, to take me out to dinner and give me platinum watches. Many overseas players never meet their agents face-to-face. It's a bit unconventional to never meet the person who's responsible for managing your pro career. But Patrick came with a great reference, and it wasn't like we were bonding our lives together in holy matrimony in sickness and in health. The contract was for one season. He was an American who had gained German citizenship and married a German woman and became an agent after a very solid playing career in Germany.

I met him when he came to a home game in February. I played terribly and only scored six points. After the game we visited in the sponsors' lounge, a small room next to the gym where players, sponsors, and families would mingle. Of all the games, he had to come to this one.

"I'm sorry you guys lost today," Patrick said.

"Yeah, me too. I didn't play that well," I said.

"Tyler, you can't have six points in a game," he said. "You're an American. You have to put up numbers each night. You are one of the main players, and you need to be aggressive every time out on the floor."

I felt lousy for my poor performance and the fact that we lost. Surely my lack of production played a role in our defeat that night. Patrick was right, and I knew it. Players got cut all the time for not living up to expectations. And it wasn't like the NBA where salaries were guaranteed. If you were released, *adiós, amigo*. You could collect what was owed through your day of departure (if you were lucky) and that was it.

"Yeah, I know," I said. "I need to play better. I've had much better games this year. This wasn't my typical outing."

"I know. As for the salary issue, I'll keep talking to the team and see what the story is. They keep telling me that they don't have money problems, so I'm not sure why they aren't paying you."

* * *

A few weeks later, I reached my tipping point. I was sick of being told that the money was coming when clearly it wasn't. I spoke to my teammates and we decided that it was time to take some sort of action. I'd heard of professional players who would sit out games unannounced if they didn't get paid. While I understood the logic, I didn't like that route because it hurt the team and the guys you go to war with side by side each day. I had no desire to sit out games, but something had to be done.

We decided that we weren't going to practice. It was a bold move on our part because we were sure that Herman would blow his lid. "Not practice?!" Herman was big on practicing, so would he take it as an insult? Would he think we were acting like immature prima donnas? Herman wasn't responsible for paying guys. His job was to coach. So I could understand if he got upset. This could potentially lead to an unprecedented number of sprints. I feared the worst of the Herminator's wrath. It was risky. But enough was enough.

We all sat in our street clothes in our locker room when Herman walked in for practice. Normally, everyone would already be dressed in their practice gear and warming up. He knew something was up.

"So what's going on fellas?" Herman asked.

"Coach, guys haven't been getting paid," Nitzan said. He was one of our captains, and Coach had a lot of respect for him. Nitzan was definitely the right man to deliver the message. "It's been going on for a while now, and we've tried to be patient. But we felt like we needed to speak up and make a stand because it's not right. We decided that we aren't going to practice today because this situation needs to be fixed."

The moment of truth had arrived. Would Herman yell and scream? Here comes two hours of lane slides. This is the same coach who instituted a one-euro fine every time we didn't touch the half-court line during layup lines before games. Anything was possible.

"Then let's not practice," Herman agreed. I almost fell off the hard wooden bench. "If they aren't paying you, then they need to fix it. I have been getting paid, but I would be upset if I wasn't. This is your job, and you should be paid what they said they would pay."

We all looked pleasantly surprised at each other. The last thing we needed was a separate battle with our coach.

We grabbed our bags and walked back out to our cars. I had a little extra hop in my step for two reasons. Number one, Herman was going to save his rage for management instead of his players. We may not have always liked his tough demeanor, but it was a great feeling when he had your back. And number two, no practice. There are few things in life that will brighten your day like the unexpected cancellation of practice.

Chapter 4

'IS DIS VAT YOUR NOSE LOOK LIKE YESTERDAY?': DUTCH HARD KNOCKS

The regular season was finished. Even though we had more losses than wins, I scored my $250 playoff bonus as we qualified for the postseason thanks to Rotterdam, who was terrible that year. They had the smallest budget, the least overall talent, and they finished dead last in ninth place. The top eight teams made the playoffs, and we were eighth, which meant we'd face the No.1 seed—the Eiffel Towers.

I know what you're thinking. Isn't the Eiffel Tower in Paris? So how and why would a team in the Netherlands name their team the Eiffel Towers? Why not the "Great Walls" or "Empire State Buildings?" It's a good question that doesn't have a very good answer other than Eiffel is consultancy firm. At first it seems strange. But after a while—well, it's still odd. We all just got used to it.

Eiffel had the biggest budget in the league and they were a powerhouse. Rumor had it that players were making between $5,000 and $8,000 per month, which was pretty impressive compared to some of our guys, who only made a few hundred euros (about $350 US dollars) per month. Eiffel had two players who were Americans with Dutch passports and were excellent post players. And they had their three regular import players on top of that, which included Ryan Robertson, a point guard who had played at Kansas. He was an all-league player every year. So they played with five Americans on the court who were experienced and talented. We hadn't come close to beating them in the regular season, losing by solid double digits every time out.

As we entered the playoffs, everyone had been paid except me. The assistant GM visited our practice following the team's mini-strike and apologized for the delay and inaccuracy in their payments. He assured us that all would be fixed. And it was … for everyone else. I was extremely annoyed that they weren't able to send all of my salary where it *needed* to go—me. I continued to hound them about it, but decided against any more strikes since crunch time was here.

The first round of playoffs would be best-of-three, with the higher seed getting the first and third games at home. Since Eiffel was the top seed, we drove an hour to their place to begin playoffs on Easter Sunday. Their home gym was smaller than my high school's. There were no parking attendants needed to guide traffic. In fact, there were probably as many bicycles leaning up against the small square building as there were cars in the parking lot. Unless you lived in one of the apartment buildings adjacent to the gym, you'd probably never know it was there.

In the third quarter we were down by about 15 and trying to keep the game from getting out of hand. My teammate Joost Ooms (YOST OHMS) and I went for a rebound, and his elbow came down right in the middle of my face. I felt something in my face crack and shift to the side but ignored it until we made it down to the offensive end of the court.

I put my hand to my nose and noticed blood coming out quickly. The refs hadn't seen it yet so I hid it from them the best I could. The ball went out-of-bounds, and it was the perfect time to signal that I needed a sub, since eventually someone would spot the river of red flowing down my face and I'd be forced to leave the game. But I figured that I could get one more shot off before exiting the floor. We ran an inbounds play, and I launched a baseline jumper. *Clank.* They grabbed the rebound and then the referee noticed my bloodied mug and stopped the game. I was escorted off the floor while holding my face.

I stuffed my nose full of tissue and went to the hospital with one of our team staff members. It was closed. Who closes hospitals on Sundays? Does no one get sick or hurt on the Sabbath? The Dutch took their off-day very seriously. Sundays were for relaxing with family or maybe a book and a cup of coffee. And for the young crowd that stayed out at the clubs until 8 a.m., sleeping.

We drove to another medical facility that had a nose, mouth, and ear specialist. This one was open thankfully, but we received bad news. "We don't fix noses on Sundays." *Are you serious?* This was getting ridiculous.

My nose is on the other side of my face and you're telling me that no one in this country can help? If a crowbar was sticking out of my ribs, would they be willing to fix that? I didn't want to find out.

Some calls were made and we found a doctor back in Zwolle who was available to help. I don't know if favors were called in, but I was just thankful that someone was going to fix me. When I sat down in his office, the doctor handed me a mirror.

"Is dis vat your nose look like yesterday?" he asked.

Dude, my face looks lopsided. I sure hope it didn't look this way before and no one told me.

In his defense, it was a fair question. He'd never seen me before.

"No," I said. "I did not have a bloodied broken nose yesterday."

"OK, we will fix," he said.

He leaned my head back and shoved two wet cotton balls into each nostril. I was forced to breathe through my mouth as my nose throbbed with pain. The liquid was meant to numb my nose so he could adjust it to its original position. I wondered if this was how they fixed noses in the States. I'd never broken a bone before in my life. I'd actually broken other people's noses. One in high school (twice actually—same guy) and one in college (also twice—same guy). Both were my teammates. Another time during my only year of playing high school football, I yanked a guy down so hard that he tore his ACL. And twice I collided with opponents on the soccer field and only one of us got up. The other two guys got their first trip in an ambulance and suffered broken legs. The time had come to pay my dues.

The liquid medicine dripped down into the back of my throat numbing my mouth and tongue. It was an awful sensation because I couldn't feel myself breathing or swallowing.

"You feel this, yes?" he tapped on my nose with his finger.

Ow! Yes!

"OK, we wait more," he said.

A few minutes later he tried again.

"Pain, you feel?" he asked as he touched my nose again.

"No, I think it's numb now," I slurred because of my senseless mouth.

I was highly uncomfortable. My nose was completely clogged with tissue, drool was streaming down my face, my head was tilted back, and I was attempting to breathe through my mouth, which I couldn't feel.

He took a step closer so that his body was leaning against mine. Then he squeezed my nose between both his hands and yanked it back into place. I started coughing and wheezing, trying to catch my breath from the force of his facial adjustment.

Thanks for the heads up.

He handed me the mirror again.

"Is dis vat your nose look like yesterday?" he asked again.

It was straighter than it had been a minute ago. But did it look like it did before the injury? I don't know. How often do you really examine your face in detail to see exactly how far one part is from another?

This was a big decision. If I said "yes" and left here without it being aligned, then I would continue my life with a crooked nose. There are more severe things, of course, like a crooked spine or leg, but that wasn't the issue here. I just wanted to be put back the way I was before. Worse yet, it might affect my breathing if the airways weren't lined up correctly. This was stressful. But I eventually conceded that it looked close enough to however it was that I looked just hours earlier.

"Looks good enough," I shrugged.

He unpacked my nose full of the numbing-agent cotton. Then he repacked it with dry cotton and taped it shut. That cotton wasn't going anywhere. Now I definitely couldn't breathe.

"Leave dis on two days, yah?" he instructed. "It help keep your nose straight."

My bandaged face looked like I just had a major nose job. *Let's get out of here before he tries to fix something else.*

The next two days ranked among the most uncomfortable days of my life. It may not have been as bad as when I was in college and had four impacted wisdom teeth removed at once and vomited blood from the meds. But it hurt, I couldn't breathe, and I had a cold. My nose was constantly running and dripping through the wet cotton and sticky tape that smothered it. Why anyone would ever get a nose job, I can't fathom.

* * *

Our next playoff game was Tuesday, and it was do-or-die. We would play Eiffel at home, and I did not want to miss potentially the last game of the season. Henk, one of our volunteer staff members, said he had a nose mask at his house that I could use. Henk was a police officer who doubled as a volunteer athletic trainer for our team. I didn't even know if he had any legitimate trainer credentials, but he was the only one who might be able to help me protect my face during the game.

When I arrived at his house, he had birdcages everywhere filled with all kinds of birds, exotic to ordinary.

"I raise these birds, then sell them," Henk said. "That bird right there is worth $2,500," he said and pointed to a large colorful bird in a cage in his living room. Then he held up a coat. "See this leather jacket? I'm going to sell that to a guy next week." Here I thought he was a full-time cop and he was actually a full-time hustler, not to mention a self-taught trainer.

I envisioned one of those clear plastic facemasks that has elastic straps and scares small children. Instead, Henk whipped out a piece of cheap-looking tan plastic in the shape of a nose with tiny holes throughout. He may have made it in his garage, but I was scared to ask. Who knows how many others had worn it before me? One-size-fits-all at Henk's pawn shop.

"How am I supposed to attach it to my face? There aren't any straps," I said. I didn't want to appear ungrateful. But I did need to be practical.

"Oh just use some tape," he said.

Just use some tape. Of course. Why didn't I think of that? I gently tried it on over my current taped-up nose. It would probably fit once I took off all the other garbage on my face. He suggested one piece of tape would go across my forehead and wrap around both sides of my head above my ears. The other piece of tape would go directly over my new nose protector and stick to the sides of my cheeks just under my eyes. It was a weak attempt at a Halloween costume. It wasn't foolproof, but obviously this was as good as it was going to get.

Had this happened the prior season while at Penn State, I would have had a custom-fit mask. An actual certified athletic trainer and expert sports medicine doctor would have treated me in a training room that was larger than many Dutch homes. I'm sure the Dutch would have loved to have access to these kinds of amenities in Holland, but clearly there was nowhere near the budget to do so.

* * *

Unfortunately, we were without Todd for the playoffs because of some terrible news. His mom had passed away unexpectedly back in the United States just days before our series with Eiffel began. I woke up one morning, and he was gone. He had received the call in the middle of the night and got on the next plane home. He left a note for each of the guys. Each one was personal and moving. On mine he talked about how he appreciated our friendship and was confident that I and the rest of our team could still get it done without him.

I was shocked and felt terrible for him. It was one of those moments where I stepped back and saw what a great friendship had developed between Todd and me. To have him leave so abruptly was sad, and it felt like things ended much too early. What awful news to receive while you are out of the country. I was glad he could get home to be with his family.

Earlier in the season, Todd had gone through another very stressful situation. His father had a heart problem that would kill him unless he received a heart transplant. He had been on a waiting list for over five years and wore a beeper every day in the unlikely event of a miracle call. Sure enough, the beeper utterly surprised him one day, and he rushed to the hospital to receive his transplant. He hadn't been at the top of the waiting list. There were others in front of him. But they didn't answer their calls, and Todd's dad was next in line. Thankfully, the procedure was successful.

It wasn't easy living overseas and being away from everyone and everything you've ever known. There is just something about being familiar with your surroundings, family, and friends that no foreign land can replace. Even though the Dutch spoke English and we were warmly welcomed by the team and made new friends, it still wasn't home.

* * *

Before game time, I untaped my cotton-packed nose and pulled the nasty snot-soaked tissue out of my nostrils. Glorious! I could breathe again. My whole head was clear after two days of fog.

We came out blazing against Eiffel in Game Two. With my new-found access to oxygen, I felt amazing. I drilled threes, the twins were throwing down dunks, and Scott was picking them apart with his precise passing. Despite my homemade garage-sale facemask, I played my best game of the season, knocking down four threes and finishing with 25 points, and we won. The series was tied now, 1–1, and returning to Eiffel. Forty minutes would determine who would move on.

If we were able to knock off Eiffel, it would be epic. It was small budget vs. big budget. Rookies vs. vets. And Zwolle might throw us a parade for taking down the mighty Eiffel Towers. Not to mention that I could leverage that for a better contract next year.

* * *

Game Three took us back to the Horstacker (yeah, pronounced just like it looks). Herman began his pregame speech in the locker room.

"I have a song I want to play for you," he said.

This was going to be good.

He pressed a button on the CD player and some cheesy '80s tune started playing. *What's this?* We all sat awkwardly, unsure of the reaction Herman was looking for. And unsure of whether to laugh, cheer, or just keep our mouths shut.

Duran Duran was filling our locker room with one of their hits, "Wild Boys."

We were stunned. This was the biggest game of the year, and he was playing a song from a quarter century ago to fire us up. And it wasn't Rocky.

"I want you to play like wild guys out there and let it all out," Herman said.

I suppressed a laugh, but couldn't withhold my smile. He knew it was funny on some level, too. But he wanted us to relax and go out there and play the game with freedom and reckless abandon.

Maybe 50 Cent or something a little more violent would have had a stronger emotional impact. We fought hard, but Eiffel was too loaded. They beat us convincingly and went on to win the championship against four-time defending champion Amsterdam.

* * *

The season was over and I was still eleven grand short. I was dying to get home to see Cara. But one thing was certain: I wasn't going home without my money. If I left the country and money was still outstanding,

I had a greater chance of starting for the Lakers the following season than recouping that salary. Until you get it, it's their money, it's their homeland, and they have control. Phone calls and emails will only do so much from thousands of miles away. A large angry man who just finished a full season battling for his team and shows up at the team's office door every day is much more influential.

NBA players didn't have to worry about their paychecks since their owners had cash coming out their ears. Their contracts were guaranteed in a league that had a players' union. Overseas, there was very little recourse as we were at the mercy of a foreign team with foreign management in a foreign country.

And at this point, I couldn't care less how I got paid. It was easiest when they transferred the money directly into my account, but obviously that wasn't going to happen now. *So pay me in pesos, cattle, or gold bullion. It doesn't matter. Just pay me so I can end nine months worth of worrying.*

Two days before I was to head back to the United States, management finally conceded to my constant nagging and realized that the simplest way to wrap up my salary issues was to pay me in cash. The financial manager sat down with me in an empty room and counted out $11,000 worth of euros. As he counted, I looked around to see if anyone was watching or might be coming through the door. I'd never seen so much cash in all my life, and it felt like a drug deal. European currency, a guy who spoke so-so English, behind closed doors—all I needed was a couple of handguns, a bodyguard named "Big Rolo," and a silver briefcase with handcuffs attached.

I'd had a solid first year playing overseas, averaging 17 points and seven rebounds per game. I was also second in the league in three-point percentage at 44 percent, just behind Todd, of course, at 46 percent. But it was for an eighth-place team in Holland, so who knew if I'd get another opportunity to play somewhere else? Unlike Scott and Todd who were unsure of whether they wanted to play overseas again next year, I definitely wanted to continue playing.

What better job could there be? All my friends back home were wearing suits and ties to work. I sported sweatpants and didn't tuck my shirt in. Who else got to get paid to live in Europe? I felt like I was still improving as a player and had so much more good basketball left in me. They'd have to break my legs to get me to stop playing. After all, I was living the dream. A different dream for sure, but a dream nonetheless. My dream.

I was hungry to play in stronger leagues and hungry for a bigger contract.

But one thing was for sure: if something was going to happen, God would have to open a door. I had zero control over the matter.

Lord, please let me play another season. Somewhere.

Chapter 5

BEST PIZZA AND PASTA ON THE PLANET: ITALY

I was unemployed again. I didn't know whether I could file for unemployment benefits, but I kind of felt like that would be cheating the system. After all, I was the one choosing to work overseas, knowing full well it's not a twelve-month job. It didn't seem right to have the government pay me while I sat around waiting for my phone to ring. Plus, the fact that I wasn't paying *into* the system via taxes made me feel even less entitled.

Other than contacting different agents and hoping they were actually working for me, I had zero control over my jobless situation. Technically, I suppose I could have started my own campaign by calling front offices around the globe. But it's awkward to vouch for yourself over the phone to a general manager in Latvia or the Philippines. "Hi, you should strongly consider signing me and all of my amazing-ness. I'm a can't-miss acquisition for your club. Consider my previous two seasons: last place in the Big 10 and second-to-last place in Holland, a proven winner. When can I expect the contract? Sorry, I don't speak Hungarian, but I'm sure we'll get along famously. You guys pay your players, right?"

A player who tries to represent himself raises a red flag to pro teams. He is: 1) not good enough for a real agent to bother with; 2) desperate for anyone to consider his plea for help; or 3) completely out of touch with reality.

I do realize that 99 percent of people in the real world of non-pro athletics apply for jobs all by themselves. For whatever reason, athletes must feel they're so special that the normal circumstances don't apply to them and other people should do everything for them. But I tell you, as odd as this whole system is, I'd much prefer a middleman do all the arguing and cursing than me. The team can shoot the messenger all they want, and I can badmouth the team and complain to the agent about how stingy management is. The agent has someone complaining in each ear. In the end, the agent's difficult role is like that of a commode: thankless and often inglorious, yet quite necessary.

Actually, I did feel my Dutch season gave me something to build on. Belgium and Germany were two neighboring leagues that were stronger than Holland and paid better. As in the regular business world, players often have to prove themselves in lower leagues before moving up. And while I enjoyed my time in Zwolle, Plan A was not to repeat my rookie year. In fact, I never received an actual offer to return to Zwolle from Herman anyway, formal or informal. Things ended well with a "Let's stay in touch over the summer" conversation, but they weren't begging me to stay. Part of me wanted at least to be asked, to validate (at least in my mind) the job I'd done there.

* * *

The summer after my season in Holland was fairly quiet. I was thrilled to be back in the United States. Pizza Hut and ranch dressing never tasted so good. My long-distance relationship with Cara was now a much-preferred short-distance relationship. I moved in with a friend of mine back in Hollidaysburg, Pennsylvania, to be closer to Cara. And yet I was anxious to discover in which language I'd next have to master "Hello," "Thank you," and "Why are you staring?" next.

During May, June, and July, I'd wake up every day and check my email immediately. My heart would leap if I saw an agent's name in my inbox. If nothing was there, I'd check my junk mail—surely something got misdirected.

Week after week, there was nothing. It was stressful. And it seemed like people would ask every hour of the day, "So where are you heading next?" *Uh, to the gym. Because I don't have a job.*

I wanted to have an answer for them more than anything. "Yeah, I'm going to France. Top League. Guaranteed six-figures with my own croissant bakery thrown in."

Patrick didn't have any takers. He mentioned that he'd spoken with a team in Belgium, but nothing came of it. Then, he was waiting to hear back from Spain. *Nada.* With every communication, my hopes would accelerate and then crash headfirst into a pit of jobless despair. I called other agents in hopes that they'd know of a secret team on an island that couldn't for the life of them find a 6-foot-8 white guy who thought he ran fast but really didn't.

* * *

August was here and I didn't have a single date to the prom. Not even from my sister. I'd been signed a full month earlier last season, and right now there was nothing to even negotiate. It didn't seem to make sense, because I had just played a full professional season in Europe. I wasn't technically a proven vet, but I was something. A somewhat controlled panic, but panic nonetheless, was setting in as I read of new European signings on the Internet everyday, and I was still sitting in the corner waiting on a miracle.

I had been praying all summer that a door would open for me to play again. I believed that it was in God's hands, whether I'd get another opportunity, and I trusted that He knew best. But there was no answer. Well, there was an answer. It just wasn't the one I was looking for.

* * *

One morning, I was alone in the house, and I'd had enough. I lay face down on the floor and prayed. I felt self-conscious and hoped that my roommate wouldn't drop in. But strangely enough, it felt good, like I was getting something off of my chest. The anxiety and tension that had been building the entire summer seemed to dissipate.

One reason I chose to have faith in God was because I had seen Him answer prayers in the past. I'd also read about how God used very ordinary people to do extraordinary things all throughout the Bible. He very well could say no and I'd have to live with that. He didn't answer "yes" to every request I ever made. But I trusted that He would lead me in the right direction. *Lord, just please don't let that direction be behind the counter at Home Depot. I'm not ready.*

One week later, I got a call from an agent named Max Raseni in Italy. A team in Italy's second division was really interested, and he expected an offer soon. Talk about coming out of nowhere. Yesterday I couldn't get the Washington Generals to sign me as a prop to get dunked on by the Globetrotters. The natural progression up the overseas basketball ladder wasn't Holland's eighth place team to Italy. How was this even possible?

Max said that the Italian team could sign three Americans this season, and he expected the contract to be in the neighborhood of $40,000 to $50,000. Work your magic Maximus! Go for fifty!

He got them to agree to $48,000. It felt like $480,000. A year ago, while I was in my unrealistic expectations mode, I would have been only semi-satisfied at that offer. Having just played for $22,000 and witnessed the reality of contracts overseas, 48-large now sounded like the offer of a lifetime. Seeing as pizza was my favorite food and Italy was perhaps the most respected basketball country outside of the NBA, what more could I ask for?

I was only in year two of my career, and I'd already made it to the place where I wanted to be. I never thought for a second that I would play in NBA. How many big, slow white dudes were in the league? Exactly. So Italy was my NBA. And I'd arrived. As long as things went well, I could spend the rest of my career there. Other than planning the next decade of life in my new Italian imagination, my mind didn't jump ahead much. *Just don't screw this up.*

* * *

Imola (E-mo-la) was a town of roughly 60,000 located thirty minutes by car from Bologna, which is in the northern half of Italy. Like many European cities, a church was at the center of the downtown area. Narrow city streets, paved in brick, curved throughout the town and the roundabouts there seemed even more dangerous than the ones in Holland with drivers paying little mind to others on the road.

My favorite part of my new city was a huge castle smack in the city center. Well there wasn't much of a castle left to it, but the outer walls and drawbridge were impressive, and it reminded me of Robin Hood.

The next best thing about playing in Imola was found just 100 yards from the "castle." It was a restaurant sponsor of the team where we could eat anything we wanted: chicken, steak, pasta, pizza, drinks, and dessert—for just seven euros (eight dollars) per meal. At first I felt guilty ordering multiple dishes. I was easily eating forty or fifty euros worth, and the last thing I wanted was to put them out of business. But there wasn't a bad dish in the entire place, and one of my most serious character flaws is my inability to turn down inexpensive delicious food.

It was open for lunch until mid-afternoon, then reopened at eight. While normal folks in America are eating at 6 p.m., we would routinely show up for dinner at eleven or midnight. Most of the tables were outside as many people preferred to enjoy the cool evenings and people-watch. I even remember driving home from dinner one night and seeing elementary school kids playing on the playground close to midnight. It seemed bedtimes were only a suggestion there.

The restaurant owner was a flirtatious woman in her forties who'd greet players with kisses on the cheek and sit on our laps with her arm around us while we perused the menu. In addition, her attire was often revealing, which many of the customers loved, of course.

"Something to drink, Caio?" she'd ask my teammate in Italian as she ran her fingers through his hair.

Half of the time, I couldn't tell if she was trying to get us to ask her out or just give her our order. I had no desire to get to know her outside of the typical server/customer relationship, as I missed Cara terribly yet again and was settling into the beginning of another heart-wrenching nine-month stretch without her.

* * *

My Italian apartment was much improved from my Dutch house and the room in an attic in Pennsylvania during the summer. Located in a quiet neighborhood apartment complex, I now had a king-size bed along with a second bedroom with a queen bed and no roommates this time. The living room looked out over a small park, and my new home felt glorious. Even the out of place turquoise couch was large and quite comfy.

While the apartment was more than adequate, I didn't yet have a phone. So I found a pay phone two blocks from my house where Cara and I could talk in the privacy of my neighborhood's main intersection. I bought some calling cards at a decent per-minute rate. The first couple of cards went quicker than I expected. All of the sudden, a week had gone by and I needed to take out more cash. I'd blown through more than 300 euros ($350) in phone calls alone thanks to the obscene pay-phone rates. I needed a landline in a bad way.

* * *

My first day of practice was going well until one of the junior players decided it would be a good idea during one of the drills to welcome the newest foreigner to the team with a careless jab of his finger (and fingernail) into my eye. I crumpled to the floor in agony and prayed that when I opened my eye that I'd be able to see something.

It was a scary moment. A burning sword of pain jabbed through my eyeball back into my brain. I withheld my desire to cry like a three-year-old, as it was only my first day on the job and I didn't want them to think they had signed a complete wimp.

When I opened my eye to test it, I could, in fact, see. But everything was fantastically blurry. *Oh great, my sight is gone. My one chance to play in Italy—gone. I couldn't even get through a single practice.*

Then I returned to a more normal state of mind to realize that maybe I had just lost a contact. It was gone and this was just my usual poor non-prescription vision. My eye continued to throb and there was a significant amount of blood coming from my eye socket, never a good sign.

They took me to a doctor who, of course, didn't speak English. We were in Italy, so I shouldn't have expected her to anymore than I would expect an American doctor to speak Dutch or Italian. But, when I was injured, I wanted some sort of comfort and to know that everything would be fine. Since I had no clue what she was saying, it only made me more anxious and frustrated.

She ran me through a series of tests. My eye was so bloodshot and irritated that almost anything she had me do only reenacted the pain from the young player's finger.

My team trainer was by my side translating roughly one-tenth of what the doctor was saying. The doctor would speak for a full two or three minutes in Italian. Then my trainer would sum it up in great detail with something to the effect of, "She is looking in your eye now." It was quite comforting.

"Tyler, I must go speak to the receptionist," he said abruptly, and he was gone before I had a chance to beg him to not leave me alone.

Then, to highlight the lousy timing, the doctor pulled out a needle. I could only hold my one good eye open, but that was plenty enough vision to confirm my precarious situation: since she and I were the only ones in the room, unless she was a psycho drug addict, that needle was not destined for her. She was clutching the syringe in front of my face and sputtering out rapid Italian that my brain loosely translated as, "If you don't run for your life, I will in fact force this needle into your eyeball and there is no one here to save you."

It instantly became a moment of faith. *Lord, please don't let this go poorly. And help this crazy doctor … not screw up … whatever it is that she's about to do.* It was the best I could summon, but I'm sure He got the drift.

A lot runs through your mind when a person of authority has one hand on your face and the other holding a four-inch needle in front of your eye with full intention of using it. *Will this hurt?* (Yes.) *Will this help?* (It better.) *Is this necessary?* (Unknown.) *Has she done this before?* (Let's hope.)

As she inserted the tip of the needle into me, there was good news and bad news. The good news was twofold. First, she did not penetrate my eyeball, for which I was quite grateful. Second, I discovered that she did speak English after all.

"Aaaaand pain," she announced as the needle pierced my eyelid and (now the bad news) released a liquid I think may only have been used on POWs in the most horrendous prison camps known to man. My eye was on fire and it was all I could do to keep from punching her in the throat. Whatever she injected did eventually numb the injured area, and she stitched me up. But I'm not convinced that it would have been less painful to simply use my mother's rusty sewing needle and thread to finish the job on my own without a mirror.

Looking back, I realize any sane person reading this might ask, "Shouldn't you have paused or waved a Dikembe Mutombo finger in her face before you allowed her to puncture any part of your body without knowing what her exact intentions were?" Apparently I'm not the quickest or wisest decision-maker, taking me out of the running to become an air traffic controller or operate nuclear submarines.

* * *

The assistant general manager approached me at the gym one day after practice. He asked me to sign another contract. This one stated that I would only be playing for 16,000 euros ($19,200). Fortunately, I had been forewarned by Max that this was going to happen. They called it an "image" contract because, like the name, it was only an image of what a team actually paid a player. Again, as in Holland, it was some sneaky way to avoid paying taxes or fees or who knows what to the governing powers that be. On paper, everyone in Italy played for 16,000 euros. I'm sure teams felt justified in some way: "Well, he does play for 16,000. We just left out the 'per month' or 'per week' part." It's all very rational if you turn off the normal thinking part of your brain.

* * *

We had a team function that included sponsors and front-office staff before our first game, and the team president got up to speak. He was a lively fellow and was very excited for the start to our season. The previous year, the team had made an impressive second-half run from near the bottom of the league to the playoffs. The head coach had been fired halfway through the season, and the assistant coach, an American named Rod Griffin, replaced him. The president spoke of the upcoming season and the team's expectations. As long as we didn't finish in one of the last two spots, it would be considered a success.

I wasn't sure the translator interpreted it correctly.

"Did I just hear that right?" I asked.

Our translator assured us that the team's primary goal was to simply stay in the league. The bottom two teams would be relegated to the third division. So, as long as we finished fourteenth or higher, we were in good shape, according to Mr. President.

It was quite odd to hear such a low goal. That's it? "Don't be last" was our rousing kickoff speech? That was like saying, "We're going to lose today, guys. Just try to keep it under fifty."

I was new there, so I kept my mouth shut. And inside, I was partly thrilled because with expectations so low, I was very confident we'd be able to satisfy them. And we'd look extra amazing when we finished near the top.

* * *

Our home gym at Imola was about twenty times better than my previous gym in Holland. It seated about 5,000 people and came equipped with a real locker room, weight room, training room, and a full-time trainer. It wasn't used for other sports and, unlike the Stilodome, I was able to detect the out-of-bounds lines at first glance.

Everything was more professional. But the one thing I was struggling with was the basketball we used. It was blue and white with the cheap feel of the free basketball you used to get from Pizza Hut with your order (for those of you who remember that promotion in the early '90s, it was a big deal to ten-year-olds back in the day). The ball was smaller than the men's ball I'd used everywhere, and the texture was more suited for outdoor play. I was surprised that the ball was used throughout the league. Surely some league official was getting paid off to promote this awful excuse for a basketball.

For whatever reason, I wasn't shooting the ball as well as I normally did. I'd catch it, and instead of instant confidence through familiarity, I'd feel uncertainty. Not a good thing for someone whose job it is to lob the ball into the basket. I worked hard at it, but couldn't shoot with the same consistency as in the past. It was especially frustrating because I'd shot the ball well from the outside the past couple of seasons and it was one of my most effective ways to score.

Hoping it wasn't only me, I looked to the other two Americans on my team, Jobey Thomas and Elton Tyler. Jobey, a 6-foot-4 shooting guard, was hitting deep threes and jumpers left and right with ease. He was a natural shooter who could have launched car tires into the net without touching the rim. Last year he played in Portugal with a different ball, but he didn't seem to be affected by this new one.

Elton was a 6-foot-9 athletic big man who could shoot from the outside and score inside. He'd played for a different team in Italy's second division last year, so he was already familiar with the ball, and its unorthodox texture didn't seem to bother him either.

* * *

Our first game was against a team from Bologna that was picked to be one of the best in the league. When I walked out of the locker room for warmups, the fan section behind the basket nearest our bench was already full. They were singing and screaming at the top of their lungs in unison over an hour before tipoff. The passion was out of control, which was really on par for Italy and many parts in Europe. They beat drums, waved flags, and charged courtside on questionable calls by the refs. This was not an alcohol-induced performance. This was just how they cheered. And I'd never seen anything like it.

Every bench on the sidelines of every gym where we played had a curved transparent plastic roof on it. The purpose was to deflect airborne items (such as beer cups, coins, and batteries) launched by unruly fans at the players and coaches. As a general truth, a stationary object is easier to hit. Hence, our sideline protection. I found it endearing that the designers of this protective force-field cared so much that they made it see-through, so that at least the fans didn't have their view of the court impaired as they hurled cigarettes at us.

I played so-so until the final seconds, when I accidentally tried to lose it for us. I fouled their big guy on a jump shot, sending him to the free throw line with us up by one and three seconds on the clock. Somehow, he missed both shots and we escaped with our first win. It wasn't the way I'd envisioned beginning the season, with an almost-game-losing mistake. But we'd take the win.

* * *

We then travelled to a road game to take on Jesi (YAY-zee). We were down a few points at halftime, and as I walked toward the locker room, someone was screaming my name.

"Smeeeet!! Smeeeeeet!!" (Obviously the "th" is a difficult sound in other languages.)

I looked up, and a seven-year-old boy hanging over a railing had a huge smile on his face, delighted that I took notice. Then, he proceeded to thrust out both his skinny arms and proudly give me the middle finger with both hands. They teach team pride and loyalty at a very young age in Italy. A proud day for his grandma, too, no doubt.

* * *

Our trainer, Gianluca (john-LOO-kah), was a pretty sharp guy and took his job very seriously. One of his favorite healing agents was a can that sprayed instant cold air. If someone jammed a finger, he was on top of him with the cold spray. Tuberculosis? Cold spray. Heart disease? Cold spray. You'd think the stuff cured cancer with the way he used it. Fortunately, he withheld the urge to spray my eye (which I'm sure was difficult for him) when it had been gouged by my teammate on day one.

The concept, in theory, was like applying an ice pack. But you're supposed to leave ice on for ten or twenty minutes, and his magical mist only lasted four or five seconds before he pronounced you healed. The Italian players loved it and were convinced of its miraculous powers. *Why couldn't I think of something so simple and useless to make me millions?* This was why some of us get PhDs in aeronautical engineering and others run back and forth with a ball until a clock tells us to stop.

My favorite example of the cool breeze was when one of my teammates turned an ankle during a game. He fell to the floor clutching his lower leg in pain, and the refs stopped the action. Before anyone could determine if the player might be able to continue or even walk off the floor on his own, trainer-man was in a full sprint toward my fallen comrade, cold spray in hand. I swear he must sit at the end of the bench clutching his prized tool waiting for his opportunity.

And here it was. The moment he lived for. Our trainer furiously sprayed the player's ankle like he was trying to annihilate a city of fire ants. The fact that the player was wearing shoes, two pairs of socks, and already had athletic tape covering his ankles did not deter him. Could the spray really penetrate those layers to the skin for maximum effect? Sure, why not? The player recovered, thanks to the trainer's swift action. Come to think of it, I think the brand name on the can says "Placebo." *Quick, Gino's down—grab the Placebo.*

* * *

Similar to my rookie year in Holland, we started off the season fairly well but quickly began going the wrong way in the standings. We lost much more regularly than we won, and I wasn't playing very well offensively. It wasn't for a lack of effort. I just couldn't seem to get in a rhythm. Jobey, however, couldn't miss and was our most consistent player, averaging 20 points per game.

After one particular bad loss at home, I went out to eat with Jobey and his wife, Kristin, at our seven-euro fantasy-feast restaurant. I was very frustrated with my recent unproductive play, and the loss had ruined my night. But I noticed something very interesting about Jobey at dinner. He wasn't sulking in misery. He was just enjoying the meal and the social setting. You'd never know if he had won or lost or even played in a game that night. While he was extremely competitive on the floor in practices and in games, he didn't let losses bother him. I saw him get in the occasional skirmish with a teammate during practice, so there was no denying his competitive drive. He wasn't putting on an act. He wanted to win as much as or more than any of us, but he truly was able to let it go when the game ended.

Jobey was a devout Christian, and his faith in Christ was his foundation in life. He strived to live a life that honored God with his thoughts, words, and actions. It carried over onto the court, and he seemed to compete with a freedom and confidence that I haven't seen in many players.

I admired that about him, because I could dwell on losses with the best of them. Show me a depressed human who just got mugged, watched his dog get hit by a car, and lost a winning lottery ticket, and I'll show you a picture of me after a loss.

I could be pitiful. People loved being around me as much as an outbreak of syphilis. But I vowed to not allow a poor performance to ruin my world any longer. Life was too short, and no one would remember or care ten years from now. Maybe not even ten days from now.

* * *

Why do teams continue to not pay me what they're supposed to pay me?

Yet again, here I was talking to my agent, Max, and the team every week, trying to convince someone that they should be paying what they owed me. The team was more than a month behind, and I started to get nervous again. How long was this going to last? Do I need to purchase a weapon? My mind conjured up images of management laughing behind closed doors at the gullible American who was currently playing for free and might continue to do so for the remainder of the season.

We returned home after another loss on the road in November, and I was summoned into the head coach's office. Since it was a day off, I didn't exactly have a warm fuzzy feeling about all of this. Sure enough, he said that since our team had been struggling, we had to make a change. He didn't want to make a change, but we were not getting the production he expected from our Italian point guard. So he was going to bring in an American point guard and let me go. Coach said that they would try and help me find another job elsewhere in Europe, and I was free to continue to practice with the team in the meantime.

I tried to muster a tiny amount of dignity from the fact that I wasn't being directly replaced by a player who played my position. But it was little consolation, and I was still getting the ax. It's like your girlfriend breaking up with you saying, "It's not that I don't like you. I do. Just not enough anymore. Don't worry, I found someone I like more, but he looks and acts completely different from you. But I might have a friend who would like to get to know you, who lives in a different country. You understand, right?"

I wasn't surprised that I was the odd man out, as Jobey and Elton had been playing well. I hadn't been stinking the place up, but I wasn't setting the country on fire with my shooting, either. Not only was I not getting paid, now I was getting fired. Max said that my contract was guaranteed. Yeah, guaranteed to be a hassle.

* * *

Since I was now fourth out of three on the priority list of Americans employed by the club, I was forced out of my apartment and into a new one shared by an Italian teammate. My king bed turned into a solo mattress that sagged like a hammock, I was no longer a three-minute walk from a gelato store, and my bidet was officially a thing of the past. Not that we ever really became that acquainted with one another (the bidet that is; the gelato store and I were on a first-name basis). We'd eye each other up each morning, but I never felt the urge to use its services. Maybe it's the American in me that wasn't as comfortable with certain customs (note also: European nude beaches and grown men wearing Speedos in public). I was perfectly content with the typical American restroom routine, and the bidet was a bit more intrusive than I was accustomed to.

One day, I came home to overhear my teammate and his girlfriend bathing together. Thankfully, the bathroom door was closed, and I sneaked in and out of the apartment without causing an awkward scene. Although, who knows, given the Europeans' freedom of expressing themselves, it's entirely possible that I would have been the only one who thought things were awkward.

* * *

With the living and playing situation going the wrong direction, I was anxious to find a new team. Our new player, Gerard Abrams, went 5-for-5 from the three-point line in his first game, and I continued to search for reasons why I seemed to be the only person not able to put that funky-feeling ball in the hoop.

Gerard played well but got injured after two games. Since I was still under contract with the team, they asked me to play again until Gerard was healthy. While I felt a bit used, I had no better options. Max hadn't found another team for me, and the positive unrealistic side of me said, "Here's your chance to play your way back onto the team. A triple-double ought to confirm that you deserve to be here."

In the next game, I barely registered a single-single in limited minutes and was no more impressive than in my previous outings. I continued practicing with the team until February, when I got a call from none other than good old Herman. He wanted me to return to Zwolle, but on a stand-by basis, as they were having an issue with their American power forward, Steve Marshall.

Holland Immigration Services had shown up unannounced at Steve's door and ordered him to leave the country. Despite him being there legally for seven months, they determined that his visa was not valid. Dutch law required that foreigners could only be hired if there is no Dutch person who can perform the same duties, thus giving their own citizens first priority in the job market. Since Steve was "working" in Holland as a foreigner, the team had to prove that no other Dutch person could play basketball as well as him.

How exactly do you measure this? For an office job opening, do they have a typing war? Most words per minute wins the job? How about a sales job? I propose a battle of selling fake sunglasses on the street corner. For basketball, it would seem simple enough. A game of one-on-one should settle the score and get the authorities off of Steve's back. Maybe the government can send out a public service announcement to all 6-foot-8, 240-pound Dutch guys to meet at the gym for their "interview." It was ridiculous.

The team lawyers were working on the situation, and I was brought in as Backup Plan A if Steve was tossed out of the country. The good news was that I had a paying job again. The bad news was that the money was half of what I made in Zwolle last year, there was no guarantee that I'd even get to play in a real game, and I had to sleep in the laundry room. A few months earlier I was living the dream, playing in Italy, making decent money, and eating the best pasta and pizza on the planet. I now awoke to crusty socks drying above my head.

During games, I only cheered and recorded defensive stops, assignments given to me by The Hermanator. In practice, I matched up with Steve, which was more game-like than him pounding against Paulo, our 6-foot-3, 175-pound backup forward. The immigration police could walk through the door at any minute and escort Steve to the airport, so I had to be ready to step in.

* * *

Steve probably wished they had cuffed him and dragged him out before one Friday practice. It was actually Good Friday, which proved to be symbolic for the punishment we were about to take. While we were not flogged, beaten, and crucified like Jesus, it was the closest I think I've ever come to dying on a basketball court.

Herman was sitting on the side of the court while we were doing some free shooting. Out of nowhere he stood up and started shouting at a couple of players. "QUIT MESSING AROUND! I'VE SEEN ENOUGH!"

And then, the four worst words you can ever hear as a basketball player:

"GET ON THE LINE!"

We ran ten full-court sprints. I was exhausted and hoped we were done. As we paused to catch our breath between each one, I'd look over at Herman to see if that was it. He'd give us three to five seconds of recovery time if we were lucky. "GO!"

Baseline to baseline. Down and back. Over and over. "GO!"

We kept running.

And running.

"GO!"

There was no end in sight. He stopped timing us. "GO!" was all he said.

After probably forty sprints, one or two guys fell down. Herman yelled at them that we weren't finished yet. My legs were on fire. I couldn't hold my head up. The only thing I saw was the ground six inches in front of me. Pretty soon, I closed my eyes while I ran because I didn't have the energy to hold my eyelids open. I hoped I didn't run into anything and I would open them just before reaching the opposite baseline so I knew when to turn around. Starbucks started looking like my new dream job.

It was one of those tests where you wonder just how far your body will go. How long will your mind continue to tell your body to keep doing what it's doing before one or the other gives out?

And I was angry. Why was I even running? I wasn't the one who had been screwing around. At best, I was only a partial member of the team anyway, since I couldn't even play in games. Shouldn't I just be watching the pain instead of taking it?

Remarkably, I did not die, nor did anyone else. We ran somewhere in the area of 150 to 200 sprints that day, without rest. I can now thank Herman for setting a new mark for how exhausted a human body can feel prior to dying.

Good Friday, huh?

* * *

The immigration authorities never did show up for Steve. I was happy for him, of course. If I had been in his shoes, I wouldn't have wanted to be thrown out of the country, either. The closest I got to playing was in a couple of second-division games on crummy floors with some teammates whose names I didn't even know. It was time to head home. A half-season in Italy where I stunk it up, didn't get paid, and then got fired, followed by being a practice player for a team I used to actually play for … I needed a summer league back in the States full of out-of-shape middle-aged guys to get my mojo back.

Back in Italy, Imola had accomplished their mission and finished "not last" by just one game. But not before they fired the coach, too.

And I was still waiting on the rest of my salary.

Chapter 6

LIFE ON A TRAPEZE: URUGUAY, ACHILLES, AND ARMEN GILLIAM

It was back to the US for another summer of waiting and praying. I went to Hollidaysburg, Pennsylvania, again to be near Cara and make up for lost time. I was in South Carolina on vacation in early June 2004 when Max sent word of an invitation to the Treviso Summer League. Calling it a league is misleading because it's really just four days of practice and games. There wouldn't be any beer bellies or guys wearing jean shorts in this summer camp, but maybe it would inspire some better play out of me. It was a highly-acclaimed pro event in the summer, and dozens of pro coaches from around Europe came to scout the eighty players who were invited. Some even signed contracts on the spot.

I had nothing to lose. Correction—I had about $2,000 to lose, since that's what I paid for a plane ticket to Italy on two days' notice. My pricey flight was leaving the next day, and I was packing up at midnight. Luckily, I had my shoes with me on vacation in case I ran into some senior citizens looking for a run on outdoor courts in humid South Carolina.

All of the sudden I froze. My stomach hit the floor. I did not have my passport. It was on a nightstand beside my bed ... in Hollidaysburg, Pennsylvania. My flight left from South Carolina in about ten hours. The plane was leaving whether or not I was on it—along with my empty $2,000 seat. The camp would begin with or without me. *Lord, please let me find a way to get that passport.*

I called my friend Jim, whose guest room I was crashing in back in Pennsylvania for the summer. It was past 1 a.m. on a weekday. You know who your true friends are and who you can really count on when you wake them up in the middle of the night. Jim arranged for a high school kid he knew to drive my passport one hour to State College, Pennsylvania. I was part-way there; my connecting flight was from JFK Airport in New York, so I just needed to find a way to get the passport from State College to JFK.

I called a couple other friends in State College without any luck. *Who do I know that isn't working tomorrow, has a car, will pick up their phone now in the middle of the night, and drive ten hours' round trip on zero notice?* As 3 a.m. approached, I felt Italy slipping away.

Then I stumbled upon a winner. A guy I went to church with was actually going to JFK that same day to pick up his wife, who was returning from Russia. What are the chances? He received my passport from the high school kid in State College, and then drove five hours, meeting me just before my flight left for Italy. That, my friends, is a small miracle.

* * *

It felt good to be back in Italy, and I played well at the camp. I personally spoke to a couple of head coaches from France and Austria. I was coming off a subpar year, and the first question every coach asks is, "Where did he play last year?" The league you were in says a lot about your ability, at least in many coaches' minds. Max did all he could to work the crowd of coaches and push my services. Even though I started the season in Italy, the follow up questions of "How'd he do?" and "What were his numbers?" didn't hold their attention for long. Unfortunately, I left the camp without an offer or even any legitimate leads.

* * *

There was one highlight of the summer, though, and that was my engagement to Cara. I remember her saying early in our relationship that she thought the most romantic place in the world would be on the beach, at night, walking with someone you loved. There weren't any beaches in central PA, so I hatched a plan.

"I'm picking you up at 3 p.m.," I told Cara by phone one day in late June. "Bring your toothbrush, a swimsuit, a sweatshirt, and a pair of scissors." I had to throw her off so I named some random things for her to include in a small bag.

"Where are we going?" she asked.

"And a pinecone, too," I said, laughing inside.

"A pinecone?"

"Yeah, it's really important," I lied. Nothing like starting out a lifelong journey based on trust and faithfulness with a couple of fibs.

I loaded up the car with a guitar, three dozen roses, and a bunch of lottery tickets. Marrying me in all of my jobless glory might be quite a gamble, so I figured it was an appropriate way to begin. Scratch and win an unemployed guy with no income or legitimate housing, whose current fail-safe plan is to wait for a phone call. Regardless, it would help pass the time as we drove the four hours to Ocean City, New Jersey, the closest beach I could think of and thought I knew how to find.

Every few minutes during the drive I'd hand her a new rose and tell her to look for another Scratch 'n Win game hidden somewhere in the car. She loved those cards and it wasn't about the winning but instead the anticipation and excitement of the games. She probably knew what was about to happen, as we had been dating for three and a half years, but the fact that we just kept driving east without her knowing our destination made the mystery that much more interesting to her.

"Oh, are we going to Philly?" she asked as signs for Philadelphia passed by.

"I don't know," I said. "Maybe."

We passed Philly.

"Oooo, Atlantic City? I've never been there."

"We will see, won't we?" I said. It was actually better that she didn't know where we were headed, because I missed a key turn and ended up in Philadelphia traffic that turned our four-hour trip into six. Of course, I acted like it was all part of the plan.

We finally arrived at the beach and it was pitch black. I parked the car and grabbed the last rose.

"Close your eyes and wait here," I said.

Cara played along. I got out of the car and ran down the beach and stuck the rose in the sand in a place where I would be sure to notice it.

I went back to the car and drove a couple blocks down the beach and parked again. I took Cara's hand and grabbed my guitar. This was about to be one special night.

We walked along the beach and were the only ones out there. The cool ocean breeze was picking up force, but I was too nervous and excited to be worried about the temperature. Now, where was that rose? It was the kickoff of my whole proposal.

It started to sprinkle. *Oh, please no.* Then it was coming down harder and the sky was pitch black. *Seriously?*

Where is that stupid rose? Man, it was dark out there. A smarter version of me would have packed a flashlight.

"Hey, what's that?" I said, finally locating my poorly placed flower. "What is a rose doing right in the middle of the beach?"

Corny, I know. There's a fine line between romantic and corny. But at the time there was too much anticipation and excitement for me to care.

I pulled out my guitar and began to sing a song that no one had ever heard but her.

Then the rain really started to pour. *Crap, this is Jim's guitar!* I didn't know what water did to guitars, but I didn't want to find out.

Cara was freezing and we were getting soaked, so I put the performance on hold and we ran back to the car. We found a restaurant and ate a good meal. Thankfully, the rain stopped and I took Cara back out to the beach. I played her the song. Told her the many reasons why I loved her. That took a while. Promised her that I had no clue what the future held but that I'd do everything I could to make her happy and love her as she deserved. And I got down on one knee, took out a ring, and asked her to marry me.

She said yes.

Then we went skinny-dipping.

Yeah, right. It was freezing, after all.

As we walked back to the car, Cara asked, "What about the pine-cone?"

"What pinecone?" I asked.

"The one you said I needed to bring."

I had forgotten all about it.

"Oh yeah," I said, remembering my romantic head fake. "That was random. I just said it to keep you guessing. Did you bring it?"

"No, I didn't bring it!" she said. "You're so weird." She smiled.

True. But you still said yes.

* * *

My nerves were acting up again, as it was August, and I had no offers yet. I had a fiancée but no job. Not the finest start to the rest of our lives together. Nothing had developed from the camp in Italy. I went to a tryout for a new ABA minor league team called the Maryland Knighthawks and played well. They asked me to sign a contract for $350 per week. I negotiated with the owner and got it up to $500 per week, but I told him that I was hoping to get an opportunity over-seas. He allowed me an "out" clause in the contract if I landed a deal overseas. I handwrote it on the official contract in my own third-grade handwriting and faxed it back to him. I appreciated his flexibility.

I checked my email multiple times per day, hoping to get some good news. None of the five or six agents I contacted had anything.

Then, out of nowhere, an email popped up one morning from Daniel Morales. *Who is Daniel Morales?*

Some people don't like getting phone calls when they don't recog-nize the number or emails from names they can't identify. I loved it.

Answering "Unknown Caller" rings and seeing mysterious names in my inbox usually meant that something was in the mix and the more consonants in the name, the better.

"Tyler, I have a team for you in Uruguay that pays $3,500 per month, meals, bonus, etc. Do you want to come?—Daniel"

This email better not be some joke, I thought. I'd already been hustled once and wasn't keen on becoming a repeat victim. While it wasn't my ultimate six-figure goal, $3,500 was more than Holland but less than Italy (who, by the way, still owed me about $30,000).

And where was Uruguay? I had to break out my seventh-grade social studies map to find it. I figured it was in South America, but I wouldn't have bet my life on it. Uruguay, Paraguay, Faraway. I didn't know many players who'd played in South America and definitely not a soul who'd played in Uruguay. Still, it was a job, and a job is what I needed.

They wanted me to fly down in two days. Our first game was in less than a week. So much for prep time and long goodbyes. I was headed to the promised land.

I asked Daniel a few more questions and signed the contract. My first contract in Holland had been seven pages. Italy was three. Uruguay ... just one.

You play well. We pay you. Then you go home. Sign here.

I said another goodbye to Cara. This one was emotional as usual, but there was hope behind it as we planned to get married the following summer. Thankfully, this would be our last season apart, which was already more than either of us wanted. Any way you look at it, long distance sucked.

After nineteen hours of traveling, I landed in Montevideo, the capital of Uruguay. I remembered the name of the city from my middle school geography classes, because we always thought it was so funny that "video" was in the name of a city. Ah, junior high humor.

My head coach, Javier, and one other guy picked me up at the airport. I was exhausted and thankful finally to be there. The lengthy trip to Montevideo made the flights to Europe seem like a quick drive around the block.

Javier was a cheerful fellow, about forty years old, short, and had a belly. He spoke pretty good English, and I got positive Latin American vibes from him right away. The driver did not speak any English and had a serious look on his face.

We merged our very old and very suspect vehicle onto the highway, and I saw a sign that said "Salto," my new home for the next eight months—"600 km."

Six-hundred kilometers? That's at least six hours, assuming we don't break down by the time we get there. The roads looked like an earthquake had cracked them in pieces and if they had used paint at one point to separate lanes, it was long gone. Pass if you feel like passing, stop if you feel like stopping. The speed limit was whatever your particular vehicle could handle. And ours was no Lamborghini. Then, I came to find out that Salto had an airport. What the —? But naturally, it wasn't open on Sundays.

Daniel said that a majority of the teams were located in Montevideo. We were one of the three exceptions. We were located the furthest from the capital city. While other teams would have a five- or ten-minute car ride to an away game within Montevideo, our trips would be over six hours each way on these awesome roads. A small detail Daniel forgot to mention.

I sat next to the driver, with Javier in the back seat. I looked back at one point and saw him holding a leather cup with a metal straw sticking out of it. Packed to the top of the cup was some kind of dark greenish herbal leafy stuff. Javier sucked on the metal straw and smiled.

"Do you know what this is?" he said.

Something illegal?

"I have no clue," I said.

"Do you think it's *drogas?*" he laughed.

Pretty sure he just said "drugs" in Spanish.

"Uh, I really don't know. What is it?"

"It's *mate* (MAH-tay)," he said. "It's what we drink in Uruguay. But it's not drugs."

Maybe. Maybe not. But one thing I do know: if you get pulled over sucking on that contraption in the back seat of a car in the US, you're gonna need a good lawyer.

* * *

We stopped for lunch about halfway through our drive at a random restaurant on the side of the road. Nothing but cow pastures in view.

"Here, you should try this," said Javier. "It's called *chorizo*."

It looked like a sausage, just with more visible fat. Let the South American experience begin. Remarkably, it was nothing short of amazing. Possibly the best sausage I'd ever eaten.

"OK, now try this one," he said.

"What is it?" I asked. It was also shaped like a sausage, but was much darker, almost black. I was 50-50 on whether I should continue with the experimentation. I couldn't imagine it tasting superior to the chorizo, but if it was anything like my first taste test, I was game.

"I'll tell you after you eat it," he said with a smile.

It doesn't matter what country you're in. That response is never a good sign and should alert the guinea pig to excuse himself to the bathroom in order to collect his thoughts. But I was trying to show that we Americans do branch out and appreciate other cultures.

I popped a fat round piece in my mouth and began to chew.

Oh no, this is not like the chorizo. It's like the dirty-sewer slum cousin of chorizo. It shares the same shape, but that's all.

I didn't know if I'd be able to swallow it in front of them.

Get it down. Get it down. Drink something. There's no throwing up in front of the coach and random driver guy within your first three hours of arriving in Uruguay.

They laughed at the look on my face.

"What was that?" I said after I forced it into my stomach, now sweating and reaching for my water.

"Cow's blood," Javier said.

"What! Blood isn't solid," I gasped. It made no sense.

"Yes, it's cow's blood, and that is how they make it here," Javier said.

I didn't want any further details. *From now on, I'll keep it simple. Chorizo good. Cow's blood bad. Check, please.*

* * *

We arrived at the Hotel Eldorado in the middle of downtown Salto, my home for the next eight months. There wasn't an elevator, but my room was on the second floor. The lobby was small. The hallway was small. The stairs weren't wide enough to place my full shoe as I ascended. I was starting to see a disturbing pattern.

When I opened the door to my room, I wanted to cry. There was a bed and a small wooden desk and chair built for a six-year-old. There wasn't room for a TV, so they bolted the tiny set to the wall up high in the corner. There was a small closet where I tried to stuff my bags without much success. The bathroom was ancient and covered in broken faded green tiles. I'd been there all of twenty seconds and was already feeling claustrophobic. Sadly, I didn't feel much hope of finding a better living situation, as the whole city seemed in dire need of a facelift.

Did they really expect me to live here all season? I might not last eight minutes. Please tell me this is temporary.

But I knew it wasn't. This was what they had. I had just flown nineteen hours and ridden another six to a glorified prison cell. Keep all sharp objects away from me.

I was desperate for a hint of hope when a verse instantly popped into my head. *I can be content in any and every situation.* I didn't know where it was in the Bible exactly, but I remembered that the apostle Paul was writing those words from prison. If he could be hopeful from a first-century prison cell, I could make the effort to find my happy place in a third-world hotel room.

* * *

Our gym was straight out of the Middle Ages minus only the moat and gallows. It was an old cement and brick building on the outskirts of town. I walked in and hoped we had come to the wrong place. A cage separated the spectators behind one basket. The playing floor was something between brick and cement. The only wood in the area was the trees outside. It was a decent size gym that sat about 3,000, but it was built to caveman standards. Row after row of cement block seating surrounded the court, the bathrooms had holes in the floor rather than toilets, and (surprise!) never had toilet paper. Super convenient on game days.

A reporter and cameraman approached me courtside.

"They want to ask you a few questions," Javier said. Naturally, the new large white American was probably big news in this small town. Maybe we should call it a village. But that implies huts and smoke signals. OK, village.

"Sure, no problem," I smiled. Part of me enjoyed being a novelty, if only in a remote place called Salto, which I think means "I jump" in Spanish. That, or "I'm salty." Given my utter lack of leaping ability, I found it quite fitting that of all cities in the world, I'd end up in the one that mocks my verticality.

The random agent Señor Morales sends me a random email to play in a random country in a random city that means "I jump," when I clearly can't. God does indeed have a sense of humor.

The reporter fired off a question in machine-gun Spanish and stuck the microphone about a half-inch from my mouth. The camera was live. And Javier suddenly was nowhere to be found.

Crap. I'm going to have to do this in Spanish? I'd had a couple years of it in high school and one semester in college. That was centuries ago. And my mind strained to remember the basics.

What did I have in my Español weaponry? I had no idea what the question even was. He could have asked any number of things, "How old were you when you began to play basketball? What's your favorite food? Have you ever owned a dog? We eat them here." *The mic is hot. Say something, Smith.*

"*Hola, me gusta Uruguay,*" I said in the worst I'm-not-from-here accent ever. Somewhere deep in the trenches of my brain's neuro-pathways, a sliver of Spanish re-emerged, and I went into some unknown monologue that included something about the library, my *pantalones*, and Cinco de Mayo.

Tonight on the 11 o'clock news: The new American basketball player claims to have ridden his bicycle to Salto and talks about not liking homework. Thanks for nothin', Javier.

* * *

"Hi, I'm Diego," one of my new teammates said.

Thank you, my friend. It was so good to hear English. While I was excited in theory about getting to use my Spanish in real-life situations, I needed some time to crank it back up to speed. Unlike Holland and Italy where there were three Americans on the team, I was the lone expat here, so the only thing I had in common with my new Uruguayan teammates (that I knew of) was that we all breathed oxygen, liked basketball, and ate food (if you call cow's blood food).

Diego introduced me to the rest of the players, a few of whom spoke a little English. Then he turned to me and said, "You will come to my house tomorrow for dinner."

Did he just invite me over for dinner? Or was that an order? It was definitely phrased as a statement. I had to laugh at this young guy telling me what I was going to do mañana. But who was I to argue? I'd been in the country all of twelve hours and already managed to embarrass all future generations of Smiths on Uruguayan TV.

Diego, if you are willing to feed me, I'm there. It beats whatever I would be making in the imaginary kitchen of my miniature hotel room. Maybe that's just how they rolled in Uruguay. You just tell people what will happen. You don't ask. "I'll come to your house for lunch today. You'll do my laundry. You pass to me, and I'll shoot the ball a lot."

* * *

Diego lived outside of town and his house was an interesting setup. The kitchen and living area were in one building, and the bedrooms were in a separate small house entirely, just a few steps away. It was one story and small but very quaint. He had dial-up Internet in his room, which was about the same size as my Hotel Eldorado accommodations, just with more basketball posters. His whole family was there, including his two older sisters, who spoke terrific English, and mom and dad.

Diego's mom was a very sweet lady who greeted me with the biggest kisses I'd had since the last time I saw my own grandmother. She had a raspy voice from years of smoking and spoke in extra slow Spanish just for me like I was a three-year-old. It turned out to be perfect since that was roughly my language level.

Diego's father owned a fair amount of land and spoke of their most recent problems. Poachers had been sneaking onto their land and killing cattle for the meat, then disappearing into the night and leaving the massive carcasses to rot. I took it all in and appreciated them treating me like a part of the family. We ate some delicious barbeque called *asado*, but of course they tried to get me to eat intestines stuffed with some sort of mysterious filling. Why couldn't they just eat the normal parts of animals? It was kind of gross and fascinating all at the same time.

"So Tyler," Diego said, shifting to the front of his seat at the table. He had an excited look in his eye. This was going to be good. "What do Americans think of Uruguay?"

He asked with such anticipation. He was genuinely interested in how his country was seen by outsiders. He had never been to the United States but dreamed of going someday. I could tell he was hopeful for a rousing answer of "It's every American's dream to visit and experience this beautiful land!" Sadly, I didn't have a real positive response for him.

What do Americans think of Uruguay? Um, we don't really think of Uruguay.

"Well," I began. "To be honest, we don't really know that much about Uruguay. We are more familiar with Brazil and Argentina because they are larger countries down here. Americans tend to travel to Europe more than South America."

The answer seemed to satisfy him.

"What do you think of the US?" I asked.

"Tyler, it's my *dream* to go to the USA," he smiled. "You have the NBA, Hollywood, and so many great things there to see. But it is very expensive to go there, and you must have a visa."

"So you can't just get a plane ticket and go visit?" I asked.

"No, we must have a real reason to go there, like for work or to see family," he said. "I cannot just go on vacation. It is a long process to get a visa, and that costs money, too. You must pay for the application, but there is no guarantee that you will be accepted. But someday I will go. I *must* go."

"Well, you can always come and stay with me," I offered. Not that I had a place to stay. But maybe by the time he finally got a visa I would finally have more than a carpeted floor for him in a friend's house.

* * *

Javier pulled me aside one day during practice before our first game.

"Tyler, you will be one of our main players," he said.

Awesome. Tell me more, amigo.

"You'll shoot about fifteen to twenty shots per game," he said.

"OK," I nodded in agreement, trying to withhold the shock that my brain was attempting to process.

I got the coveted green light, every player's dream. Fifteen to twenty—I had never shot that much for any team since gym class in high school. Even when players have the freedom to shoot, there isn't always an outright discussion of it between player and coach. It's often just a silent understanding. Here we were, not having played our first game, nor had Javier seen any film on me, and I was handed the title of first option in the offense. All he had to go on was a few practices during my first week. They expected a lot from their lone American. But now in my third pro season I was more comfortable being aggressive and not worrying about taking too many shots. I was more than ready to get my Kobe on. Let it rain.

* * *

We pulled up to our first home game and were greeted by thirty fully armed police decked out in riot gear with shields, batons, and helmets. Is there something I should know? Is the president coming to the game or is there a chance we will be attacked by lions? I'd left my Glock at the hotel.

We opened up the season against a team from Montevideo named Welcome. Welcome to what? How about Welcome to the greatest show on earth?

If I thought Italy had rowdy fans, they were like little school kids compared to the Uruguayan crazies. Their drums and chants were deafening thanks to the rockin' acoustics in our brick-and-concrete bunker. Midway through the game, some fans ran onto the court and I discovered why we had invited the riot police. Fans were threatening the referees. Coaches were screaming at the fans. Not exactly the family-friendly atmosphere you'd find at Disney. It took about fifteen minutes to get everyone off of the floor and back to some sense of organization before resuming play.

I turned to Edmund Saunders, the American on the other team. "Is it always like this?" I asked.

"Don't worry," he said. "It gets worse. Welcome to Uruguay."

* * *

Our second game was a 9 p.m. tipoff in Montevideo against Cordón. We left Salto on game day at 10 a.m. and drove six and a half hours to some random house in the middle of downtown Montevideo. We sat around for a couple hours and munched on some questionable sand-wiches and snacks for our pregame meal.

When we arrived at the gym, I had to use the bathroom. This had been my pregame routine for the last ten years. Somehow, my body always knew it was time to go about ninety minutes before tipoff. I can't explain it.

I found the restroom at the gym, but there was a problem. No toilet paper. What is the big deal with toilet paper? Is it expensive or rare? I found my teammates in the locker room and explained my pre-dicament.

"Johnny!" shouted our team captain, Bicho (BEE-cho), across the locker room. "Tyler needs the toilet paper!"

Johnny was our team manager and he dug in one of his equipment bags and handed me a fresh roll. Am I the only one who found it strange that we carried our own toilet paper to away games?

Bicho wasn't his real name. Bicho is best translated as an annoying tick that clings onto a dog or some animal in warm climates. His real name was Luís, but he earned his nickname when he was young because of his feisty and relentless way of playing. He had endless energy and he'd make many key plays that changed games. He could score off drives, from the three-point line or from flopping to get to the free throw line. At 6-foot-2, he was built like a tank, strong and fearless. He'd get into scuffles nearly every single game because of his rough style of play. But he was also clever and always seemed to get away with questionable antics that the refs either didn't notice or simply ignored because he was something of a legend.

Bicho's signature move was to shove a defender into one of our teammates as we were shooting, drawing a foul on the other team and sending us to the free throw line. Most of those plays would never have resulted in free throws, as the defender was far enough away not to touch the shooter. But Bicho would nudge him as hard as he needed, often with two hands to the defender's back, to make sure that the defender collided with our player who had the ball. He was one of those players you hated to play against but loved when he was on your team. Opponents despised him for good reason. As far as I was concerned, he was our X factor. I'd never seen another player like him who could hit big shots, make huge defensive plays, and get into the other team's heads. There wasn't a more appropriate nickname on the planet.

After I successfully navigated the restroom situation, I dropped 34 points on Cordon. It earned me the respect and credibility with my team that I needed. And I even convinced myself that 15 to 20 shots per game were now necessary. We drove through the night back to Salto and arrived home at 6:30 a.m. One eventful road trip down, about twenty more to go.

* * *

Possibly the best part of my contract was the free food. As in Italy, my team had a restaurant sponsor—La Caldera ("The Black Kettle"). It was a ten-minute walk from my hotel, and I went there every day for lunch and dinner. I could order anything I wanted, and the owner, Eduardo, was a terrific guy. He was gregarious and full of life. There must be something in the water down there, because I had yet to meet a shy Uruguayan.

As I ate my meal at the bar one day, a guy pulled up to the restaurant on a scooter and carried in a noticeably heavy clear-plastic bag with something messy and bloody inside. He walked right through the restaurant and greeted Eduardo with a kiss on the cheek, the standard greeting among friends (we'll come back to this). Eduardo smiled as he grabbed his delivery bag and then looked at me.

"What's that?" I asked. I'm not sure why I inquired. Maybe I was curious or maybe I was just being polite. The bag was even bigger up close than when it had first appeared. Delivery Dan needed two hands to hoist it up over the counter.

Eduardo was beaming.

"*Lengua*," he said and pointed to his tongue. Then he opened the bag for me to see. I definitely could have done without the visual, but it was too late, as I'd made the mistake of asking, and Eduardo was obviously enthusiastic about showing me.

Massive cow tongues.

My face somehow gave away that I wasn't used to seeing detached cow tongues on the counter next to me while I ate lunch. Eduardo found it all quite amusing.

"Quieres comerlo?" he asked.

I'd rather eat the waiter's socks, but thanks.

"No, gracias, Eduardo," I said.

He laughed again.

This became the running joke between us, and he asked me every day from then on if I wanted to eat his cow tongue delicacy. As much as I wanted to appease the locals, I was quickly discovering that I needed to hold my ground on certain issues.

* * *

I was having a hard time getting used to the kissing greeting. A handshake or hug seemed perfectly acceptable. But I wasn't used to the greeting *and* getting pulled in for some kissing. If I started kissing all my guy friends and every woman I was introduced to upon re-entry to the States, there would be rumbles.

I mean, I get it. It's a much more intimate sign of "hello" than a handshake. The kiss says, "I care about you so much that I'm willing to kiss you publicly, even if you really smell or have not shaved since the late '80s." That's called love.

The handshake says, "Listen, it's nice to see you and all, but let's keep our distance in case things get awkward. I might not like you tomorrow, and it will be better if we didn't get too involved." The Uruguayans had no problem expressing their passion. The kiss made sense to them.

Eventually, I became more comfortable and figured "why not?" I started kissing everybody, and the locals thought it was great. I was kissing my agent, guys on the team, and basically anyone I greeted. I was half-Uruguayan at that point.

One thing is for sure. Americans aren't ready for the kiss.

* * *

Besides La Caldera, one of my other favorite spots in Salto was the Internet café. For less than fifty cents an hour, I could stay in touch with everyone back home. I think every kid under twelve in Salto visited the café on a regular basis, as well, to play video games. These kids didn't have the money to buy their own gaming systems at home, so they would visit the café to get their fix. With almost no living expenses to speak of, it seemed insane that one of my big expenditures was three dollars worth of Internet, even after tossing in an extra hour or two for a couple of the boys I'd gotten to know who were avid gamers.

My other splurge was fresh orange juice. Our main sponsor was Caputto, a massive fruit-exporting company. It exported fruit to countries all over the world except for the United States because our regulations were too stringent. Caputto was a big employer to many citizens of Salto and, as a result, there was no shortage of fresh fruits and juices in local stores. I regularly brought home a three-gallon jug of freshly squeezed orange juice for about $1.75. Since fresh OJ runs about four dollars per glass at most breakfast places back home, this was the citrus deal of a lifetime. Pulp and I get along famously.

* * *

One afternoon I was reading a book on my stroll to La Caldera for lunch. It was one of John Feinstein's captivating works on basketball, and I was completely in the zone. I was using my savvy peripheral vision to navigate while I read and walked along the crumbling city sidewalk toward the restaurant.

Suddenly, I felt a sharp pain along the side of my face. Something had sliced my cheek and ear, and I jerked my head away from the pain. It was as if a razor blade had sheared off eight layers of skin. The side of my head burned and I wondered if I had lost an ear. I'd run into a store sign hanging out over the sidewalk. A rusty metal sign. Perfect. When was my last tetanus shot?

I put my hand up to my ear and it was bleeding like crazy. *Real smooth, van Gogh.* Fortunately, my ear was still attached. But it turned out that a mole I'd sported for years had been ripped clean off. I never liked that mole anyway, and I often considered having it removed. But slashing my head against a corroded South American sign wasn't the procedure I'd envisioned. So much for my peripheral vision and secret dreams of being a point guard.

* * *

We played a team called Unión Atletica at home a short time later. Everyone was raving about a thirty-five-year-old Cuban named Richard Matienzo on their team. He was a rock star in Uruguay and a big-time scorer.

I found out quickly why he was always one of the top scorers in the league. He shot *every time* he touched the ball. He was strong and still fairly athletic for a guy born in the 1960s. He tried to post me up and jump into me to draw a foul each time. I was doing back bends on defense for the first fifteen minutes of the game trying to avoid him hurling his body at me.

Offensively, I was having another great game, with almost 20 points already in the first half. With three minutes to go in the half, out of nowhere, one of Unión Atletica's team directors walked out onto the court screaming at the refs while the ball was in play. He was furious at one of their calls or no-calls or missed calls. It all ran together, frankly.

The refs in Uruguay were beyond horrendous, so I understood Unión Atletica's frustration. The game was stopped and attempts were made to get the lunatic off the floor. He screamed at one ref, then another, and another. He threw his hands wildly all over the place and pointed fiercely at each of the refs. His own team tried to get him off the floor, but he wouldn't budge. Our home crowd whistled and chanted and tried to threaten him off the floor. The riot police even came out and tried unsuccessfully to reason with him. I stood sweating a few feet away, amused at the whole circus.

Then the head referee, who had been taking the majority of the verbal thrashing, cleared himself of the small melee at half-court. He faced the scorer's table, blew his whistle three times, and waved his arms above his head.

Game over.

That's it?! He can do that?

He walked out with the other two refs. Since we were ahead at the time and it was their fan who caused the problems, we won. There would be no rematch. Classic.

Again, I understood the anger over the referees. To quote my high school baseball coach, "If you look at a map, here's brutal ... they were three states away." Refereeing is a difficult task, for sure. I'd get a taste of it a few months later, and it's one of the toughest jobs in sports.

But c'mon. Can we get a little self-control? This was a basketball game. No one's life is at stake ... I don't think. It appeared that everyone lost their sense of reality (and manners) as they walked in the gym doors.

The previous season, an American player in Uruguay lost his cool and decked the referee with about three seconds left in the game. The ref's face was crushed and he needed major surgery. The player was thrown in jail and told that he'd be there at least six months. About the last place on earth I'd ever want to be is in a third-world prison. Reportedly, if you didn't know somebody inside, you didn't eat. The player got lucky, though, and was bailed out less than a week later before he starved. Needless to say, he never set foot in Uruguay again.

* * *

I was having the best basketball season of my life. Our team was in first place. I had the green light and was in the top three in scoring at around 22 points per game, depending on which scorekeeper you talked to. "The White Tower," as Diego told me the papers had nick-named me, had found his groove. (And with that third-person refer-ence, I'm officially a cocky full-of-himself athlete.)

There was only one problem.

My right Achilles tendon was killing me.

I had the worst tendinitis I had ever felt, and with no trainer to speak of, ice and Aleve were the best treatments on hand. And they were proving to be as useful as a snow blower in the summer.

I went to see the movie *Troy* starring Brad Pitt on a Friday night. Movies ran about two dollars and were shown in English, with Span-ish subtitles. At the end of the movie, an arrow pierced the back of Pitt's character's (Achilles') heel, and I felt his pain. Mine would not go away.

That Sunday, we practiced in the oldest gym known to man. My tendon was still screaming at me, and the gym floor wasn't helping. Although the playing surface was surprisingly made of wood, there were literally holes the size of shoes in multiple places. We simply steered clear of them during drills. About a dozen birds flew overhead, in and out of the broken windows. And my favorite part of the gym was the old-school game clock on the wall with the revolving second hand. Straight *Hoosiers* style. The coach tried to convince me that back in the '50s the "world championship" was held there. I'm not sure which world championship he was referring to. *Sure, Javier. And I was the No. 1 pick in the draft. The Lake Bluff, Illinois, Precision Lawn Mower Drill Team Draft.* (Hometown reference.)

On Monday, we drove to Montevideo to take on Defensor. They played in a tiny gym on a concrete floor just as rock-hard as our home court. The perfect place to injure backs, ankles, knees, or any part of the human body. The only plus was that the court was about thirty feet too short. The three-point line was within a step of the half-court circle. It was like playing on the side rims at a YMCA. You never got tired.

My Achilles continued to throb during warmups on the granite-like surface, but once the game started, the adrenaline took over and I didn't notice it.

I scored 10 quick points in the first quarter and was feeling great. Then I caught the ball in transition and pushed off my right foot to go to my left and ... bam! I collapsed to the floor and was livid.

Who tripped me? Uruguayans are such dirty players! Forget the players, that had to have been a fan! All these thoughts raced through my mind in an instant, and I looked behind me to find the culprit so I could chew him out.

Then the pain hit. The worst pain of my entire life. While I will never give birth to a baby, childbirth would have to be the only comparison to the excruciating pain I was feeling. To all the female readers who brave childbirth, I humbly tip my cap.

It felt like someone had sliced my Achilles in two with a samurai sword. My tendon rolled up my leg like a window shade made of razor blades. I screamed and clutched my leg until the pain subsided. Thankfully, it wasn't fourteen hours of labor. Because fourteen seconds was plenty.

I spent the next week in a hotel room in Montevideo that was twenty times nicer than the one I called home in Salto. Seeking medical advice, I called the United States directly to speak with my trainer from Penn State, which was probably costing a fortune, but our team sponsor said not to worry about it. The team offered to pay for my surgery there in Uruguay, or I could have it done in the United States and I would have to cover the difference.

But one problem was that I didn't have health insurance back home. While I didn't want to shell out five to seven thousand dollars in the States for a surgery that would be free in Montevideo, I also didn't feel comfortable with a surgeon who didn't speak English opening my leg. How do you say "It's the *right leg*" in Spanish? Our team doctor, while not a surgeon, was a chain-smoker, for goodness sake. Who knows what the guy in the operating room is on?

It ended up being an easy decision. Thankfully, I was able to arrange to have the surgery at Princeton University's medical center, where I knew one of the team physicians, Margot Putukian. She set me up with their orthopedic surgeon, Jeffrey Bechler, who operated on all of the Princeton athletes.

As I lay there by myself in a Uruguayan hotel room for five days without so much as taking a single step outside, I had plenty of time to consider my not-so-promising future. The team still owed me my salary since I had been there for almost two full months and hadn't been paid yet. I was facing surgery that would cost more than what I'd made to that point in the season. Then, there was the minimum of nine months of rehab. Who was going to want me next year after a major injury?

Maybe this was it. My season, and possibly my career, were completely over just as I was playing the best basketball of my life. I was headed into marriage without a job, plan, money, or an Achilles. My fiancée sure picked herself a winner.

Stupid *Troy* movie.

* * *

And yet in some strange way, I was really at peace with all of it. I truly felt that God had His hand on the situation despite it seeming like a crappy one. This was an opportunity to really put my faith to the test. Did I really trust that God could take the bad and turn it into good? Or would I dive into depression and paralysis with a "Why me?" attitude? Clearly there was plenty to worry about, but I trusted that He already saw this coming miles away, and I believed that He would lead me to better places.

What were the chances of *Troy* being released that week in Uruguay and me seeing the invincible Mr. Brad Pitt-Achilles get taken out by his heel, his only vulnerable spot, three days prior to tearing my own tendon? It was too eerie to pass it off as a coincidence. If the Lord saw this coming, then surely He knew what would happen next. While I believed that He had good things in mind, I wasn't naïve enough to think that I was immune to the bad. This was real life. Jesus doesn't promise to steer us around every challenge life throws at us. But He does promise to walk with us every step of the way. Maybe I just need to stay away from the theatre.

One other small issue was that while my current Montevideo hotel was a half-hour from freedom, otherwise known as the airport, all my belongings were six hours north, strewn across a much uglier hotel room in Salto. I had to trek six hours on a bus back to Salto, pack up, limp around to say my goodbyes, and bus six more hours back to Montevideo.

As I checked out of the Montevideo hotel to make my way back to Salto, one of the bellhops I'd befriended came over. He loved basketball and I had given him my basketball shoes the day before when he saw that I was going to throw them in the trash. They were completely shot in terms of foot support and smelled as fresh as the landfill on a hot humid day, not to mention the fact that I had just suffered a major injury while wearing them. I had no intention of bronzing them and couldn't imagine someone else finding any value in them. But if he thought they were worth keeping, who was I to steal his dreams?

"Señor Smith," he said as he handed me a pen and piece of paper. "Can you please sign this and write a short note that says it is okay that I take these shoes? I do not want anyone to suspect that I stole them without your permission."

"Absolutely," I said.

What a fantastic young man. I admired his integrity, character, and work ethic. There was no way my size 14's would fit him. Maybe it was just a souvenir to him. But I wouldn't be surprised if he considered wearing them to play pickup ball. Basketball shoes were very expensive in Uruguay. And I had witnessed a similar situation a few weeks earlier, when I gave away a pair of my ankle braces that had seen their last day. Or at least I thought so. My teammate was thrilled to have another pair of braces, no matter how ancient they were. The rest of our team secured their ankles with Ace bandage wraps that looked like they'd been passed down three generations. It was unbelievable to me that these guys who were pros wrapped their own ankles with shredded old Ace bandages.

* * *

After arriving in Salto by bus, I packed my things and said a cheerful adios to my hotel room, thankful that I would never have to spend another night in that tiny place. Not only was it small, but a band played full blast at a bar right outside my window the night before every home game from 10 p.m. to 4 a.m. Oh the memories we made together, Hotel Eldorado.

Diego's sister drove me around town to say goodbyes. I had come to know a fair number of people pretty well in a short amount of time, and I wanted them to know that I appreciated them welcoming me so graciously in their town.

When we reached the Salto bus station where I'd catch my lift back to Montevideo, the place was packed. Camera crews and photographers were there, along with a large crowd. They had come to say goodbye to me.

I was blown away. People were smiling and shaking my hand. I may have kissed over half the town goodbye. Some people were even crying. The Pope did not die, my friends.

"Tyler, you must come back to Salto," one man said with a smile.

"I'd love to," I replied.

"No, no. You *must* come back next season," he insisted.

"OK," I smiled. "I'll try. Let me get healthy first."

And tell our team president to pay me. That would help things.

Actually, he did pay me for one month in cash on my way to the airport. Nothing like traveling with $3,500 in your pocket. I hoped I wouldn't get mugged, because I couldn't have chased down a vending machine. He assured me the rest of the payment would be wired to me.

Sure it would.

* * *

In terms of comfort level, the Achilles surgery sucked. Getting my right leg numbed was as much fun as being struck by lightning over and over. Then, the night after my surgery, I woke up screaming for help after the pain medication wore off and it seemed like a knife was slicing through the back of my leg again. But as for repairing my tendon, Dr. Bechler said it had been a success. You can really only take a doctor at his word on these things. He could have wrapped it with duct tape, for all I knew, and thrown a cast on. He also said the tendon looked like it had gone through a shredder, but that it had been a "pretty standard" procedure.

Standard.

Standard is getting water with your dinner at a restaurant. Standard is commercials during a TV show. When "standard" means tying pieces of the inside of another person's body back together, you are carrying a completely different skillset than the rest of us.

* * *

I moved back to State College to do my rehab at Penn State with the basketball trainers there. Jon "Saz" Salazar took great care of me during my senior year at PSU, and he was gracious enough to let the insurance-less nomad come in and do rehab there with him. He had a full plate already, managing fifteen players' daily health issues and the occasional coach who needed mending. Nevertheless, he and his grad student from Japan, Sumie (SOO-me-ay), got me moving again.

* * *

I needed something to do besides rehab so I didn't lose my mind and start doing heroin or stealing little kids' bikes. Preferably, something legal that paid in dollars. Italy still owed me about $30,000 and Uruguay owed me $10,000. But it wasn't like I could send Dog the Bounty Hunter to go collect. My agents were working on it, but at the end of the day, if a team didn't want to pay, I was stuck with an empty wallet.

I put my Telecommunications degree to use and started working the men's and women's basketball games as a camera operator. It paid *something*, which was more than what my rehab was paying, and I got to be a part of the production crew, which was enjoyable, because I was part of a new kind of team.

But the best part about being home was getting to spend more time with Cara. She was working an hour away in Hollidaysburg, so we usually hung out on the weekends. One day we were walking to a local restaurant when a car pulled up beside us.

"Hey man, do you play basketball?" the driver said. He was African-American and looked pretty big jammed inside his sedan.

Kind of random. Especially at 8 p.m. on a weekday when other cars were driving past. But my ego was happy to answer affirmatively.

"Yes, I do," I said. The more truthful statement would have been, "Yes, I *did* play basketball up until a month ago when my leg blew up. Now I just limp."

"Where do you play? I'm the coach over at Penn State-Altoona," he said.

That's cool, but is he really trying to recruit me on the side of the road in a random neighborhood?

"My name's Armen Gilliam," he said.

The name rang a bell and I explained my lame-duck status.

"Hey, come on over to campus and visit me, because I could use a good assistant coach," he said.

And just like that, my second job was born.

* * *

Armen was one of a kind. He was 6-foot-9, 250 pounds, and in great shape for a forty-year-old. He played racquetball, was really into nutrition, and had a genuine love for basketball. He was the No. 2 pick in the 1987 NBA draft and played thirteen years in the league, for six different teams.

And here he was in Altoona, Pennsylvania, trying to breathe some life into a struggling Division III program. Clearly he didn't need the money. But he needed to be around the game. Armen loved being in the gym and would play one-on-one against anybody. He was friendly and very intelligent.

On our first road trip, we stopped to eat at Cracker Barrel. He challenged me to a game of checkers. I took it seriously and beat him the first game. He couldn't believe it and then began to take it seriously, too. He put on a checkers clinic the next three games and destroyed me. Thankfully, our food came before I was embarrassed any further.

On another road trip, we were in the middle of who-knows-where Pennsylvania with only a couple of fast-food options for our meal-stop. The players chose McDonald's, and after they hopped out, he told the driver to head over to the grocery store. Since I was the assistant, I went with what he wanted. My Quarter Pounder would have to wait.

"Hey, you guys have any vegetables?" Armen asked the first employee he saw.

"Yeah, over in the deli," the employee said.

On a road trip where you just got hammered by 20 and then stop to eat, who's in the mood to go the extra mile for soggy spinach? Armen, that's who. He took care of himself and it showed.

We talked pro basketball a lot, and he still had the itch to play.

"If you hear of anything good come up, let me know," he told me.

"Armen, you're coaching now," I said. You're *forty*. You haven't played in *five* years.

"Yeah, but you never know," he smiled.

One agent in Europe that I knew had an open job for $10,000 per month in France. To me, ten grand a month was unfathomable. I'd play at the North Pole without shoes for that money. It was three times what I was making in Uruguay. And I bet they ate a lot less intestines in France. Maybe even got paid in full.

I knew it would take a big offer for him to even think about going. I thought that he might go for it.

I mentioned it to Armen.

"Ten-thousand, huh?" he asked.

"Yeah, plus all the bonuses and usual stuff," I said.

"Yeah," he said thoughtfully. "I think they'd have to sweeten the deal a little bit."

Sweeten the deal? It's already got eight layers of hot fudge and a cherry on top! Then again, during his NBA days he probably made $10,000 during his commute to practice.

* * *

In February, my Salto team (that still hadn't paid me) flew Cara and me down to cheer for them since they had advanced to the playoff semifinals. They said they wanted me there as "inspiration," and I found it to be a kind gesture on their part. Funny, they wouldn't follow through with my salary payments, but they spent a couple grand on plane tickets for us.

After I had been injured in October, the team asked me to recommend a power forward to them. I suggested my former college teammate, Gyasi Cline-Heard, who was very strong, athletic, and dunked way more than I did. Truthfully, I didn't think Gyasi would take the job because he could make more money in other places. But he was available and accepted their offer. Gyasi had been tearing up the league since he arrived and here they were, just two games from the finals.

When Cara and I landed in Montevideo, we had that six-hour drive ahead of us, and I needed to prepare her for the insanity that was driving in Uruguay.

"Cara, listen," I said. "It's going to seem like we will crash and die multiple times during this trip. But we won't."

"Great," she said. "I came to Uruguay to die."

After five minutes in the back seat and numerous near misses already by our driver, Cara turned to me. "You weren't lying."

Salto won both semifinal games while we were there, and Gyasi hit the game winning three-point shot to send them to the finals. The town went bonkers.

Cara and I flew home, and I followed the finals series online. Bicho and Gyasi led Salto to the championship. They had braved the brutal floors of Uruguay and were campeónes!

Let's hope they got their dinero.

* * *

My rehab went well until March, the fifth month. I had started running and was feeling really good. Then I began to have pain in the top of my foot and the trainers and doctors couldn't give me a clear answer why. It prevented me from continuing my rehab at a consistent pace. My right calf atrophied so much that it looked like a chicken leg. I had zero muscle definition, and I couldn't do a single-leg calf raise. I would stand on my right leg and my brain would tell it to push up onto my toes but there was no response, my muscles were still so weak. It was a bizarre feeling.

At seven months from the surgery, with my leg still unable to do simple functions and sharp foot pain that would not go away, I began to question if this was the end of the road. I was praying one day and asking for God to show me some sort of sign, good or bad. I wanted to be hopeful, but my progress was not moving very well.

Lord, please heal me. Help me to accept whatever Your will is for my life and for the outcome of this injury. I want to play again, but I know that Your plan is ultimately the best one. Help me to remember and trust that.

I picked up the Bible and turned randomly to the book of Job. "For He wounds, but He binds up. He shatters, but His hands heal" (Job 5:18).

I felt a surge of hope fill my heart and my mind. I didn't know when I would get better or what exactly was going to happen next. But those verses were more than enough to lift me and help me continue striving toward my goal of getting back on the court. Jesus is a God of hope. He is a God of second chances. And third, fourth, and fifth chances. Lord knows I needed them all.

* * *

While my leg wasn't game-ready, it was fit enough to get me down the wedding aisle to marry my sweet Cara at the end of June. We took our honeymoon in the Dominican Republic where the resort had a rock climbing wall, a trampoline, and a trapeze—none of which I'm any good at and all of which Cara could practically teach. God humbles us all. Some of us just look dumber than others when it happens. Let's all watch the cute young woman do backflip twists while the big guy debuts on *America's Funniest Home Videos*.

The world quickly learned why there are no 6-foot-8 trapeze artists in the circus. I'm no fan of heights, which may seem odd since I am already closer to the sky than most people. But it's completely different when you're climbing a ladder with no security belt to a two-by-four plank that's already holding another person and is as high as the hotel you're staying in.

While I was convinced that my experience was scarier than anyone else's due to my size, I couldn't start out our marriage being shown up by my wife and having the story repeated for decades to come, "Hey, remember our honeymoon when you were such a baby that you couldn't even swing from a rope?"

So I stepped off of the trapeze ledge. My sweaty hands somehow didn't slip off the bar and hurl me into the safety netting below. I swung forward, then back, then hooked my legs through my arms and onto the bar. *Hey, I think I got this.*

On the second swing, I released my grip and flung myself through the air toward a guy dangling from a different swing who was half my size but apparently twice as strong. He grabbed my wrists midair and I clung on for dear life.

It was at this point I was certain it wouldn't end well. I'm not your average 120-pound tourist he could toss around. Yet somehow this beast held on to my large frame for a full swing before throwing me back toward the empty swing I had just come from.

Or at least he tried to throw me. I came up well short of the bar and landed in the safety net. Certain that I had been soaring impressively high above the buildings and palm trees, I was a little disappointed to see the video replay a few weeks later showing my toes mere inches from dragging on the safety net below as I swung like a monkey. I definitely didn't feel I was that close. Then again, how would I know? I was way too scared to look down.

Cara did so well on her attempts at hurtling through the air that they asked her to be in the show they put on in the evenings at the resort. Surprisingly, I was never asked. No matter: I accomplished my goal. Cara couldn't say she married a chicken. At least not after day four of our marriage.

Chapter 7

HOMEMAKING AND HOMECOMING: URUGUAY YET AGAIN

"YeshelloTyleritsDanielfromUruguayhowareyou?" It was Daniel's usual rapid-all-in-one phone greeting.

"I have a team for you," he said.

Really? After my injury?

"You remember Malvín, yes?" he asked.

Oh, I remembered Malvín (mal-VEEN). Their floor was just as hard—but perhaps a bit smoother than ours—up in Salto.

"The coach and president like you and want to sign you," Daniel said. "How is your leg?"

My leg had gotten stronger and the foot pain finally subsided. I even refereed an outdoor men's league that summer. Baby steps, but I volunteered partly to get used to running on the court and making sudden starts and stops on a controlled blacktop environment—perfect prep for Uruguay—and partly because I enjoyed exposing myself to the criticism of middle-aged men who liked to miss shots and then complain about getting fouled. *You know what? You did get fouled. Tell your teammate to get out of your way next time.*

"Daniel, my leg is doing better," I said. "But I don't know how it will respond to practicing every day and playing in games. I'm working out and playing again now, but the season could be a different story. Are they OK with that uncertainty?"

"Yes, it is OK," he said in his Uruguayan accent. "The team know you are very good player, and they hear about how Salto loves you, and the coach and president want you to come."

I was glad to have an offer, but I wasn't crazy about playing again on floors that tore up my Achilles in the first place. It seemed kind of stupid on my part to go back to the place that contributed to my injury.

"Any chance they will get a new wooden floor this season?" I asked.

I heard laughter on the other end of the line. Apparently, I was on speakerphone and the head coach and president found that question quite amusing. I know, what a ridiculous inquiry. A professional basketball league playing on wooden floors—who does that?

I should have been the one laughing at their offer. The contract offered the first two months at just $2,800 per. My yearly salary wasn't exactly on an upward swing. But I couldn't be too choosy; I didn't have any other potential takers. And clearly the way they structured the contract protected the team in case my leg was a liability. By the last three months of my contract, my salary would go up to $4,000 per month. But until that money was sitting happily in my bank account, it was nothing more than an idea floating out in space.

Salto had never paid me the remaining three months of the contract that we'd agreed to last season. The one month's worth of cash that I carried back on the plane after my injury wasn't even enough to cover the surgery I'd paid for out of pocket. I was trying to recoup the balance from Salto, but I knew the odds of them settling the debt were as good as the Timberwolves replacing Kevin Garnett with me.

* * *

I accepted the Malvín offer, unsure of whether I'd be able to play well enough to survive a full season. Cara stayed back in Hollidaysburg to continue teaching until I gave her the go-ahead to come join me. I needed to feel confident enough in my leg before she quit her job. It didn't make sense for her to give up a secure full-time job when my situation was so unstable.

Malvín was a neighborhood in Montevideo located on the beach. My apartment, fifty feet from the sand, was five stories up, overlooking the water. A small island, home to only trees and birds, rested a short distance from shore. Simply beautiful. It was spring in September below the equator, and I was going from summer in the United States to summer in Uruguay. I could get used to this.

The league changed the rule to allow two American players per team that season. Curtis Marshall was my American teammate, from Texas Tech, where he'd played for Bobby Knight. There was no shortage of entertaining Coach Knight stories, my favorite being about a Thanksgiving Day practice where the first three hours were spent without basketballs.

We walked twenty minutes through a residential neighborhood to practice each day because we didn't have a car and the weather was usually nice. Most houses we passed had a small patch of grass that could be mowed in under a minute. Gates surrounded many of the single-story homes because break-ins were not uncommon. A taxi ride to the gym was only four dollars, but why spend money when you could stroll broken sidewalks and count stray dogs on the way?

* * *

"*Ty-lair, soy Tito*," my coach introduced himself.

This was going to be awesome. First Herman. Now Tito. How do you not love a guy named after Michael Jackson's forgotten brother?

I later discovered that Tito was actually his last name and Álvaro was his first. But who's keeping track? Given the choice of what I'd like to be called, I'd probably go with Tito also. Way cooler. No one called him "Coach" or "Álvaro." This was going to take some getting used to.

Where do you want me on this play, Tito? I'm sorry, I wasn't paying attention and was picturing you singing ABC *and doing the moonwalk.*

Tito was 6-foot-7 and quite friendly. He was also the assistant national team coach, so he knew the game pretty well. Our team was a blend of talented young guys and a few vets. We had two guys named

Gastón on the team, which was pretty impressive, since the only other Gastón I knew was the bachelor egomaniac from Disney's *Beauty and the Beast*. And I swear, one of *our* Gastóns looked eerily like Disney's, minus the cartoon muscles. The other Gastón had blonde hair and actually was as strong as the animated version.

Our point guard was named Daniel, and he reminded me every day that the Spanish emphasis was on the second syllable of his name— dan-*YEL*. He was one of the smallest guys on the team, but definitely the fastest and our best shooter.

Augustín (aw-gu-STEEN), or "Gus," played some college ball in the States and spoke fluent English, so we became fast friends. He had a twenty-five-minute car ride to the gym—the only problem being that he didn't have a car. Instead, he took a ninety-minute bus ride to and from practice. Sometimes twice per day.

Another player was named Sebastián, but everyone called him "Gordo." You mean like "Fatty"? Sadly, yes. He wasn't even that big—more like chubby on the weight spectrum. But he was strong and could really play, as evidenced by the team's investment in him. They bought his rights from another club for around $20,000, which was big money there. I don't know if he liked his nickname, but I couldn't get myself to call him Fatty, so I stuck with Seba. Guys tried to correct me all the time.

"Ty-lair, he is 'Gordo.' His name 'Gordo,'" they would say.

"Yeah, it's a crappy nickname," I'd say. *How about we call you "Hideous"? It's English for "Can't-Get-A-Date." You're not really that ugly, but it's just fun to say.* I wasn't into it.

* * *

Just like my teammates in Salto, these guys were full of life and fun to be around. They worked hard but didn't take themselves too seriously. Our assistant coach, another Daniel, owned a restaurant named "Veintitres," or "23," and the logo was Michael Jordan's dunking silhouette. I can almost guarantee you that MJ saw no royalties from

Daniel's business venture. Too bad for Mike, because the restaurant did so well that Daniel opened a second one. A part of my contract that helped make up for my skimpy salary was that I got to eat there for free. Even if it hadn't been free, I'd have eaten there every day. I could get an entire meal with drinks and dessert for five dollars. Food was so cheap there, it was crazy. They had my four favorite food groups: pizza, chicken, steak, and pasta. Whatever I wanted. Twice per day.

Our basketball gym was part of a health club—Club Malvín. Every night the fitness area was packed with weightlifters, spin classers, swimmers, and the typical people hanging out doing nothing. The actual playing gym was decent, accommodating about 1,500 fanatics at every home game. It was literally standing room only on one sideline that didn't have bleachers—just a rope courtside that people could stand behind and drink, spit, and curse: key ingredients for a good time. And I am dead serious when I use the term *fanatics*, as they'll kiss you and give you their first born when you win.

One big "negativo" was that there was no heat or air-conditioning in the gym. While in theory it should have been warming up as winter was over, it was still freezing on some days, and good ol' Tito wore his winter coat during practice for the first few weeks.

The rims on the baskets were in terrible shape and screws fell out of them twice during the first week of practice. Thankfully neither rim fell. One basket stood 9-foot-9 and the other was generously tilted down to 9-foot-5 and softer than church music, thanks to too many dunks. You could almost throw the ball straight in. Who needs arc? We started our games going toward the shorter basket and often jumped out to big leads, as the ball always seemed to find a way to go in.

In an effort to bring a small amount of professionalism to the situation, someone had the bright idea to restore the rim color with a fresh coat of bright orange paint about thirty minutes before practice started one day. They did not use a quick-dry formula. It could have been house paint or car paint for all we knew. Either way, why let a little fresh paint stop anything? If that wasn't enough, we simultaneously broke out brand new basketballs that day. Paint all over the balls. Paint on the court. Paint on our hands, jerseys, and shorts. Nice.

* * *

We won our opening game at home, as Curtis dropped in 35 points in an impressive first outing. The fans were psycho as usual, singing, chanting, and beating drums the entire game. I played well, but Curtis was our game MVP that night. We went out to dinner after the game, and agent Daniel was there with us. Daniel was excited that we got our first win, too. He represented Curtis also, and he was proud that two of his players were off to a good start.

"Tyler, do you know that there have been many good American players to play in Uruguay?" Daniel asked.

"Really?" I said. Before last season I had heard of zero. Had he told me I was the first one, I would have believed him.

"Yes, even the head coach of Ookla played here twenty years ago," he said.

"Ookla?" I repeated. Even though many people I conversed with in different countries spoke English, this misunderstanding was practically an everyday occurrence. I'd have to translate, consider the context, and then read people's minds to figure out what they were talking about. Communication was hard enough with language barriers, and I didn't want to seem like an idiot when the person was actually speaking a language I understood. Still, "Ookla" wasn't ringing a bell. My only clues to go on was "head coach" and "American" from twenty years ago. Nada.

"Very famous coach," Daniel explained. "Ookla won many championships."

"Professional or college?" I asked. I needed more clues.

Daniel was getting annoyed that I wasn't following.

"Ooo-Klaaa," he said slowly.

Dude, it's not your pronunciation. No one has ever heard of your made-up Ookla team.

"In California," he said.

"Ooooooh!" I said. I finally got it. "You mean UCLA?"

"Yes!" Daniel gasped. "Ookla!"

Of course. Ookla. UCLA. Potaytos. Potahtos.

"Ben Howland is their coach," I said. "He played here in Uruguay?" I played against Ben Howland's Pitt teams before he went to UCLA. But I couldn't imagine him playing in Uruguay. But maybe that was Howland's big selling point in his interview with the Bruins. "Well, back in the day I did dabble in pro ball in Uruguay ..."

I liked Daniel a lot. But sometimes I didn't know when he was exaggerating. So I looked it up. Sure enough, if you Google Howland's résumé and look far enough down, "played professional basketball in Uruguay" is right there. Next time I see Coach Howland we'll have plenty to talk about.

* * *

My Achilles was feeling good enough that I thought it was time for Cara to submit her teaching resignation. I forced her into early retirement so she could roam the streets of Montevideo with me. We scheduled her flight for the end of September, and the team assured me that they would find a new place for Curtis to live. Curtis and I had been roommates in our beachfront apartment for a few weeks and got along very well. But seeing as Cara and I were still newlyweds, I wasn't real keen on having a roommate when she arrived. And she wasn't big on the idea of picking up after two guys instead of one.

But that's exactly what happened. The team casually neglected to get Curtis a new place to live, despite a full month's notice from me.

Cara's first morning in Uruguay didn't exactly get off to a friendly start. Apparently I wasn't the only one to get excited for her arrival. An army of ants greeted her at 7 a.m. with a parade all over the bathroom. Throw in a bed made for Smurfs and a small, hot apartment without air-conditioning, and she was now living the dream.

My new bride acclimated well, though, and would go for walks on the beach and work out at the club when I had evening practices. Cara came to all of my games, even the away games, which were usually within ten or twenty minutes by taxi. We even walked to one away game, as it was only a couple blocks over in the next neighborhood.

One game she wasn't able to attend because she wasn't feeling well. We were playing on the road against Bohemios (bo-HAY-mee-ohs). Their court had four rows of cement seating on one side and six rows on the other. A waist-high wooden railing surrounded the court directly above the out-of-bounds lines—the perfect height for angry fans to lean over to berate players and referees. The railing was very dangerous for players, as it was unpadded, and anyone going after a loose ball would certainly lose the war with it. And any fan could crawl under or over it if they pleased. It was symbolic, I guess.

The backboards may have been transparent at one time, but those days were long gone. The floor, of course, was some solid mass that was significantly smaller than a regulation court. At first it would have been hard to recognize the smaller size. But when you tried to shoot a three-point shot from the corner and realized that only someone with a size-13 shoe or smaller could fit their foot between the arc and the sideline, you discovered what a special place this was.

I always tried to make it a point to say hello to the other Americans on the opposing teams. It was an easy ice-breaker, as we automatically had a few things in common such as basketball, America, and teams not paying us. Even if we never would've been friends in the States, there was plenty to laugh and complain about right where we were.

Americans were always easy to spot, and one of the Bohemios Americans was probably the easiest. He was a big, strong white guy and he was the only one jumping rope on the court an hour before the game began. Who jumps rope before games? I had to meet him.

"Hey, I'm Tyler," I said reaching out my hand. There would be no kissing during this greeting. My Uruguayan-ness only went so far. When Americans meet in foreign lands and have a conversation, the ground they are standing on automatically becomes sovereign land and local rules like kissing don't apply.

"I'm Ben," he said. "Hey, you're not married are you? Because I am. And my wife really needs someone to hang out with."

Now, that's a greeting. Or possibly a cry for help. Either way, it sounded great to me, as Cara hadn't had much female interaction and I was sure she needed someone to relate to.

"Are you kidding? *My* wife needs someone to hang out with," I said.

"Is your wife here tonight?" Ben asked.

"No, she wasn't feeling well," I said. Must have been the cow's blood. So much for 'trying new things.'

"Is your wife here?" I asked.

"No, she doesn't like basketball," he said.

"Oh, that's rough," I said. It wasn't like people frequently came from the United States to vacation in Uruguay. So if you didn't like basketball and that was your husband's job, living there may not be the time of your life.

Ben's Bohemios team beat us that night, but I was happy to have made a new friend and a potential friend for Cara. Ben Sturgill, who had played college ball at New Hampshire, seemed to be someone I actually would hang out with back home, so we exchanged numbers.

* * *

Our team, Malvín, had started the season by winning our first couple games. Our first loss felt awful. We played like garbage and lost by 20. The day after, I was expecting Tito to declare war on the entire team with defensive slides, sprints, and outright beatings for such a lame performance. Instead, he sent us to the hot pool. No practice, just a little relaxation. I was dumbfounded. We got destroyed the night before and there were no verbal thrashings or physical abuse. Just warm bubbles.

We won a few here and lost a few there. We looked like the Lakers on some nights, or at least the Spanish-speaking version, and on other nights we were like an old ladies' knitting club. There wasn't much consistency, but we always managed to stay a couple games above .500. When we went to eat at the Veintitres restaurant, the fans were usually supportive. But when a big game was coming up, they'd put the pressure on.

"Ty-lair, we must win this weekend!" one older guy would say in Spanish, giving me a high-five.

"We'll do all we can," I'd reply with a smile.

"No, no. You *must* win," he would repeat, a little more seriously this time.

I don't know if he had money on the game or what.

"Sí, sí," I said. "We will play well for you."

"No 'play well,'" he'd say, getting more serious. "Must win!"

Got it. Is this a subtle death threat? Or do you just put way too much importance on a random upcoming game? These weren't playoff games. This was like game number eight.

I was never one to talk trash and make a bunch of outlandish predictions. But this one particular group of fans kept nagging me every time I saw them with "You *must* win." They were never satisfied with my answers of "We'll do our best" and "I'll play really hard." These people wanted results.

So I began doing what I never thought I'd do. I guaranteed victory. Every time. And they loved it.

"Ty-lair, you must win tonight!" they said.

"We are going to win," I said in Spanish. "Of course we will win! We are going to win always." It was the best Spanish guarantee I could muster.

"¡Sí!" they cheered. They smiled and high-fived. I gave high-fives, too, and acted crazier than them. Why not? It got to the point where I figured *Who cares? Guarantee away. Declare victory before the battle.* It's not like this was on ESPN and the other team was putting this on their chalkboard for inspiration against us. I was the cocky heavyweight boxer saying all kinds of ridiculous nonsense before the fight and acting so confident that other people thought I really knew something that they didn't.

I didn't know jack. But it was much more fun to get everyone all riled up. All they wanted was to feel that we were ready and excited to play for their beloved Malvín. And I was. So yes. Bet the house on it.

* * *

One gym actually had a half-decent floor, and I was looking forward to playing on a normal surface for once. It was the home court of Aguada (ah-GWA-da). They had arguably the wildest crowds in the country. Someone was reportedly stabbed in the stands a couple years back. That fan didn't die, though—so the team was allowed to continue playing in the league.

My American friend, Jason Osborne, played for Aguada and told me that one of the fans threw a live chicken on the court just before tipoff of one game. Jason literally had stepped off of the plane that morning from the United States and it was his first game in Uruguay. Priceless. Was the guy who checks tickets at the door like, "Oh, just a chicken? That's fine. Does he cheer for Aguada?"

It rained the entire day we were scheduled to play Aguada. By the third quarter we were up by 15 points. That's when it started raining again. The gym had a leaky roof, and one of the holes dripped water right in the middle of the lane in front of the basket. After five players wiped out, they decided to suspend the game. My first basketball rainout.

Three weeks later, we travelled back to Aguada to finish the game and we picked up right where we left off in the middle of the third quarter. It was quite odd warming up for a "game" when we were already ahead by 15 points with only fourteen minutes left. One would think we pretty much had it in the bag. Sadly, they went on a huge run and *we* lost by 15. A 30-point swing. Stupid rain.

* * *

Cara and I began hanging out more with Ben and his wife, Shannon. Ben and I had a lot in common. The 6-foot-8 Midwestern-white-guy-in-Montevideo-club was pretty exclusive. We were both newly married, had a strong Christian faith, and were trying to convince our wives that these were the best days of their lives. Ben had a great sense of humor and didn't take himself too seriously, which was really refreshing in the athletic world where guys thought they should be treated as gods.

When Ben first landed in Uruguay and his team picked him up at the airport, he was wearing a cowboy hat and thick-soled shoes. He stuck out his chest with an exaggerated posture that made him look almost seven feet tall. Ben knew that the team would eye him up the instant they saw him, and he didn't want to leave any hesitation in their minds that he was as big as they were expecting. He had heard how quickly Americans got cut for all sorts of dumb reasons. So he made sure that his size, or at least their perception of it, wouldn't be one of them.

His living situation was similar to mine, minus the roommate. Ben and Shannon had a small apartment, but the furnishings were modern. Bohemios didn't have a big budget, and it turned out that he was lucky to even have an apartment. His American teammate lived in a glorified janitor's closet at the gym. They threw a cot in there for him and wished him luck.

Ben and Shannon came to our apartment one day to hang out.

"That's a cool island," Ben said looking out our window at the water. "I wonder if we could swim to it?"

Cara rolled her eyes. "Here we go again with the swimming to the island idea," she said.

The debate had gone back and forth between Cara and me for a couple of months. Every day we looked out that window, and the island taunted me.

Could I make it? Maybe. *How far was it?* I didn't know. *And why even try?* Just because it would be fun to do.

The "fun" factor wasn't my most rational thought, as it could leave Cara a widow. Tides. Currents. Choppy waters. Whatever; I was on the swim team when I was eight.

"We should totally do it," Ben said.

"Definitely," I agreed, thrilled to have an eager partner. "Are you a good swimmer?"

"I was a lifeguard for a few years," he said. "You?"

"I've dabbled in the aquatics," I said with confidence. "My friend was a lifeguard." That should count for something.

I didn't want to be outdone, and Ben sounded like he was a really strong swimmer since he was trained to save lives. I considered myself an above-average swimmer for no reason other than I had spent many youthful summers in pools and in a mucky Rappahannock river in Virginia on family vacations.

Well, we decided not to conquer the island that day. But it stayed on the Uruguayan bucket list. Right up there with win more games than we lost.

Shannon was a sweetheart and very pretty. Ben and I were Double-A ball players married to Hall of Famers. Like Cara, Shannon never envisioned married life beginning in rowdy South American gyms. Shannon wasn't as interested in basketball as Cara, but she went to the games to support Ben. Cara went with her on occasion to Ben's games, as they were more interesting for Shannon to watch with a friend.

Cara couldn't make it to one of Ben's games and she called Shannon to ask how it went.

"Well, I think he played well," Shannon said. "But then, toward the end, he got tired and went and sat on the bench."

"He got tired?" Cara asked, surprised. "Ben is in really good shape." He also played every minute because the team desperately needed him on the floor if they were going to have any chance to win.

"Yeah, well he looked worn out and needed a break," Shannon replied. "He sat on the bench for the rest of the game."

Cara looked up the box score. Ben had fouled out.

"Shannon, Ben fouled out," Cara said. "He wasn't allowed to keep playing."

"Oh, OK. That makes sense," Shannon said.

She was a wonderful girl. But she wasn't going to be working for ESPN Deportes anytime soon.

* * *

With all of the games and practices, even on awful surfaces, my Achilles was holding up well beneath the skin. The problem was the outer layer of skin and scar tissue. I get pretty ugly keloid scars, which are raised above the skin and appear inflamed and discolored. The one I got from my surgery was a beast.

The raised scar was rubbing against my shoe and ankle brace, and the skin's soft scar tissue had torn completely open. The skin never had a chance to heal because I played every day, coming home with bloody socks and lots of pain.

We had a team doctor, but he didn't have anything that could act as a cushion to protect it. An open wound with sweat and bacteria pouring into it every day was a ticking time bomb. The doctor told me if it became infected, it could lead to something even worse than just tearing my Achilles.

Worried, I called home to a couple of different trainers in the United States to see if they had any ideas. I emailed them pictures to understand what I was talking about. The photos were pretty gruesome, like something in a medical textbook. "Pictured here is what happens just prior to a lower extremity amputation due to massive infection. Commonplace in dumb American basketball players in Uruguay who don't have proper medical support."

The trainers from Drayer Physical Therapy in Pennsylvania mailed me three options for padding on the back of my leg. One of them, a gel pad, did the trick. The rubbing stopped and the skin began to heal slowly. Unfortunately, the gel barrier broke down after a couple days, and I ran out of my supply quickly. They sent me another shipment with a more stable version of the padding, and I had a little less fear of losing my leg.

It was very frustrating to have to get treatment from trainers on another continent. Something that could have been solved in four seconds back home took longer than four weeks to figure out in Malvín. I would need to start bringing my own first aid bag overseas. The first thing I'd throw in there: cold spray. Not.

* * *

Curtis and I were playing well together. He was one of the top three-point shooters in the league. I was scoring and rebounding well. But every game was an adventure. We could never settle into a routine of just playing basketball. Every gym had its own shenanigans for us to deal with.

At Biguá (bee-GWA), we shared a locker room with the other team. Awkward. With the opponent on the other side of a row of lockers, Tito had to keep his voice down as he whispered our pregame strategies. It's not much of a pep talk when you're using your library voice.

Soriano (sor-ee-AH-no) was one of the four teams outside of Montevideo, and they played in what looked like an airplane hangar. It was shaped like one with the high, curved roof. The scoreboard was a half-mile away it seemed, with plenty of missing light bulbs, so you never knew if you were winning, losing, or tied. Very handy in fourth-quarter crunch time. What's more, there wasn't a locker room for us to use, so before the game we had our pregame talk outside on some broken concrete steps with fans walking by and yelling at us.

One of the creepier moments of my pro career happened during a game against Soriano when I was guarding a huge, overweight Uruguayan player. He was running down the court toward me on defense. The guy was 6-foot-6 and easily 300 pounds. His jersey was more like a Spandex top than a uniform.

I watched him as he rumbled toward me. All of a sudden, a cockroach ran right across his stomach and disappeared under his shirt. *Did*

I really just see that? Unfortunately, yes. I wish it had been a hallucination. It was straight out of some horror film. Now I had to push against chubby sweaty cockroach boy in the post. *Sub!*

At Atenas (ah-TAY-noss), a visible mixture of cigarette and unmistakable marijuana smoke clouded the gym as we came out for warmups. Who doesn't love a good buzz in layup lines? The kids there were way more obnoxious than normal, too. Either their parents weren't there or they were too high to drag them off the court during the pregame shootaround and timeouts. There must have been twenty kids on our half of the court before the game. They were running around stealing our balls and then shooting them. It was cute for the first shot, but it got real old real fast. How do you say, "Gimme my ball before I throw you over the scorer's table" in Spanish? They were running between my legs, and I had to avoid trampling them for forty-five minutes before the game started. Then the refs had to shoo them off the court after each timeout. Who needs halftime entertainment? It was a free-for-all.

One kid yelled, "Smeeth! Smeeth!" I ignored him at first because I was getting agitated and began to worry that I might drill one of these little punks into the wall. But he kept calling my name. "Smeeeeeth!" I reasoned with myself that I was being a little ridiculous. These were kids. They loved to play basketball and be around the players. I needed to chill out and quit being such a stuck-up prima donna. Acknowledging a young boy was the very least I could, and *should*, do. Even if he was hurling basketballs at our heads while we were trying to prepare for the game. *Be the bigger man, for goodness sake.*

I looked over at him. He must have been eight years old and he had a huge grin on his face. I waved. He held up both hands and gave me a double thumbs-down sign. It was his non-English-speaking-little-kid-way of saying, "You suck." Hey thanks. Better than the double-fisted bird I received from the Italian kid. Maybe I'm growing on them.

The court itself at Atenas was comical. First off, whoever was in charge of the whole "check to make sure a basketball court can fit in the building" part must have been one of the same ones smoking the herbal medicine. The baseline was painted literally directly underneath the basket instead of a few feet back. If you came down with a rebound near the hoop, you'd be out-of-bounds. It had to be this way, because otherwise the wall would have been our out-of-bounds marker. It was where the baseline should have been.

The flooring was some sort of imitation wood with holes scattered throughout. Not holes that dropped down into a large pit of lions, though that would have been way cooler, but openings and cracks large enough to get stuck in. On one possession during the game, Tito screamed for our point guard, Daniel, to get back down the court and play defense. It appeared he was being lazy and not hustling back to cover in transition. But Daniel yelled back at him and pointed to his foot. His shoe had become wedged in the floor somehow, and he was held captive. Daniel finally broke free, but not before Atenas capitalized on their five-on-four fast break.

Some call it poor facilities. Others call it home-court advantage.

Even at our home court, the opposing fans packed their section of the gym. We played Unión Atletica once at home, and they stood about five people deep along the sideline for the entire game. There were a good 200 people jammed into a small roped-off section across from our bench.

Lucky me, I got to take the ball out-of-bounds directly in front of the belligerent Unión fans during the third quarter. As I walked over, they were howling and waving their arms at me like I was an animal. Their hatred was impressive. You'd think I'd just shot their dog and kidnapped their favorite kid.

I stepped out-of-bounds to receive the ball from the ref and I was an arm's length in front of them. I made the mistake of looking up, and all I saw was a wall of spit raining down on me. I turned my shoulder to catch most of it on my back and the top of my head and neck. Some got on my face, definitely one of the most disgusting moments of my life. I was only able to reason that at least I was already a gross, sweaty mess in that humid gym. What's a small bucket of saliva? I threw the ball inbounds and got out of there before I was sprayed with something worse.

* * *

One of the things I did love about Uruguay was the low cost of living. Cara and I went to almost every movie that was in English with Spanish subtitles. Sure they were four or five months behind the original release date in the States. *What,* Karate Kid *is playing?* But the two-dollar price tag was worth the wait.

You could get a lot of things for two bucks in Uruguay. Men could buy a ticket to our game. Women and children could purchase four tickets. For kids, I can understand the lower price. But I never understood why a woman's ticket was fifty cents and the man's was two dollars. Maybe they were trying to grow their female fan base to attract more males to the gym. Not a bad marketing ploy.

A two-dollar tip would be huge for most meals. There wasn't the 15- to 20-percent tipping rate that Americans are used to. So a couple of random coins from your pocket would do. The delivery guy from Veintitres came in the restaurant one night before it closed, and he was beaming. He couldn't believe his good fortune on one of the best nights he'd ever had. After really hustling out countless deliveries all over Montevideo on his motorbike, he accumulated ten dollars in tips that night. I'd never seen him so happy.

* * *

We met some American Christian missionaries there who lived near the gym. They invited us to Thanksgiving dinner, which was delicious, although the main course was chicken as there weren't any turkeys in Uruguay. Or if there were, no one knew where to find them. Chicken was close enough. It was still a feast that we enjoyed with other English speakers. Cara and I considered it a victory.

Charles and Karen had given up a comfortable life in the United States to become missionaries in South America. They immersed themselves in the culture and mastered Spanish as they served the community by providing food for a children's home, offering a mentorship program to young men and women, and supporting local churches. They were called to share the teachings of Jesus. I was called to share the rock.

Wherever I went I knew that I was a representative and I tried to always keep this in mind. I represented my country and all of its wonderful and baffling diversity, my family with its solid, Main Street middle class, Midwestern values, and my church, which encourages us to love our neighbors as ourselves even and especially in distant lands such as Uruguay or Holland.

I was one of two Americans on the team, and I might be the only American some people would ever get to know. Would I be loud and obnoxious, as the American stereotype goes? Unwilling to appreciate the new land I was living in? Or could I appreciate a different culture and not act as if the whole universe revolved around the United States? Simply treating others the way you would want to be treated can go a long way.

This is especially true with referees. Refs get zero love. It's the nature of the game. It's easy to be a jerk to them. I don't pretend that I always act perfectly towards the refs, but I do make a conscious effort to show them respect and interact with them in a courteous manner. Not so I can get calls, but because they are humans, too, and they miss fouls just like I miss jumpers. Jesus brought hope and encouragement to everyone. The least I could attempt to do was demonstrate this and share it with others during my journey. It's hard to believe at times, but Jesus died for everyone. Even refs.

* * *

Ben's team hadn't been winning many games since beating us. As a result, their season would finish earlier than the rest of the league's. They wouldn't just miss the playoffs, they were going to miss the whole second half of the season.

Uruguay had some ridiculous rule that allowed only the top ten teams to advance to the next phase of the season. The bottom six teams were automatically eliminated in December. Even though there were three more months of basketball to play, if your team wasn't in the top ten, you were on your way home.

Ben had a team lined up in Australia for a league that started in February. So even though his Uruguayan glory days were coming to an end, he had another continent eager to accept his services.

I, on the other hand, was growing more nervous by the week. As the top-ten team deadline approached, we were slipping closer toward the elimination line. It was unbelievable to think that we should be anywhere near it, given our talented team. Yet, here we were, facing possible doom.

We were tied with Aguada for the final spot. It would come down to one game. We were 15–14 and would play them at home. We could have beaten them earlier in the season at their place had we not been rained out. We always played better at home anyway. So I liked our chances.

I was guaranteeing victory all over the place in the days leading up to the game. What else could I do? The entire Malvín community was gearing up for the first do-or-die game of the season. If we lost, I was out of a job. Again. I wouldn't even make it to the $4,000 per month part of my contract. I'd be home for the holidays and sitting on Santa's lap at the mall asking for a contract sans loopholes. I'd never been to a Christmas party as an unemployed newlywed. Could be fun. *Hey, I thought you guys were supposed to be in Paraguay or something …*

If we beat Aguada, I'd continue on for three more months and then playoffs. Bonuses. Maybe a bigger contract for next year. Possibly a statue outside the club. Winning was preferable.

* * *

A couple days before the Aguada game, there was a knock at our door. It was Ben and Shannon. Ben's season had finished and they'd come to say goodbye.

"We're headed home tomorrow," he said. (Shannon's grieving over not continuing in the Uruguayan league was short-lived.) "So I had to come by and do one last thing."

"What's that?" I asked.

"We're swimming to the island," he said with excitement.

"Awesome!" I said. "Are you sure?"

"Yeah, we're doing it," he said.

"Let me get my suit," I said.

The island had laughed at us for five months. Maybe the reason we hadn't swum to the island yet was because I didn't know deep down if I could do it. Not making it wasn't a good option. There are things in life you can fail at. Skydiving, bungee jumping, and swimming in open waters without a life jacket are not some of them.

But there was no better time to conquer the island. If Ben felt confident that we could do it, then I felt confident. If I didn't believe myself, I chose to believe Ben. I'd faced challenges as big as this. And when had I ever failed? Don't answer that.

There was a part of me that would only believe it was possible when we were standing on that rocky shore looking back at our own beach. And if I did make it to the island, there was another important question: Could I make it back?

Cara grabbed the video camera so she could document our triumph or our death. We walked across the street to the beach and approached the water.

It was windy, the waves were choppy, and it was anything but an easy day to swim an unknown distance in rough waters for no particular good reason. Yet the decision had been made.

Ben and I waded out into the water laughing about our current challenge. The island looked a heck of a lot farther from the beach at eye level than it did from five stories up in our apartment. Oh well. We were on our way.

I was feeling good for the first couple minutes. However, I quickly noticed that the winds and current were stronger than I anticipated. I put my face in the water and swam hard, but the island only moved sideways. I was putting a lot of energy into my strokes and fighting off the waves splashing over me. I stopped every few moments, treaded water, and tried to gauge my progress, which sapped even more of my energy. I had to wipe my eyes all the time since I wore contacts. A slightly smarter version of myself would have worn goggles.

Ben was ahead of me. He wasn't lying when he said he was a lifeguard. The guy was a freakin' dolphin. He'd swim out in front and then wait for me to catch up. Only I'd never catch him. I was trying to, but I realized quickly that basketball shape and swimming shape were two completely different things.

"You doing OK?" Ben asked.

"Yeah, I'm good," I lied. "You?"

"I'm good," he said.

And he really was.

I, on the other hand, was pretty sure that the island was moving farther away every time I looked up. It reminded me why I was never a big fan of water polo in gym class during high school. In basketball or football, if you got winded you just stopped and put your hands on your knees between plays. I wasn't a big fan of sports where, when you got tired, you drowned.

I tried to mix up my strokes. A little breaststroke. Some back-float-stroke. Pretty much anything to keep me moving somewhat toward the island and still have access to oxygen. Ben remained ahead of me by about ten or fifteen yards. *Ben, don't you dare leave me.*

We were getting closer, but my arms were exhausted. My legs were running out of energy quickly, fighting the resistance of the water. Maybe I could make it. It was still at least 150 yards away, but it felt like 1,500 with the powerful waves and current pulling us away from our destination. I had to make it.

There was no way I would be able to make it back, though. Someone would need to air-drop a few meals and a sleeping bag, as I would need three solid days to recover before I attempted to swim back.

This wasn't good. *Don't think about it. Just get to the stupid island so you can breathe.*

Unlike in basketball, I wasn't catching my second wind. My first wind had evaporated long ago. I was in pure survival mode. We were over halfway there, so it didn't make sense to go back. But every wave seemed determined to be the one that put me under for good.

I kept fighting. My original goal was to make it to the island. My new goal was not to die.

I didn't have the energy to tell Ben that I wasn't doing well. He continued to seem fine as he cruised along like the current was somehow carrying him and burying me. So I churned slowly at the water, hoping that somehow the island would start swimming toward me. *Oh, what I would give for something that floated right now.*

As my brain debated back and forth over whether it thought I would make it out alive, I heard a voice.

"*Hola!*"

I looked over to my left and a kayak was approaching. A lifeguard was yelling at us and waving his arms as he paddled toward us.

"You cannot go to the island," he said.

After all this! You're not going to let me finish my death swim?

"Why not?" Ben asked since he was the only one between the two of us who could speak comprehendible words.

"No one can go to the island," the lifeguard guy said. "It is not allowed."

Great explanation. Who cares? Can I hold onto your boat?

"You must go back to the beach," he said.

Go back? Guess who couldn't make it back to the beach if there were $10 million waiting for me in gold? The island was within 100 yards at this point. Let's go there.

"Do you want to hold on to my kayak?" he asked us.

Dear God, yes.

I latched on.

"Sure, gracias," I mustered. I had never felt such relief in all my life.

"No, I'm good," said Ben.

Are you kidding me? He's going to swim all the way back? Ben was insane.

I clung to my new best friend's kayak as it dragged me through the water toward land. Ben swam behind us the entire way.

The island claims that it won that day. Technically, however, since our voyage was interrupted by *mi amigo* before we either completed the journey or I died in Uruguayan waters, it was a draw. We will never know who won. My endless ego calculated that with my body not sinking to the bottom of the Atlantic or washing up on shore a week later, I was indeed the winner. Take that, island.

* * *

On December 15, we played our do-or-die game against Aguada at home, the last game before Christmas break. The winner moved on with nine other teams to the second half of the season, and the loser went home. Literally.

I played my best game of the season, 33 points and 11 rebounds. I was even 10-for-10 from the free throw line until I had to miss a foul shot on purpose near the very end of the game as we scrambled to catch up.

It wasn't enough. We lost by a few points, and our 15–15 record wouldn't allow us to advance. My second consecutive season in Uruguay finished prematurely. Thankfully, both Achilles were intact for the plane ride home this time.

Chapter 8

"THEY WANT MY SOCKS": ARGENTINA

Six months into marriage, most of which was spent in Uruguay, I was unemployed and living with my mother-in-law. *Just like we planned, right, sweetie?* What a provider I was turning out to be for my lovely spouse.

It was Christmas break, and I emailed and called every agent I knew, desperately hoping to get a job for the second half of the season. Malvín was the first team that actually paid me what they said they would, although in December, they didn't pay me for the entire month—only up to our final loss on the fifteenth. I'll call that progress.

If there was a bright spot about being jobless at Christmas, it was the timing. Many teams made changes over the break, so there was a chance I could be one of those changes. Some teams overseas told players to not bother returning to the club after they'd gone home for the holidays. Other times, players were the ones who stayed home and broke the contract without saying goodbye.

Max called from Italy.

"*Ciao*, Tyler. How are you?" he said in his jovial Italian accent. His English had improved dramatically from the first time I spoke to him. "I have new team very, very interested in you here in Ee-taly. You can send me new video very quickly? Maybe through Internet?"

"Max, that's great news," I said. "But I don't know how to send you a video over the Internet." It was 2005 and online video was just starting to become more popular.

"I need it tomorrow because the team must make a decision right away," Max pleaded. "You are one of top two guys they consider." He was pushing me pretty hard, and I could feel the urgency. I desperately wanted a second chance in Italy. I'd blown it the first time, and if I got another opportunity, I wouldn't screw it up this time. Oh pizza, come to me.

"It's on the way," I promised, as I'd move mountains to get them my film.

I made a DVD copy of one of my better games and drove directly to FedEx. After a failed attempt to get them to fly the cargo plane directly to the Italian team's office and air-drop it onto the roof of their building, I forked over sixty-two dollars and settled for their "fastest service"—two-day delivery. I should have gone *Con Air*, hijacked a plane, and delivered it myself. How hard could it be to fly a plane? I'd played *Asteroids* for years in Pizza Huts all over America.

The Italian team chose the other guy.

I understood that you had to spend money to get game video to agents and teams. But it was getting to be such a waste. Every summer I mailed out hundreds of dollars' worth of DVDs without a guarantee that a team would even watch it. I liked Max's idea about having it available to send online, but I had no clue how to do that. YouTube offered about ten minutes of grainy video, and you couldn't even read the jersey numbers in most games. There had to be a better way.

* * *

My French agent, Fred, emailed with an offer for me. A real one. *Yes! I won't be homeless for long.*

It was my best offer so far—$5,500 per month. More than I "made" in Italy per month. And twice what I had made in Holland and Uruguay. They were even going to throw in a car … and a personal driver!

There was only one problem. It was in Saudi Arabia. Yes, they play basketball there, too. Even the Saudis like their roundball.

Single Tyler may have taken it. Married Tyler had to consider whether he wanted to … stay married.

Maybe a bit dramatic. But the reality was that bringing a woman to the Middle East is not like driving up to Canada. Some countries didn't allow women to attend games or stay in certain hotels. Would Cara have to cover herself head-to-toe during their 110-degree summer? Additionally, there was a war going on in Iraq, and the nightly news never made you think words such as *vacation* or *holiday* when you heard the phrase *Middle East*.

Googling "Riyadh" didn't help either.

Another Seven Dead in Random Bombing. Ambassadors on Stand-By. Basketball Players Should Never Come Here.

12/31/05
Dear Fred,
Right now, I am having a hard time convincing my wife to go to Saudi Arabia. I think it could be a nice place, but I have some concerns also. I think we will wait for now. Thank you.
All the best,
Tyler

French Freddie, thanks for trying. It just didn't feel right. I wasn't a big fan of turning down high-paying jobs to accept a non-job. While it was a good salary for me, didn't they have enough oil money there to buy their own planet? It seemed that $5,500 was almost a bit low for such a rich country. Now, if they had thrown in free gas for life, *that* could have been a game-changer.

* * *

Daniel called from Uruguay.

"Tyler, I have a team that very much likes you in Argentina first division named Central Entrerriano," he said. "They pay $4,500 per month plus bonus."

Leaving Malvín might not have been a bad thing after all. Argentina was a stronger league and the pay was better. But the real question was: Were there any islands to swim to?

Here's where things got tricky.

I received an email the same day about a job in Argentina from a different agent we'll call Juan. The team: Central Entrerriano. Offer: $4,000 per month.

Crap.

To this point, I had worked with several agents and had exclusivity with none. It had worked in my favor, as a different agent every year found me a job. I was lucky that no two agents had shopped me to the same team successfully, because that was when things got messy. Who really reps the player? Who got the deal first? Most importantly, who gets the commission?

Now, two different agents (who apparently didn't like each other very much) were both shopping the same player (me) to the same team (Central).

Juan was furious and sent me one of the more hateful emails I've ever received. *"YOU ARE KILLING ME MAN! . . . THIS IS BULL—. . . I'M NOT MAFIA MAN . . . MAN I'M RELIGIOUS . . ."*

Yes, you sound very devout and I appreciate you not feeling compelled to rip out my fingernails one by one with pliers. But let's slow down here.

He was e-screaming at me one day, and then the next day he was pleading with me to sign with him. I have to give him some credit for his passion, as he was treating this deal like it was the last deal of his life and his entire family would be burned at the stake if he didn't complete it.

Juan was putting the screws to me. But I had worked with Daniel twice already for Salto and Malvín. We had bonded over Uruguayan McDonald's and he had educated me about Ookla's coach's Uruguayan stint two decades before. How do you compete with that? I had a strong relationship with Daniel, and I didn't know Juan at all.

Plus, somehow Daniel's offer was $500 more per month than Juan's. I went with Daniel.

The funny thing was, two months later, I helped Juan get in contact with a couple other American players he was trying to get signed in South America. We don't exchange Christmas cards, but I think we hugged it out.

* * *

I was scheduled to travel by myself to Argentina the first week in January 2006 to play for Central Entrerriano. I signed my shiny new contract in Spanish on a Tuesday, and my flight left on Wednesday. I would land in Argentina on Thursday and within twenty-four hours I would play my first game, in which I planned to dazzle my newest Argentinean teammates and fans. That's right. Dazzle.

The plan was for Cara to stay behind until I cleared out all the cockroaches in the apartment. Their size and speed would determine how quickly she could get down there.

My plane in the United States was delayed, and while I was waiting at our gate I noticed a tall black guy wearing a basketball sweatshirt. His presence piqued my curiosity. Maybe we'd be playing against each other.

"Hey, what's up?" I said.

"What's up?" he replied, uninterested.

"Do you play basketball?" I asked.

"Yeah," he said.

Not the biggest conversationalist I'd ever met. Sadly, this I found to be par for the course with many pro basketball players. They're not always the spunkiest bunch.

"Where do you play?" I asked.

"I'm going to Argentina," he said.

"Cool, me too," I said. "What team?"

"I don't know," he said.

I was slightly shocked. "You don't know?"

"I'm just joining them now. But I don't know the name of the team," he said matter-of-factly.

"Do you know the name of the city?" I asked. I was trying to help the guy figure it out. Not that I could really help. What did I know about the cities of Argentina?

"No," he said coolly. "But I think it's near Buenos Aires."

Yeah, that didn't narrow it down.

There were two leagues in Argentina. First division was called LNB—Liga Nacional de Básquet. Second division was the TNA— Torneo Nacional de Ascenso. My team was in the first division, the LNB.

"Do you know if you're playing in the LNB or the TNA?" I asked, reaching for something.

"Nope," he said.

He was essentially saying: "My agent sends the plane ticket. Sometimes I look to see where I'm going. Sometimes I don't. I fly down there. The team picks me up because I'm the tallest guy getting off the plane. And then I get buckets. Now, go away."

There's no way. I couldn't do that. When I heard where I was going, I researched that place like a madman. I wanted to know what to expect in my new country. I could tell you what they ate for dinner, which players I knew who had played there, and the birth rate of the city I'd be living in.

My fellow passenger couldn't care less. He had no clue. Nor did he want one.

"Well, good luck with that," I said.

* * *

As I boarded the plane to Buenos Aires, I noticed another tall athletic-looking guy about my size sit down in the row behind me. We started talking and, sure enough, it was my new Argentinean teammate Dionisio

Gomez from Central. Nichy (NEE-chee), as he liked to be called, was originally from Panama, and he was the other import player.

"How is the travel down there?" I asked.

"I hope you like buses," he said.

That's not good.

"One trip is thirty hours," he said. "That's one way. Then we drive another eight hours for the next game."

"They haven't heard of planes?" I asked.

"It's Argentina, man," he said. "Nobody can afford planes."

"How does the team make money?" I asked. "Who is our sponsor?"

"It's this big parade thing," he said.

So Macy's is our sponsor?

"You mean like with floats and bands and stuff?" I asked, trying to make sense of this conversation.

"Yeah," he said, "and if they win against the other two competitors, then the team makes a ton of money."

I'd had some odd sponsors in the past. A school, a fruit company, and now a parade would pay my salary. Move over and hand me the papier-mâché.

* * *

Nichy and I landed in Buenos Aires on Thursday, and we were picked up by our team driver nicknamed "Vaca," or "Cow." He wasn't particularly fat and had no visible udders, so I'm not sure how his stellar nickname came about. Maybe he really liked milk.

We drove three hours to Gualeguaychú (gwal-ay-gwi-CHU), recently the bonus-round word on the ESPN2 spelling bee. I stayed that first night at the Grand Hotel Berlin, as my apartment wasn't ready. (I made up the "Grand" part to make myself feel better. But "Hotel Berlin" was the *actual* name.)

When I stopped by my apartment the next day to scope out my new place, two workers were taking a jackhammer to my concrete bedroom wall. I had a broken shower and one working light in my spacious two-bedroom apartment. But I didn't care if I was dirty and blind, I *needed* AC or I would die. Since it was over 110 degrees and in the midst of summer, the team was kind enough to hire someone to cement an AC unit directly into the wall next to my bed. Plugging in a window unit would have worked, too, but I appreciated the finality of my new wall decoration.

That night I played in my first game at home after being in Argentina only twenty-four hours, and we won. I came out feeling great despite playing in the hottest gym known to man, and I made the first three-point shot I took. The crowd went crazy. The new *extranjero* (foreigner) was going to be fine. It was a huge adrenaline surge to knock down my first bucket. Maybe it was the real wooden floor that we were playing on, my new best friend.

* * *

On Saturday, the madness truly began. Coincidentally, my twenty-sixth birthday. Like Nichy said, this town, Gualywhatever in the middle of almost nowhere Argentina, basically survived on a huge parade. Forty-thousand strong came out to see one of the largest carnivals (called *carnaval* and pronounced "carnaVAAAAAL") in the world on eight consecutive Saturday nights from 10 p.m. until 5 a.m. Permanent stands were set up on both sides of a long runway, and you had to buy tickets to enter. Floats were fifty or sixty feet high, some looking quite rickety, with people dancing and singing all over them.

The women in the parade wore gigantic and elaborate outfits, none of which covered much of their bodies. The men also wore as little as possible. I think whoever sang the loudest and wore the least was declared the winner. For every tan, almost-naked woman shaking it up that my single (or married) teammates screamed at for photos, there was a smiling hairy, sweaty guy doing the same for all the women in the crowd.

"Ty, you think that woman is sexy, no?" our shooting guard, Edu, asked, pointing to one of the glamorous female performers.

"C'mon, Edu," I said smiling. "I'm a married man now."

Edu wouldn't leave it alone.

"Ty, Ty," he insisted. "She is beautiful, no?"

"Sure, Edu," I said to get him to leave me alone.

"Yes! I knew this!" celebrated Edu, smiling. "She is beautiful!"

"Yeah, great," I said.

"And guess what?" his smile broadened.

All of my teammates were now listening closely and watching our conversation.

"What?" I asked.

"It's a man!" he yelled. My entire team roared.

Haha, very funny. You got the new guy. But just for the record, it was the most womanly looking dude I'd ever seen in my life.

If you have been to Mardi Gras in the United States, you have seen a smaller and calmer version of carnaval. People *lived* for carnaval in Argentina. Many of my teammates were drinking and smoking like the country was about to adopt prohibition. Never mind the fact that we had a game the next day. This was CARNAVAAAAL!

* * *

My coach's name was Fabio, like the international model. Except that my Fabio never had his shirt tucked in and his beard was always confused with the in-between phase of not really a beard, but not neatly trimmed. He had a bit of a belly and a laid-back personality. At thirty-nine years old, he didn't even have a driver's license. No one on the team could give me an explanation why. Even though he didn't speak English, my Spanish had improved to the point where I could understand most of his main points before games and during practice. Nichy also helped translate since Spanish was his native language growing up in Panama. Cheater.

I liked Fabio for many reasons. Number one, he let guys play. He kept things very simple and allowed players to make decisions on the court without trying to control everything. Second, he maintained his composure and rarely raised his voice. He didn't have to use scare tactics to get guys to play hard, they just did. Fabio had a relaxed confidence about him and he always seemed ready to draw up a play during critical moments in a game.

I was brought in to replace another American. I heard he was more athletic but wasn't a big scorer or shooter from the outside. As long as I put up decent numbers I figured I'd be safe from being cut like my predecessor. It wasn't uncommon for a new American player to show up and try to destroy the other guys in practice and be ultra-aggressive during his first couple of games. It set the tone for everyone in the organization and it said, "This guy's got it." If there was any doubt in a coach's or general manager's mind about whether they brought in the right guy, the player wouldn't be around for long.

Another team in our league also brought in a new 6-foot-8 white American with a similar skillset to mine in the beginning of January. In my second game we played against each other. I scored 25 points and we won again. The other American didn't shoot the ball particularly well in his first couple of games, and a week later he was released. I was fortunate to play well enough right off the bat to solidify my place on the team. One or two bad games can cost you your job. In fact, Nichy played in Mexico one year and upon arriving, he helped his team win eight games in a row. They lost the next game and he was fired. So much for job security.

Cara flew down and joined me a week later. There wasn't a fitness gym where she could work out, so we went for walks almost daily. Within a mile of our apartment was a river that had a beach area where many of the locals would relax. The water didn't seem particularly clean, but the waterfront made for nicer scenery than the fractured sidewalks of downtown. The streets of Gualeguaychú were laid out in a grid but there were no stoplights and few stop signs. Drivers yielded seemingly in random fashion to one another, but I never even heard of a car accident happening.

Like Uruguay, there were numerous stray dogs throughout the town that needed an animal shelter in a bad way. Various shops lined the main drag leading down to the river—a travel agency, convenience stores, small boutiques, cell phone shops, Internet cafes, and a few restaurants. No building was higher than three stories high and each business occupied only a small space as there weren't any big box stores like Best Buy or Lowe's.

There wasn't a single American fast food chain to be found either, but on each of our walks it became our mission to taste-test every ice cream shop that we could find. We could buy two large cups for less than two dollars, all the more reason to support the local ice cream economy. Cara usually ordered "dulce de leche" which the locals always smiled at with pride because apparently it was the flavor of choice among the Argentineans. Personally, I thought it just tasted like vanilla ice cream with caramel. But we made a lot of friends by ordering the local flavor.

We stopped at an ice cream shop one evening, and an older woman approached me while we were waiting in line. She was smiling and started speaking rapidly in Spanish. I didn't catch all of it, but one phrase clearly stood out.

"*Tu hija es muy bonita,*" she said grinning and looking at Cara.

Excuse me?

"*Tu hija ... ella es bonita,*" she repeated.

"*Um, muchas gracias,*" I stammered.

Then, the woman turned and walked out the door. I burst out laughing.

Cara understood some of the language but confessed that she slid her way through high school Spanish. As a result, she often asked me to translate. (See, kids? Do your homework.)

"What did she say?" Cara asked.

"She said you were very beautiful," I said, still laughing.

"What else?" Cara pressed. She knew I wasn't telling the whole truth.

"She thought you were my daughter," I said.

"What! How old do I look? Twelve?" she said.

"Well, what does that make me? Some creepy old man?" I said. "I should have pulled you in close and said, 'Yes, this is my *beautiful* daughter. I love her *so* much.' And then given you a huge kiss on the lips."

Cara laughed. "You're gross. But that would have been funny."

Oh well. Next time.

* * *

Argentina reminded us a lot of Uruguay. While the two countries aren't exactly best buds and probably wouldn't agree that they had anything in common, to an outsider there were plenty of similarities. Both were very inexpensive compared to the United States, and both used the peso, although each had a different value. Both countries spoke Spanish faster than I could understand. Everybody kissed each other upon greeting. No car went above 15 mph driving through the small towns, probably so that men could shout obscene things at women walking on the sidewalks. The cars were ancient, and I don't think I rode in one that didn't have a cracked windshield. Maybe they were just sold that way as a standard feature—the same as wheels or a gas tank.

Like Uruguay, we received our meals for free as part of the contract. Lunch and dinner were actually delivered to our door. There wasn't a restaurant, but rather a family who simply ran a business out of their house. They cooked food and delivered it to customers around town. We never had to cook or even go out to eat if we didn't want to. But we were at their mercy when it came to what we ate. Sometimes it was way too much of something that we didn't like or recognize. Other times it was a delicious pasta that barely filled Cara. So I would often go around the corner to a small café and order two *panchos* (hot dogs) with melted cheese and a crispy potato topping and a Fanta for $1.50. Despite the uncertainty of our meal deliveries, it was Fabio-fabulous having meals dropped at our doorstep every day.

* * *

There were dozens of kids who hung around our basketball club and went to our games. Before one game, I picked up some candy at a convenience store so I could hand it out to the kids after the game. I handed the store owner a few pesos, worth about a dollar, and figured he would give me ten to twenty pieces of candy. Instead, he filled up a huge bag with well over a hundred pieces in it.

Following the game, I walked out of the gym and through the crowd of people hanging around the club. We had won again and everyone was in a great mood. There were men smoking and drinking at tables outside. Another group of people were having a barbecue. And all the kids were running around a large outdoor area, throwing balls and acting insane, since it was about 11 p.m. and Argentina doesn't have a word for *curfew*.

I handed the first kid I saw a piece of candy and his eyes lit up. He started yelling and jumping up and down, which was like a dog whistle to other kids in the surrounding areas. Within seconds I was mobbed by hot, sweaty *niños*. I handed each kid one piece and they'd circle back to get more, swearing they hadn't received a piece of candy yet. Even the old guys called for me to toss them some of the good stuff. Shortly thereafter, I became known as *El Caremelito*. "The Candyman."

* * *

I had been there less than a month, and Daniel's partner agent in Argentina, Nino, called me and asked if I wanted to play in the All-Star Game. One of the American players didn't accept his invitation, and they were short a player. Not the most glamorous way to make an All-Star team, but who cared? It wouldn't affect my endorsement deals. I hadn't been there long enough to justify my election one way or another. Plus, since I hadn't played on an All-Star team since little league and was allowed to bring Cara, I accepted.

We drove seven hours on a double-decker bus, and Cara got a first-hand glance at the way we travelled as a team. For weekend road trips we would leave on a Thursday and drive between six and twelve hours to our first game. We'd play on Friday and then bus another three to eight hours on Saturday to the next city. We'd play again on Sunday and then drive five to eight hours home following the game. Gualeguaychú never looked so good as at 5 a.m. on Monday mornings.

On our "All-Star" bus, we met some of the other Americans I'd be playing with. Tim Jones was the epitome of an All-Star. He wore his sunglasses everywhere he went and was decked out in the latest Nike gear from head to toe. Tim was hilarious, often unintentionally. Listening to Tim talk made the hours go by a lot faster for Cara and me.

"Ty, I visited my friend playing in Israel one time," Tim said. "And I heard all these big 'booms' off in the distance. I'm like, 'Yo, what's that?' He tells me it's bombs. *Bombs*, Ty!"

"That's crazy," I said.

"*Bombs, T*," he said. "I had to get outta there. I mean, I can dodge a bullet." He faked left and right in his seat like a fighter in the ring. "But I can't dodge no bomb."

While he was known for his scoring and showboating style of play, he insisted that all he wanted to do was win.

"Ty, man," he said, "People don't respect scoring."

"No?" I said.

"No," Tim said. "People respect championships."

"True," I said.

"They respect championships," he repeated. It was like he was trying to convince me that all he cared about was winning. But when a guy looks into the stands after every basket and makes gestures all game long to players, refs, and fans, people have a hard time believing he's only about winning championships. Tim was an amazing athlete and the most exciting player in the league. At 6-foot-3 he could dunk over 6-foot-10 guys and then drain four threes in a row. He played with a swagger that his team's fans loved and others hated. He was on his way to the perfect place for a guy who wore sunglasses indoors. The All-Star Game.

It was Americans vs. Argentineans. In many countries this wouldn't work because the Americans are often much stronger players. But

Argentina had some of the best talent in the world. They had just won the Olympics in 2004 with Manu Ginóbili leading the way. Granted, most top Argentineans played in the NBA and Europe, where they commanded bigger salaries. But the top national players in Argentina were still fantastic. Manu's brother Sebastián was actually one of the Argentinean All-Stars. He was a point guard and a righty. Not quite as lethal as his little brother, Manu, but still one of the top players in the country.

We (the Americans) were loaded with talent as well. We had experienced players and more athleticism than they did. Basketball was invented in our country. We thought for sure we'd win.

We were wrong. It was close the whole way, but we lost by a few points at the very end of the game. The fans loved it of course, seeing their homeland heroes take down the Americans. I was a little embarrassed and felt like we should have won. But big props to the Argentinean players. They earned it.

After the game we were swarmed by fans. The kids were relentless and we could barely make it to our bus. I signed as many autographs as I could, but it was impossible to get to everybody. Kids were begging for anything as a memento from the players. Some of my teammates who wore headbands and wristbands threw them to the kids. I had nothing.

"¡Una media! ¡Una media por favor!" the kids screamed.

"What are they asking for?" asked Cara.

"They want my socks," I said.

"Your socks?" said Cara. She knew all too well how disgusting my socks were.

"Yeah," I said.

"Oh, please don't," she said.

Trust me, kid. You do not want these socks.

* * *

Our team continued to play well and we were in the middle of a winning streak when my parents and sister came to visit from the United States. The weekend they were there was a road weekend for us. But my family didn't mind traveling, and they came to our game versus Ciclista (see-CLEE-sta) in a town called Junín (hoo-NEEN). Cara made the trip, also by bus, with them. I had been warned that Ciclista had the rowdiest fans in the league, known for attacking referees, players, and anyone who didn't wear their red and white. Perfect for Martha, Lindley, and Allison. They'd get a true taste of the madness.

Our team president came to the game and sat with my family up in the top corner of the bleachers in the least dangerous section, which is like saying the safest part of a riot. My family hadn't seen me play in a couple of years and were very excited for the game. But they were under strict orders from the president that they were not allowed to clap or cheer no matter what happened. The Ciclista fans were simply too erratic, and he didn't want anything to set them off.

At the end of the fourth quarter, the score was tied and we had the final possession. I received a pass with three seconds left. I took one hard dribble against my defender, who was on me like a leech. Then I went up for a shot. And missed.

But the whistle blew—foul. Two shots. One second on the clock.

The crowd went berserk and the ref had just invited about 2,500 death threats on his head.

When I'd gone up for the shot, there was enough contact to warrant the foul. But at the end of regulation with the game on the line, I wouldn't have been surprised if the ref had let it go. It was a gutsy call.

My family and the president were going crazy trying to control themselves. They wanted to scream and cheer, but it was too risky. They kept their arms tight by their sides, as they were already getting scowls from the home fans—as if my mom had been the one who blew the whistle.

I stepped up to the line. The crowd was deafening. I couldn't even hear the ball bounce as I took my four dribbles. It was an odd sensation, but I was having a hard time even really feeling my body with all of the noise. I had to rely on my muscles remembering what to do since the gym was one giant mega-scream.

Thankfully, my first free throw went in. We were up by one. With one second left, I didn't want to give them a chance to set up a Hail Mary play. And in international rules, you can't call a timeout while the ball is in play. So I missed the second free throw on purpose and the clock ran out.

Game over. We won.

The Ciclista fans were furious. It looked like a revolution was about to begin. The refs sprinted off the court to avoid getting mobbed.

Fabio screamed for our guys to get into the locker room immediately. He didn't have to tell me twice. There were no handshakes or nice game or good lucks. We raced into the locker room and locked the door when the last guy made it in. We could hear the fans stomping above us and screaming for justice. Many had begun to storm the court just as we were leaving.

A police escort entered the building and surrounded my family. They created a barrier between them and the loonies and helped my mom, dad, sister, Cara, and the president navigate their way out of the gym. People were pointing and shouting at all five of them. My family didn't exactly blend in and everyone knew that they belonged to the enemy.

It wasn't even safe for them to stand outside the gym and wait for me. So the police flagged down a taxi and sent them back to their hotel.

Later, my mom said, "Oh Tyler, it was crazy. One lady was looking right at me and kept screaming '¡(foreign expletive)!' '¡(repeat foreign expletive)!' at me in Spanish. But I didn't know what it meant."

Cara and I looked at each other.

"Yeah, we'll keep it that way," I said.

Meanwhile, our team got nice and cozy in the locker room because we weren't allowed to leave until every single fan was gone. Who knew how long that would take?

Basketball is exciting enough, especially when games come down to the last second. But throw in the element of potential bodily harm from irate citizens and you've got yourself one exhilarating show.

* * *

For each home win, I received a $100 bonus. Away wins were a little bit sweeter at $150. We went on a seven-game win streak that paid for a lot of ice cream and panchos, and we climbed a few spots in the standings.

The cost of living continued to blow me away. I dropped off my nasty socks and other disgusting practice gear at a laundromat on the corner and a woman would wash, dry, and fold each smelly load for under two dollars. God bless her. Cara and I hardly spent any money, and I felt like the richest guy in town. One month we really lived it up, going out to eat a lot, playing pool in a café nearby, and even visiting the local casino. Our total expenses were under $500 for the entire month.

We became good friends with one family in town, the Greccos. We would go over to their house for dinner and to watch the NCAA tournament since they had satellite TV. They even invited us waterskiing one day. Cara and I were shocked that anyone around Gualeguaychú had a powerboat, since it seemed like such a luxury in a fairly simple town. We jumped at the chance and were having a great time until the rope snapped when the boat tried to yank my huge butt out of the water. As I floated there with the rope's handle in my hand, waiting for my boat crew to secure a new line, I spotted something moving pretty quickly in the water. The boat was about fifteen yards in front of me, and I was a very easy target with my life jacket on and two water skis weighing me down.

It swam closer. A snake. A fat snake that was longer than me and moved much faster in water than I did. Who knew if it was a biter or a strangler? Snakes freaked me out. Especially Argentinean ones that swam towards me.

Fun's over, guys. You can pick me up now.

Thankfully, I did not have to wrestle the slimy reptile (or scream and cry like a five-year-old) as it decided against feasting on the foreigner.

Ricardo Grecco, the father, was a doctor and happened to be a superfan of our team, sitting in the front row of every game and giving the other team and the referees all the verbal abuse they could handle. I never paid much attention to him during the games, but Cara was highly entertained from her seat across the gym. He was the nicest man you'd ever meet off the court, and his wife and three boys were wonderful as well. But somehow he morphed into Loco Ricardo on game nights.

I have a theory. And it goes for more than just the Argentineans. It's commonly known as NFAWD. Nice For A While Disorder. During the week, people like Ricardo are very professional and polite in their jobs and with their families. They smile and serve. They laugh and joke. But something is churning inside on a deeper level. By the end of the week, they've had enough. All the pent-up aggression toward ungrateful patients, idiotic customers, and nagging spouses has to be released before the person explodes. It's a self-preservation matter. Sometimes people can go a month or even a few years before D-Day. Eventually though, all of the suppressed emotion will pour out. It's just a matter of time.

For Ricardo, it was twelve days, max. That was the amount of time between home games, when he would go about his daily business in a friendly manner before he blew his lid sitting courtside across from the visiting team's bench.

Ricardo was nice. Until Friday night home games.

* * *

Central finished in fourth place during the regular season, which meant we should have received a bye in the first round of playoffs. However, because our fans attacked a referee earlier in the season, we were penalized and knocked down two spots to sixth place. It happened before I arrived, but I was not shocked to hear of such an occurrence. Horrendous refs + basketball maniacs = very bad things.

We swept the first round of playoffs, 3–0.

The second round matched us against Atenas and Mr. All-Star himself, Tim Jones. Atenas had been playing very well and was really talented. Tim had some great national players on his team, and they had very few weak spots. It was not going to be an easy series. We were extreme underdogs, as Atenas had championship banners hanging in their gym. Our banner had a picture of a chicken.

Before every game when the starters shook hands at half-court, the Americans on the other team would always say the same thing to me and Nichy. "Be safe."

Not "good luck" or "play well."

Rather, "Be safe."

I had never heard that before in all of the countries I'd played. But I liked it and quickly adopted it. Only the American guys would say it to the other Americans. It was kind of like our own little brotherhood mantra. We all knew how insane things could get during the games, with the outrageous atmosphere in every gym. To me, the message between Americans was, "Look, we are going to compete and try to beat each other tonight. But whatever happens, nobody wants to get hurt. This is how we feed our families."

The series was best of five and the first two games were at Atenas. We lost both as Tim Jones and company showed why they were one of the best teams in the country. Even though we lost both games, we had played them pretty well on the road and knew that we could get them at home.

In Game Three, we jumped out to a big lead with our fans pumping the place full of energy with songs I couldn't understand but loved to hear. The words didn't matter. The message and emotion were all we needed, and we won convincingly.

Down 2–1 in the series, we were still one game from elimination, but that first home win gave us a lot of confidence. With Game Four on our home court again, the momentum had swung back in our favor.

* * *

There was one day off between playoff games, and Ricardo and Elina Grecco invited me out to dinner. Cara wasn't feeling well and couldn't come. I let the Greccos pick the restaurant, as this was their hometown and they knew the best places to eat.

Where did they pick? None other than the hotel restaurant where Atenas was staying. Hey, this won't be weird.

Of all of the restaurants in this city, did we really have to walk into the tiny restaurant of our current playoff rival?

When we walked in, the restaurant was full except for four tables that were reserved for Atenas. And lucky us, we were seated close enough to lean over and eat off their plates.

We ordered our food and had begun eating when Atenas walked in. They walked right by our table, and every player looked at me like, "What the…?"

I gave a half-hearted wave.

I know, I know. I didn't choose the place.

The table right next to us was full of players and they started to get loud as some sort of argument was brewing. One of the players was pointing at our table and raising his voice in Spanish.

Just what I was hoping for. A large public confrontation with the entire Atenas team the night before our next playoff game. If this went down, I didn't like my chances with the 150-pound doctor and his 110-pound wife against twelve large angry Argentineans.

The player who was making the most commotion next to us pushed his chair back, stood up, and threw his napkin on the table.

Great, here we go.

He took two steps and was standing next to Ricardo, who was seated directly across from me. The Atenas player looked right at me with a scowl on his face. Then, he looked down at Ricardo and began cursing at him and shaking his finger in his face. The player pressed his finger against Ricardo's head and shoved him hard. Ricardo's head wobbled to the side.

"Hey relax, man!" I said. "Chill out."

The entire restaurant stopped eating and was watching the drama unfold.

The player pushed Ricardo's head to the side again and continued cursing at him. Ricardo just threw his hands up and kept looking straight ahead as if to say, "I'm innocent." The player leaned down and got right in his face. Clearly the player had a personal issue with Ricardo.

"Relax man!" I said again.

The player looked at me. "He curse me, my family, and my Jewish people," he raged. "Now I curse him."

I knew Ricardo could go overboard in his Spike Lee courtside seats. The Ricardo I knew didn't have a bigoted bone in his body. But the chances were high that he said some very colorful—even unacceptable—things at the previous night's game, including toward our new friend from the table next door. And Mr. Backup Atenas Guard was not going to miss his opportunity to fire back.

Some other Atenas players jumped in and pulled the crazy guard away from Ricardo and yanked him the whole whopping four feet back to their table.

Ricardo, you're killing me. First you insult some benchwarmer at our game, saying who knows what, and then you bring me to the restaurant where he and his entire team are dining? "Nice Ricardo" would never have done this. Please bring him back.

Then, something very interesting happened.

The entire restaurant began yelling at the Atenas player. It went from silent to shouting in a split second and every Gualeguaychuan was waving their hands and napkins towards the Atenas team. The restaurant was rallying behind Ricardo. They weren't going to let an opposing team come into their town and bully one of their people in their restaurant. They wouldn't have cared if Ricardo kidnapped the player's entire family. They were going to stand behind him. It was a fascinating moment.

Check, please.

* * *

Game Four started with a bang. Tim Jones got hot in a hurry and already had 15 points midway through the second quarter. But we were playing well, too, and were up by eight.

Tim drove baseline and *boom!* He dunked right over our big man, something that no one had done all season.

Tim jogged coolly down the court nodding his head with pride over the ridiculous play he just made. It certainly was impressive, and if I had the athletic ability for such feats, I can't say I wouldn't suggest my sheer awesomeness to the crowd as well.

Suddenly, he turned and bolted toward his bench. The assistant coach and players intercepted him. At first I thought he wanted to fight his coach, whom he'd clashed with in the past. But it turned out he was taking on the entire fan section behind his bench instead. His girlfriend had been standing up and yelling at some of our fans, and Tim was trying to defend her honor mid-game.

Only Tim would have even noticed the scene, because he looked into the crowd so much. There could be unicorns and kangaroos in the stands for all I knew. I was way too focused on the game.

Tim never did make it up into the stands, but he did receive his very own technical foul. His coach received one during the fracas, too. We sank the free throws and scored on the possession, which gave us some huge momentum. We went on to win by more than 20 points and even the series at 2–2. I should have thanked his girlfriend and given her some candy after the game.

Presumably, Ricardo was somewhat more under control during the game. At least our new dining buddy didn't throw any balls at him during warmups, so I assume Ricardo was on his "best" behavior.

Game Five at Atenas proved to be too big of a challenge for us. Atenas hit big shot after big shot on their home floor to beat us by 12. Our season was finished.

We had a lot to be proud of. We finished fourth (if you don't count our "ref mauling" incident) and took Atenas to five games in the second round of playoffs. It was the best finish the team had ever achieved.

And most importantly ... Central won Carnaval!

Which means I received every peso the team said it would pay.

I need to shake that transvestite's hand.

Gracias.

Chapter 9

RICK BARRY NOTICES: CHINA DRAFT CAMP

Max convinced me to go to Italy again for the Treviso Summer League. He felt that because I'd had a strong season in South America, particularly Argentina, it would help my stock among the European coaches.

I remembered my passport this time, and I brought my wife and her cousin, Anna. Riding in a Venetian gondola wasn't a bad way to spend our one-year anniversary. Anna even paid for it as her gift to us, making it that much more romantic. In exchange, we took Anna to see the Pope in Rome. He didn't recognize us and call out to us by name outside the Vatican, but we were pretty busy anyway. You know how it is.

I played well at the camp once again, and Max was working the Italian teams hard. My phone rang.

"Tyler, I have a team for you," Max said with his usual excitement.

"How serious is this, Max?" I asked.

Quit playing games with my heart, Maximus. I knew he was doing his very best and would never mislead me on purpose. He would often flat out tell me that there was no news or that I didn't play well enough. I respected his honesty and appreciated him coming clean.

"This is a very serious offer," Max continued. "The GM likes you. The president likes you. And the head coach likes you."

That's the golden combination right there. All it takes is for one of three not to be in agreement and I'm out of luck. So unless they needed the equipment guy to sign off on it, I was in line to head back to Italy. Oh, fresh gelato, I can taste you now.

"The team will give you a two-year deal," he continued. "The first year will be $75,000 and the second year will be $100,000."

I'd have played for half of that offer. *Max, don't tell them that.*

"If they choose to not keep you for the second year, then they will pay $85,000 for the first year," he added. "This is 99 percent sure right now. I will call you tomorrow when I have the contract."

Ninety-nine percent sure felt like 100 percent. I had been hoping and waiting for more than two years to have another shot at Italy. This time, it really felt good.

The next day came and I checked my phone every eight seconds. Nothing.

Two days after my dream phone call, Max rang again. This was it!

"The team is waiting to sign another Italian player first," he said.

It wasn't it.

Two weeks went by and the team wasn't able to sign the Italian players it wanted. As a result, I wasn't the right fit with the players they brought in. The deal was off. Italia, where's the *amore*?

* * *

We returned home to Pennsylvania, and Cara's wrist was giving her lots of pain. She had been having problems with it for the past year, and a cyst had developed. It was drained, it reappeared, was drained again, and returned, like a bad movie trilogy. Each one worse than the one before. Keep in mind that there was a theory in play that the cyst was actually my fault. Truthfully, I don't know how forcing her to carry countless kilos of luggage to foreign countries repeatedly could have any effect on a wrist. But if so, such is the price of global domination.

Cara endured surgery in July 2006 to remove the cyst and had a terrible reaction to the anesthesia, becoming very sick for longer than expected. She also learned first-hand what migraines were, unfortunately.

Four days after surgery she was still not doing well. Sure enough, that's when I had to leave for a tryout camp in Oregon. You can see where my priorities were that week. Thankfully, her mom came to the rescue and nursed her back to health. Note: it required me *leaving* for her condition to improve.

The China Basketball Association (CBA) paid an organization called the United States Basketball Academy (USBA) to hold an exposure camp in the States. The Chinese teams would then draft American players from the camp to be the imports for their teams in the CBA. Since all of the NBA teams had made the biggest mistake of their lives by not drafting me out of Lake Forest (Illinois) High School or Penn State, I figured a draft for China was a close second.

At the time, this was the only way you could get into the Chinese pro league. Eight hundred players applied to get into the China Draft Camp. Only eighty were invited. I was not one of them. Instead I paid $500 to go to a guard/big man camp the week before the China draft camp, and if I played well enough, I could earn one of the four spots reserved for the actual draft camp. In other words, I was the back-up date to the dance. There were lots of better-looking guys in line ahead of me with better hair and better moves.

Since the Chinese paid about ten times what I had made in the past, I figured it was worth a shot. My only other job lead was down in Uruguay. One of the old sponsors at Salto was now with Unión Atletica. He asked me to return to Uruguay and play for his new team. I informed him that Salto still owed me a fair amount of money and if they wanted to settle that first, then I would be happy to discuss a possible return to Uruguay. He said that if I came down there and signed with his team, *then* Unión Atletica could arrange settling former debts.

So you want me to come back to Uruguay when the team you sponsored before didn't pay me? How about you pay me first, then we can talk?

I don't think it was his fault that I wasn't paid in Salto the first time around. It was the sketchy management who didn't honor their agreement. He wasn't the GM or in charge of those things, so I had to cut him some slack.

I really liked him and appreciated his offer. He even dangled the possibility of helping me get a Uruguayan passport. It sounded far too easy for me to gain citizenship there, seeing as I had spent less than eight months total actually within its borders. Did they sell passports in vending machines? Uruguayan citizenship would certainly increase my value quite a bit and guarantee me a job playing into my forties. But it might also guarantee I'd require knee replacements every three years from the lousy playing surfaces.

I think I'll take my chances with the Chinese.

* * *

The China camp was located about one hour from Eugene, Oregon. Picture a beautiful campground retreat-style location in the middle of the woods with a pond and mountains looming in the background. Then add six full-size basketball courts (four outside, two inside), cabins to hold 250 guests, a dining hall, state-of-the-art weight room, and a thirty-foot Yao Ming banner … and you've got yourself a place where literally the only thing you could do is play basketball. Or chop wood. All while admiring the scenery.

Only Verizon users had cellphone service. And that was within a ten-square-foot area. Internet wouldn't be out there for another fifty years, mark my words. But there was running water, and when the toilets were not clogged up, everything was cool.

Bruce O'Neil, the former head basketball coach at the University of Hawaii, founded the USBA. He put together an impressive board of supporters that included basketball legends such as John Wooden, Kareem Abdul-Jabbar, Rick Barry, Shaquille O'Neal, and many more. Hall of Famer Rick Barry was scheduled to make an appearance for the last two days of the China Draft Camp.

* * *

I played well enough in my first week there (the tryout for the try-out camp) to be selected to stick around for the China Draft Camp. I was in. Then, the real test began.

The word was crystal clear from the get-go. The Chinese were looking for *big* and *athletic* guys as their foreign players. I fit about one-fourth of the criteria. There were more than twenty guys who were 6-foot-10 and taller. Numerous players had NBA experience. A few were former NBA draft picks. Plenty had big contracts overseas already playing for $30,000 to $50,000 per month and beyond. I was coming from Uruguay and a freshly healed Achilles. Bring the ruckus.

I was one of eighty who were vying for twenty-one draft positions and guaranteed contracts worth up to $25,000 per month. A few Chinese teams would keep one of their American players from the previous year. Every other team would draft two new players.

The draft would be four rounds, with the first two rounds of picks receiving guaranteed contracts. If a deal could not be reached with the team and player from the first two rounds, then the third- or fourth-round pick would receive the contract. That particular year, the Chinese had a rule that a team was not allowed to change its foreign player during the season. Once you were signed, it was guaranteed. It was better job security than the post office. To my knowledge, China was the only country that did not allow replacement players, even if some-one got injured.

From day one, I knew I pretty much had the award locked up for lowest vertical leap. Five-foot-ten-inch guards had sweeter dunks than me. Out of eighty players, there were six white guys. I was No. 80 in terms of athleticism. I'm pretty sure a few refs even had me beat. But there's a little Rudy in all of us and I was dreaming, baby. Oh, was I dreaming.

The camp was five days long. Since I had already been there for a full week for the guard/big man camp and had adjusted to peeing in the woods, I had an advantage over the stronger and faster players. The shock and awe of the unconventional environment had worn off. Many of those guys were completely out of their element. No TV, no women, no video games. It was borderline prison camp for some. At least a few brought their stash of weed to endure the punishment. It's a miracle a forest fire was not started that week behind the cabins.

Being secluded didn't bother me one bit. It helped me focus on basketball, and I'd be back to reality soon enough. If other guys were miserable and it affected their play, then that just meant a better opportunity for me to move up the depth chart.

I had to find ways to separate myself from the pack of ultra-athletes. Despite many players' natural athleticism, it was incredible to me how lazy guys were when there were jobs on the line. I played really hard and was more vocal than other guys. My pasty white skin tone even helped me stand out. It didn't hurt that I was making shots from everywhere and outplaying guys I knew were more talented than me. It was probably the best basketball week of my life.

Lo and behold, I was chosen to play in the "Projected First Round Picks" game on the last day. I had arguably the best game of anyone on the floor and put myself in position, potentially, to be a lottery pick. What's up with a shoe deal?

After the game, Rick Barry walked up to me.

"You know, Tyler," he said. "It's a shame that you aren't in the NBA right now."

Pardon? You mean like a mascot or the beer guy? It sounded like you said something about me and the NBA in the same sentence. And since you're in the Hall of Fame, I'm going to assume you haven't been smoking up with some of my teammates over in the woods.

"Wow, Rick . . . Mr. Barry," I stammered. "Thank you."

Yeah, because I was just thinking that if Kobe would just get his act together and send Phil Jackson to sign me, they'd have way more championships.

"I'm sure you'll be going to China, as there are some teams that really like you," he said. "But if you don't, I'll make some calls for you. The NBA needs more guys like you that can play smart and really understand the game."

I've always felt the NBA wasn't maximizing their market potential by me not suiting up, as well.

Talk about a vote of confidence. I was completely shocked at his words and his willingness to help an unknown player like me. Bruce O'Neil also had some encouraging words for me after the game. Another coach even went so far as to say, "Start thinking about how much you want to ask for." I was sky-high headed into the draft.

On draft day, the players went to the cafeteria in Nike shorts, cut-off Ts, and flip-flops. Standard non-NBA draft attire. The draft began, and before each team announced their pick, the team would show a two-minute video of their city. It was pretty cool until all the cities you couldn't pronounce began to look the same. And sure enough, big athletic guy after big athletic guy was drafted. Even some who didn't play particularly well that week.

The tension in the room grew with each pick that went by. *Would they call my name? I couldn't play any better than I did this week.*

"Tyler Smith."

Too late. I was selected by Dongguan with the number two pick in the third round which meant I wasn't offered a guaranteed deal. They handed me an 8XL jersey and a hat. I posed for a picture while shaking hands with the coach. But it was all for show. I missed a guaranteed deal by two measly picks. The players selected by Dongguan in rounds one and two were quite content with their large contracts, so there was no need for me to hang around.

Ironically, the two players picked immediately before me and after me in the third round were given contracts. Even though they went in the same round as me, their teams couldn't reach an agreement with their first- and second-round picks, so the third-round guys signed deals. I was headed home with the consolation prize of being the first white guy picked out of the six of us.

Something shady was going on. I was told by multiple American coaches at the camp that there was, in fact, a reason why I wasn't picked higher. Not because of production. Not because of attitude or effort. But because I was white.

Before the draft, one Chinese coach called home to his team's president in China and said that he'd found their guy (me).

"Is he white or black?" the president asked.

"He's white," the coach said.

"Pick somebody else."

They were looking for a different kind of player, and I just wasn't it. They had slow guys who could shoot, hustle, and defend. They wanted someone who could play above the rim.

I think I just got discriminated against by the Chinese.

All I could do was laugh. When things are not meant to be, they just are not meant to be. Some things just aren't in God's plan for our lives.

Fortunately, Rick Barry didn't forget about me.

"I'm going to make some calls for you," he told me before I left.

You're my new best friend. Can I call you Ricky?

He contacted a couple of teams and I received my first phone call from an NBA team, the Utah Jazz.

Naturally, I downplayed the phone conversation with the team as if I received those calls all the time, because that's what you're supposed to do instead of giggling like a little school girl hopped up on Pixy Stix. They invited me to a workout at the end of September in Salt Lake City. And … now I need new underwear.

As Ben Sturgill, my swimming buddy from Uruguay, put it, "Man, I'd be psyched if the Jazz called just to wish me happy birthday. I'd be happy just flying out to meet their mascot."

Whether an angel visited Jerry Sloan in a dream or Rick Barry lost a bet with someone, it looked like I'd have a shot (however small) at the big time.

Hold on.

OK. I just threw up.

Chapter 10

GOD, JERRY SLOAN, AND $412,718: THE UTAH JAZZ

For the next six weeks. I worked out like a madman. I lifted and ran. I shot and played. I ate a strict diet and even took creatine. Every day. I had never been so focused on getting ready for anything in my life.

My trainer in State College was Rob Oshinskie, who owned Victory Sports. He played a huge part in preparing me, down to every detail.

"Why am I doing twice as many sets of calf raises on my right leg as my left?" I asked.

"Because your right calf is smaller due to your Achilles surgery," he said. "I can see that easily. You don't want to be walking away from a coach and he sees one of your legs is muscular and the other looks like a chicken. You don't want to give them any reason to have a negative thought about you."

That was the kind of attention to detail that Rob maintained. He and his staff helped me add fifteen pounds of muscle and drop to 6 percent body fat. Cutting out ice cream for the Jazz was easier than when I gave it up for Lent one time. Sorry, Lord.

* * *

Another small miracle happened during this time. My old team in Italy, Imola, had been dragging their feet about paying me what they

still owed me. Max had been all over them for the past three years, trying to recover what he could. The team had said they would pay "next
month" for years now, and it never came. They still owed me a few
thousand dollars, but I had lost track of the exact amount. It may not
have been much to some people, but I needed every dollar.

One day in church, I wanted to put some money in the offering
plate with some type of meaning behind it instead of a random five-
or ten-dollar bill. I happened to have exactly forty-two in cash. Two
twenties and two singles.

I prayed.

*Lord, this is all I have in my wallet today. If you multiply this by
10,000, then that would equal the amount of a rookie contract in the
NBA. I don't know if that is what you have in mind for me, but I ask that
you would do something great with this meager offering.*

Listen. I don't believe that when you give money, you should
expect God to give you back more money. And my request may not
have been the most holy. God's not an ATM in the sky or a piñata that
you can whack until you get what your selfish desires want. God calls
us to be generous because He is the most generous of all, and we need
to reflect Him in that sense. By His grace I was trying to be generous,
but none of us will ever out-give God.

It's okay to pray for big things. I was pursuing an NBA contract.
Sometimes the answer is yes. Sometimes the answer is no. I wasn't
quoting scripture and demanding that God do what I said, because
that's not how it works. Forty-two dollars was a drop in the bucket to
the church, but it was a fair amount for me at the time. So I prayed and
asked God to bless the small amount that I had.

Three days later, on Wednesday, I received a bank transfer: $4,256.
It was from my team in Italy, finally settling its three-year-old debt with
me. It was money I never thought I'd see. It was also a hundred times
what I had put into the offering plate on Sunday. And God even threw
in an extra fifty-six dollars to cover the wire fees. Now, that's generous.

The fact that Imola paid me was pretty much miraculous in itself.
Then add in the timing, and it really amazed me and strengthened my

faith. Not because I received the money, but because it gave a small glimpse into an infinite God who knows every single detail of our lives down to how many hairs are on our head and how many pennies we have in our bank account or couch. He knows and loves us deeply. That's a beautiful thing.

While I had asked God for one thing, the NBA contract, he had given me something else.

And who knew: the contract remained to be seen. He is a big God after all.

* * *

My relationship with the NBA was very one-sided, like the nerdy guy who's in love with the smokin' hot model. She has no idea he exists, and he's a borderline stalker. But one day a friend sets her up on a blind date with the nerdy guy. And he gets his shot.

I was the twenty-six-year-old nerd. But my game had come a long way in four years since I graduated college. I was much more confident in myself as a player. If everything went well during my three days of workouts, just maybe I'd get a shot at a second date. Training camp.

* * *

The Jazz flew me first-class to Salt Lake City on September 22, 2006. I don't know if the whole first-class thing was a standard NBA rule or if the Jazz felt bad for slow white guys who didn't have much of a chance. They didn't have to spend all that money for the upgrade. I would have ridden a mule to Utah if they'd sent one.

I arrived three days early because I wanted to get acclimated to the higher altitude of Salt Lake City and meet up with my old friend's family, the Rabetoys. I hadn't seen them in over a decade.

Joe Rabetoy and I had gone to junior high together in Lake Bluff, Illinois. His family moved from California to Lake Bluff, and Joe and I became instant friends. He was the best athlete and most competitive person I had ever met in my life. He was a really passionate guy and

Holland, 2002. Who says we don't have style? Todd, Scott, me, and Ivan (from left to right). Our tiny car behind us was plastered with sponsor logos, making it difficult to speed and park illegally.

"You shoot it!" I'm passing to Jobey Thomas (#9) which was probably wise since I couldn't make anything that year (2003) and ended up getting cut partway through the season. I loved Italy, but I hated that blue and white ball. *Photo courtesy of Imola Basketball.*

How about some mate (MAH-tay)! Outside Diego's house in Salto, Uruguay, with Bicho, Diego, and his mom (from left to right). Bicho claimed this drink gave him super powers. Given the way he played, I believed him.

Americans vs. Argentineans All-Star Game, 2006. Tim Jones, in true form, is front and center. We had incredible talent, but actually lost to the Argentinean team which included Manu Ginobli's brother, Sebastian.

The world is not built for tall people. This was in Italy, but it could have been in most any country. During my time in Japan, I stayed in hotels for over 200 nights and I wasn't able to stand completely upright in a single shower.

About as close as I'll ever get to the Hall of Fame. Rick Barry (NBA Hall of Famer) and I at the 2006 China draft camp in the woods of Oregon. While I didn't get picked up by a Chinese team, Rick connected me with someone way better—Jerry Sloan and the Utah Jazz.

Snapped this pic in the Jazz locker room just before the VP came in. Derek Fisher's locker was next to mine. I'm pretty sure he requested it.

With the Anaheim Arsenal in the NBA D-League (2007). Seven-foot-three Ha on my left and MaJic sporting his signature headband on my right. We are wearing Clippers jerseys playing in the Staples Center against the Lakers' D-League Team, the D-Fenders. Roughly twenty-eight people were in the stands—possibly there by accident.

"Get outta my way!" One of the few awesome pictures of my hang time in Holland. The shot went in and my song started playing—"Ice, Ice, Baby." *Photo courtesy of Brigitte van Heeswijk.*

Cara and I sporting our Matrixx Magixx lime green on our home floor (The Horstacker!) in Nijmegen, Holland, 2008. Baby Hannah is inside, flipped the wrong way.

I actually dunked this one! It didn't happen often which, in a way, is kind of nice because then they are easier to remember. *Photo courtesy of Hitachi SunRockers.*

For THREE! This one went in. My third year with Hitachi (2011) and we are playing in Tokyo in our "home" gym called Yoyogi. Notice the handful of fans wearing the "dentist masks" in the stands. Safety first! *Photo courtesy of Julie Zamorano.*

Cara, Hannah, and I at the All-Japan tournament in 2011. I looked like Big Bird in all my yellow. But, I did bring home a shiny trophy for making the All-Tourney team—one of the first Americans to do so, I was told. *Photo courtesy of Hitachi SunRockers.*

Can you guess which one belongs to me? Hannah (four) singing her heart out at Sunnyside International School in 2012. She was the only non-Japanese kid in the entire school, thus making it "international."

My coach (and Kobe's dad), Joe "Jellybean" Bryant, and me at a tournament in Bangkok, Thailand, in 2013. We didn't have enough players for one game, so Coach Joe suited up and played forty minutes. He out-scored me. At age fifty-seven. The guy can play. And no one loves the game more than Joe.

Look who just walked right into our restaurant in Thailand. Out for a casual night on the town. Justin and I were fascinated while the Thai players weren't that impressed.

very inspiring. I felt like there was nothing he couldn't do. If there was an MVP award for football, basketball, and baseball, he'd have won it for each sport during our eighth-grade year.

He was funny, the girls loved him, and he had no fear.

No one was tougher than Joe, and I'd have bet on him in any fight.

Unfortunately, Joe moved away once high school arrived. He suffered a nasty knee injury playing football, and he wasn't the same. But he taught himself how to play lacrosse and became an All-State player in his very first year, and he went on to play lacrosse in college.

Joe only knew one speed—100 mph—which was great for sports but bad for life. He got caught up in a bad scene of drugs and alcohol after college and almost threw it all away. One night, things had become so bad that his dad and brother, Tim, literally dragged him away from that lifestyle before it killed him.

I stayed with Joe's dad, Gary, in Salt Lake City. He explained to me that while Joe was doing better, he was still getting his life in order, and I wouldn't be able to visit with him. I was disappointed because I hadn't seen him in over ten years, but happy to hear that he was doing a little bit better than before.

I left a letter with his dad to give to him.

Joe,
I'm sorry that we didn't get to see each other this time. I'm glad to hear that you are doing better. If you ever want to reconnect, I'll be here for you. No matter when that time comes. Please know that Jesus loves you and I love you.

Your friend always,
Ty

Joe's brother Tim drove me to the Jazz practice facility the day before my official workouts would begin. I wanted to get some shots up so I could get a feel for the court and the balls before my big interview. The assistant trainer, Brian Zettler, let us in the building and showed us to the locker room.

It was huge and amazing on every level. None of my locker rooms in Uruguay had vending machines in them. Or saunas.

I looked at the names above the lockers. Carlos Boozer, Andrei Kirilenko, Deron Williams.

"Your locker is over there," Brian said.

On the outside I said, "Great, thanks."

On the inside, *Holy crap, I have a locker?*

He pointed to the corner.

There was my name. Not scribbled in Sharpie on a piece of shredded athletic tape, either. It was on an official Utah Jazz nameplate. Spelled correctly. And laminated. I guess word got out that I was coming.

Next to my locker: Derek Fisher.

Yep, awesome.

Brian said to make myself at home and that I was free to shoot and use the facility. Then he left the locker room.

"Tim, quick, I need some pictures," I said. I handed him my camera. Before I appeared as some gaudy tourist rather than someone trying out for the team, I had to get some photos while I was alone in the locker room. Who knew how long I'd last? I needed evidence that this was really happening.

Tim snapped a couple pictures. Then we heard the locker room door open. The vice president of basketball operations, Kevin O'Connor, walked in.

Tim. Camera. Away! Oh please don't let management have seen me posing like an idiot.

I don't think O'Connor saw my modeling moment, thankfully. Tim was a smart guy and was thinking the same thing that I was. He slid the camera into his pocket nonchalantly.

We went out to the practice gym where I got some shots up and took a few more pictures while no one was around. I couldn't believe I was playing in the same gym where Karl Malone and John Stockton had practiced. Nor could I fathom that I was wearing legit NBA clothing that my mom didn't buy me at Target.

* * *

The next day I began the workouts. The other young Jazz players were there, who had just been drafted—Ronnie Brewer and Paul Millsap. C. J. Miles, a second-year Jazz player, and Roger Powell, a rookie free agent, showed up as well. Assistant coaches Ty Corbin and Scott Layden put us through different drills and I performed well. I was a fundamental player who could shoot well and was skilled, so I generally looked half-decent in drills as long as dunking wasn't the main objective.

Jerry Sloan and his top assistant, Phil Johnson, walked in and sat courtside. I tried to continue to act cool, but let's be honest. Up until this point I'd played for Herman, Tito, and Fabio, not an NBA Hall of Fame coach. I was slightly more nervous.

At the end of the workout we played one-on-one to five baskets, with each player rotating into the game. I am not the world's greatest one-on-one player, but I won the first game pretty handily. In the second game, I was the first one to four points, but couldn't finish it off. Still, having beaten the new Jazz draft picks, a second-year player, and a very talented Roger Powell, I was starting to feel like I belonged.

After the workout, the veterans showed up. Carlos Boozer, Andrei Kirilenko, and most of the rest of the team. We scrimmaged five-on-five with the coaches watching. I definitely felt the eyeballs on me whether they were there or not. Fortunately, I did not trip over any lines or throw up any memorable air balls. Nor was I dunked on, which would have shattered the meager confidence I was slowly building. I just played my butt off and tried to show effort and enthusiasm, and fake the fact that I wasn't moments away from collapsing in the oxygen-deprived city of Salt Lake.

Coach Sloan approached me after the games.

"Rick Barry had some nice things to say about you," he said as we shook hands.

I don't know what prescription medications Rick was on at the time, but here I am. God bless his soul.

"Thanks, Coach," I said. "I hope to prove him right."

Guilt suddenly rushed through my entire being. I had cheered like mad against Coach Sloan and the Jazz two years in a row when the Chicago Bulls beat them in the 1997 and 1998 NBA Finals. Growing up just outside Chicago, I was a huge Bulls fan. Nobody in Chicago liked Stockton's shorts or Malone's dunks. We loved the Triangle offense and hated the pick-and-roll just because Utah ran it.

Now here I was—face-to-face with the man I had wanted to see lose more than anything else in the world as a teenager. A few years later and I'm dying to make his team.

I felt awful. Mike and Scottie had five rings going into the 1998 Finals. Standing in front of Coach Sloan at that moment, maybe it would have been nice for me if they'd let him have just one. Then I could say, "Hey, congratulations on that title, Coach. It feels like I was watching it just yesterday." Which it did. I had great memories of those Bulls championship runs, but they probably weren't so fond for Coach Sloan. Not the best conversation piece.

I briefly considered confessing my blatant anti-Jazz past to purge myself of the guilt and come clean. I was a Jazz player now. Or at least I really wanted to be. Purple and white for life! Who needs the Bulls?

But the smarter version of me stopped short of a confession, as I didn't see any productive way that nervous conversation would have ended. "Yeah, I saw all those championship games against Chicago. Too bad you guys lost. Twice. In a row. Great last shot by M. J. though, right?" I'm an idiot.

Instead I shifted the meeting to a more personal level.

"Congratulations on your new marriage," I said. Coach Sloan had remarried just two weeks before. His first wife passed away from cancer in 2004.

"Thank you," he said. "It feels good now. I was lonely."

He said it in a very touching way. I was surprised at his candor seeing as we had just met. But Coach Sloan is a very straightforward person. From his answer it appeared that he must have had a heavy heart for quite some time. Understandably so. Now he seemed to have moved into a happier season of life.

Let's keep him that way. Maybe I can stick around a while.

* * *

I was expecting some sort of defining moment from the coaching staff after my three days of workouts were complete. That was the agreement: they'd watch me and then give a yay or nay. But no one said a word to me. I showered up. Hung around.

Nothing.

So I went back to the hotel where I waited for a phone call. Still nothing. Not really knowing what to do, I figured I would just show up at the gym the next day like I had the past three days and see what happened.

Scenario A: "Hey, Tyler. Great to see you. Stick around ... training camp is on its way."

Scenario B: "Why are you still here?"

Worst case was that I would be sent packing after three great days with an NBA team. That was three more than I ever thought I'd have.

Sure enough, at 9 a.m. my phone rang as I was in the car on the way to the gym. And the news was ... *good.* They invited me to training camp, and I was to be put on the payroll and sign my first NBA contract.

Thank you Jesus! How can anyone not believe in God now? This was as big a miracle as Moses parting the Red Sea.

A lot of hard work had paid off. And somehow I had found great favor in the team's eyes.

Hours later I sat down with Kevin O'Connor to sign a one-year deal for $412,718. Kevin was very gracious and gave me some time to look through it. I don't know why I felt compelled to read all of the legal jargon. Maybe because I had never seen an NBA contract before and my previous contracts had been written in foreign languages. I guess I just felt it was responsible to give a quick read to what I was signing.

Obviously there was nothing to worry about. It wasn't like they were going to slip some clause in there that read, "We reserve the rights to your first born child and all of your family-owned property dating back to the 1800s. And you'll have to drive the veteran's kids to school three times per week."

I signed for the NBA minimum. Better than the Gatorade summer job minimum. Compared to Boozer's six-year, $70 million deal, it felt a little low. But let's be real. I didn't exactly hold many chips at the table.

And the contract was contingent, of course, upon me actually making the final cut at the end of October. Details.

* * *

Training camp was easy. If you were a "multi" player that is. Multi-million, multiyear.

Well, maybe it was easi*er*. At first, it was a little intimidating playing with guys who had been first-round picks, had won NBA titles, and owned more cars than I did shoes. A year ago I was carrying my own toilet paper to away games.

But once I got out on the court and was in basketball mode, all those insecurities went away and I focused on playing as hard as I could. There was no slacking with Coach Sloan in charge. I definitely couldn't go half-speed in a drill or pace myself at any time, because I'd be sent packing. The Jazz took eighteen of us to training camp, held at Boise State University. The team could keep fifteen, max. It was fascinating to get to know the different personalities on the team.

Deron Williams was in his second year as the Jazz point guard and he was an absolute stud. He would make crossover moves at full speed and never miss a beat. Every time he shot, I swore it went in. He was extremely competitive and played with a chip on his shoulder. Now that he wasn't a rookie anymore, he also made sure that the new guys unloaded the bags from the plane.

Carlos Boozer was a great communicator on the floor. He was always talking on offense and defense. "Booz," as everyone called him, was one of the friendliest guys on the team and treated everyone with respect, from the GM down to the managers. He even left me with a sizable slash mark on my shoulder that I can tell my grandkids about.

"AK47," Andrei Kirilenko, had one of the most interesting skillsets I had ever seen. His arms were unbelievably long, and he seemed to somehow get a deflection on every possession. He could do everything. He was a very smart player and always made subtle plays that were crucial in games but easily went unrecognized if you weren't on the floor with him. He also owned the largest laptop I had ever seen—some elite Russian super machine.

Derek Fisher was the classiest of them all. He was the definition of a professional who had a great attitude and kept himself in tremendous shape. Before training camp even started, he was one of the first players in town. His personal trainer flew in just to train him for a few days. I even saw Fish make nineteen NBA threes in a row during a drill. And it was one random drill on a random day, which means … he could make a lot more than that.

I became closest with Roger Powell, who was not only a Christian but also an ordained minister. We were both from Illinois and had each renewed our faith in God during college as we realized there was more to life than just basketball and girls. Roger was a terrific guy and an intense competitor. We had some great theological discussions with another rookie, Frans Steyn, about what it meant to honor God with the abilities He gave us. Measuring a legitimate 7-foot-2, 290-lbs, Frans was one of the biggest guys I had ever played with. He took away just as much spiritually as he did from basketball in his time with the Jazz, which was great to see.

Every player on the Jazz was a nice guy who had a brain in his head. I'm sure that was by design, as Coach Sloan wanted intelligent, hard-working players to fit his system.

The first two weeks were very draining for me. Just about every muscle in my legs was strained and screaming. The trainers became my new best friends. I couldn't stop working though. Even on off days I went in to shoot because I had to show that I was willing to work harder than anyone.

* * *

The NBA had no shortage of perks. Nearby BMW dealers tracked us down in the parking lot after practice and offered to open up the dealership after hours for us if we were interested. I never did take them up on it, but I should have at least taken one out for a test drive.

Nor did I buy a suit from the rep who knocked on my hotel room door during training camp and did custom measurements for players on the spot. This way, we didn't have to actually visit a store. How inconvenient that would have been.

The trainers handed out our meal money of $106 per day. I'm a big eater, but I had never spent $106 on just myself at a restaurant. I even tried one day, but I got full and fell short.

On top of the meal money, they also handed us an additional check each week.

"What's this for?" I asked. Not that I was complaining. But I wasn't familiar with the payment protocol.

"It's your 'walking-around money,'" they said.

Walking-around money? It was over a thousand dollars. Walking-around money is having just enough to buy a Coke. And maybe a Snickers. Apparently I don't walk in enough expensive places.

We played the LA Lakers in our first exhibition game, in Fresno, California. One of the proudest moments of my basketball life was pulling on an NBA uniform with my name on the back. My sister flew out to the game from Phoenix and scored a seat in the top section. So there are witnesses. She tried to get herself kicked out though when she sneaked in a video camera and got some footage of me during pregame warmups before security made her shut it down.

I went through layup lines like an animal. Warming up to play against the Lakers was pretty incredible. Granted, Phil Jackson and

Kobe Bryant weren't there, but I didn't let that curb my enthusiasm. Jackson was recovering from hip surgery. Kobe had a court date in Colorado. At least that's the story floated by the media. But we all know the truth: they were scared of me.

It turned out that they didn't need to be. I sat on the very end of the bench the entire game. Check that: on the *floor*. Being low man on the totem pole, I got cozy next to the photographers on the baseline, but never checked in. Even without Kobe and Phil, the Lakers beat us. Would things have been different with my uncanny screening capabilities and swarming white-flash defense all over the floor? We'll never know.

Two days later we held an open practice and intrasquad scrimmage at the Jazz's main arena in Salt Lake City. We interacted with the fans and I got to pretend I was a famous NBA player and sign autographs for a few minutes before the game. Then we scrimmaged, and I even got in the game during some meaningful minutes—as meaningful as preseason open scrimmage minutes can be. I did nothing spectacular, but I didn't make a fool of myself either. The Rabetoys came to the game and it was gratifying to have some familiar faces there.

After the game, Coach Sloan and Coach Johnson pulled Frans and me aside.

"Guys, you did a nice job for us and we've enjoyed having you," Coach Sloan said. "But we're going to have to let you go."

And with that, the dream was over.

"I really appreciate the opportunity," I said. "Is there anything in particular that you think I should work on?" I asked. It was the nicest way I could inquire without saying *Why??? Why now???* Just two more weeks. You can cut me right before the season starts and I won't feel bad.

"You're a very good shooter, but you need to work on your foot speed," he said.

I wasn't the fastest guy in the world, I'd give him that. But I also felt that if my legs were fresher, I would have put up a better performance.

"Thank you, Coach," I said.

I hit the showers and got a bit choked up. In the locker room, everyone heard that Frans and I had been cut. Each player gave me a hug and wished us the best. Cuts happened every year on every team, but these guys were friendly and their sympathy felt genuine. Rafael Araujo even sent me off with two of his old suits. He's 6-foot-11, 280 pounds, so his suits were a little big on me, but I could get them tailored. Or just eat three dozen donuts a day.

It was disappointing to have it come to an end. I would miss the ribs and Dove bars on private jets. I'd miss all the free gear. Brian Zettler, one of the trainers, did send me home with my jersey, though, a thoughtful and perfect parting gift. I didn't leave empty-handed, either, as my suitcase looked like I straight up robbed the Jazz Fan Club store, with all of my Utah gear jammed inside.

I had given it everything I had, and it wasn't enough. The outcome wasn't in my control. But in life, what is? What do we really have control over? As far as I can tell, we can only control two things: our attitude and our effort. Other than that, there are too many other influencing factors for us to think we can be in command of things.

We can't even control our own bodies. It gets sick when we don't want it to. It falls asleep and wakes up on its own. It digests food without us and our hearts beat on their own. Only God is truly in control. And it's a good thing, because I would never have even had a shot with the Jazz without Him.

Chapter 11

GOING TO DISNEYLAND: THE NBA D-LEAGUE

You'd think that coming out of an NBA vet camp would open up some more serious job offers overseas.

It didn't. Not for me, anyway. Maybe it was poor timing, because it was October and all the overseas rosters were full. Or maybe teams thought I'd be out of their price range. That must've been it.

Whatever the reason, I had two options. Sit around and wait. Or give the NBA D-League a shot. I had never really considered the D-League (now known as the G-League due to its relationship with Gatorade), because if I really wanted to make minimum wage, I didn't have to move to North Dakota, where one team was located. There was a McDonald's right down the street that I like to think would have been happy to have me. And I had never really considered the NBA to be a viable option anyway. Until now.

Since I had just been with the Jazz, it now made more sense to see if I could push a little harder and see if there might be another shot at the big time. Maybe it could lead to an NBA Summer League invite. Or, if all thirty NBA teams somehow had five players get injured on the same night, it was conceivable that I could secure a coveted ten-day contract worth 30,000 US dollars.

Truthfully, I knew I was still a long shot to make the NBA. But even if I never received a call-up, the D-League was such a high-profile league that it could significantly boost my stock overseas. The D-League was respected worldwide, as it was the only minor league tied directly to the NBA and there was so much high-quality talent.

When I was with Utah, I certainly didn't dominate. But I felt I'd held my own and could play with those guys. There was no better time to give the D-League a try and capitalize on recently getting fired by an NBA team.

* * *

I put my name in the D-League draft and was picked first! Well, first in the third round. Seeing as there were ten rounds, I felt pretty good about it. Round three, pick one was one spot higher than when I was drafted by China. And I was headed to Anaheim, not Dongguan. More progress.

Cara and I packed up my 1998 Jeep Grand Cherokee and headed west. After three consecutive twelve-hour days behind the wheel and crying through the ending of our audiobook on CD, *Marley & Me*, we arrived in Anaheim, California. Still married. A Dr. Phil success story.

* * *

Joining an expansion team is always an adventure. It was Anaheim's first year in the D-League, which, by the way, technically stands for Developmental League. Although, I can think of some other words that start with D that might be more fitting. But in order to keep this family-friendly, we'll stick with DevelopingMentals.

Any genius with an IQ over twelve should know that it wouldn't be smooth sailing with an expansion franchise. Everything was new to everyone, from players to coaches to the front staff. If only the reality show cameras had been rolling.

To start, we had two guys named "Magic" on the team. Unless they could do some amazing card tricks, it seemed pretty bold for a basketball player to assume the same nickname as the legendary LA Laker, Magic Johnson. One guy was a strong power forward with gold teeth. The other was a 6-foot, 180-pound point guard. The point guard spelled his version of Magic differently. It was "MaJic," and he was not amused when it wasn't spelled correctly in the media guide.

"I paid $1,500 for my name," MaJic said one day. "They better not to mess it up."

Point taken. "Tyler" has just one R, by the way.

Fortunately, he wore a headband each practice and game with "MaJic" stitched across the middle, and that helped everyone remember. Legend has it that the spelling and usage of "MaJic" was even copyrighted by him. I might need a good defense lawyer when this is all said and done.

I really liked MaJic and was amazed at how he could finish tough shots in the lane among the bigs. He was almost always the smallest guy on the floor, but he was very creative with the basketball. A clever passer, MaJic was never afraid to be flashy, which surely carried over from his days with the AND1 Streetball Tour. He even invented his own move, known as "The Tornado," where he did some sort of spin-fake-dribble-through-the-legs thing that worked well on guys who played no defense. Not having any patented moves of my own other than "surprise lefty running hook," I didn't bring nearly the entertainment value to the table that MaJic did. Allegedly, his action shot is even on the sides of buses in some town in Mexico, where he played for a while. MaJic was talented and fun to watch. And probably thanks to his smaller stature, he played with the hungry attitude of an underdog, never afraid to prove himself.

The other Magic was cut in training camp. Maybe he should have spelled his name with two M's and a K.

* * *

The egos on the team were highly entertaining. Some guys felt that they should be in the NBA and had no qualms expressing it.

"I don't plan on being here very long."

"My agent says I'll be with the Knicks next week."

I could appreciate their confidence, but it seemed to me that if you were in the D-League, there was a reason. I heard someone say, "Every guy in the D-League is missing something. Otherwise, he'd be in the NBA." Some guys had the talent but might not have had the right timing or situation come their way yet. There are a limited number of jobs available in the NBA and lots of players who can score and defend. It will always be a buyer's market.

I made the final cut of training camp with the Anaheim Arsenal, and we had ten players on the roster. Our games were held at the Anaheim Convention Center, which was a great venue—if people showed up. A few did on most nights, but even a crowd of 1,200 looked pretty sparse in an arena that held five times that.

At first glance, Anaheim appeared to be a great place to have a team. We were within thirty minutes of Los Angeles, where there were two NBA teams, the Lakers and Clippers. Disneyland was around the corner, so there was plenty of activity in the area.

But maybe that was the problem. Maybe there was so much activity that our team got overlooked by fans. When I wore my Arsenal sweatshirt around, people asked me if I played for the soccer team in England.

"No. Do you play polo?"

"No, why?"

"Well, there's a picture of a guy playing polo on your shirt."

C'mon, people.

I went out to eat at the ESPNZone with two of my teammates who were even taller than me. When the waitress first came to our table, I jokingly commented that I was in the company of not one, but two professional basketball players. I asked if the restaurant had any specials for pro athletes. She asked what team they played for and I said, "The Anaheim Arsenal." Not only was she not impressed, she hadn't heard of our team and sarcastically replied that she was a professional server.

Did I say "pro" athletes? I meant *poor* athletes. The league had three salary levels: $12,000, $18,000, and $24,000. Before taxes. Eight out of 10 of those contracts were in either $12,000 or $18,000. It wasn't like overseas where the salaries were "net." Some of my team-mates, being the geniuses that they were, would go to the casinos to try and supplement their income.

I told one guy, "Man, we don't make any money as it is. Why are you going to a casino?"

"I'm gonna flip it," he said.

In case you hadn't noticed, the casino is always bigger than your house. Trying to double your money at the casino is crazy talk. But we were talking about guys who had even higher odds stacked against them as they tried to make the NBA. Risk was all part of the game. At least roulette was almost 50–50.

* * *

Our first six weeks in Anaheim, the entire team stayed in a hotel because apartments had not been arranged for us yet. Since I was mar-ried, Cara and I had our own room and it was bigger than the others. Every other player shared a standard room with a teammate.

Life was grand. There was a pool downstairs, our room was cleaned almost every day, and we didn't have to cook. We used our thirty dol-lar per diem to eat out most nights and had cereal for breakfast and sandwiches for lunch. It wasn't the $106 I had with the Jazz, so we ate at IHOP instead of Japanese steakhouses.

We finally got notice that our apartments were ready. When we pulled up to the apartment complex, it didn't have the cozy feel of our hotel one block from Disneyland. We walked into our new apartments to find roaches, both dead and alive. The place reeked of paint fumes from an oil-based paint they had just slapped on the walls. That might have explained the dead pests.

No one got a warm, welcoming feeling from the neighborhood. A guy knocked on one teammate's door selling DVDs out of a shopping cart. We saw another character trying to pawn off fishing poles. The woman at the front desk told me that gangs lived across the street in housing that should have been torn down already by the city.

"One gangbanger stuck his gun in my face," she said, as if it was no big deal. "I told him 'I'm not scared of you.' And he left me alone."

The look on Cara's face was priceless. *So we just tell them we aren't scared of getting shot in the face. How did you word it exactly again?*

Comforting.

Somehow, I reasoned that maybe these things weren't a big deal and that we should give the apartment complex a try. Bloods and Crips need love, too. Maybe we could bake them a fruitcake. And we could get an exterminator for bugs and open the windows to air things out.

We stayed for one night.

And that was more than enough.

The next morning we packed up and went right back to the hotel.

A few weeks later, the team placed us in a much nicer apartment complex owned by one of our team owners. The next question would be, "Why didn't we go here in the first place?" Who knows? Maybe it was a test. "How bad did those minor league NBA-wannabes want it?" Nobody on our team got a call-up that season. So apparently, not bad enough.

* * *

The competition was incredible. Every night we were playing against NBA draft picks and others who just as easily could have been. The Bakersfield Jam was loaded at point guard. With Gerry McNamara (Syracuse) and Mateen Cleaves (Michigan State), they had two guys who had each won an NCAA championship. Then throw in a Japanese point guard who had played for the Phoenix Suns. That was just one team at one position.

But along with all of that talent, there were egos as big as elephants. Every player knew that NBA scouts were watching every game, which lead to a lot of selfish play. The guards would jack up shots from any-where. They'd often "miss" the wide-open big guy in the post who had his man sealed behind him. *Extra pass? Why would I make an extra pass when the rim is right there in front of me, forty feet away?*

Guys were so worried about themselves that it sometimes would hurt the team and it ended up hurting them as well. NBA teams didn't need more scorers. They have their superstars, so they need solid role-players. Every guy in the D-League would be a role-player at the next level. But that message was nearly impossible to beat into the brains of many of these minor league superstars.

One classic example of the selfishness happened in one of our home games. We were down 51–50 near the end of the first half. We got a defensive rebound with four seconds left. Our guard dribbled toward our basket, and I was running beside him. No one was in front of him. He had just enough time to get a shot off as he crossed half-court.

3 ... 2 ... 1 ...

Shoot it!

He kept dribbling until the buzzer went off. Then, he picked up his dribble and heaved a shot toward the basket, about two seconds too late. Maybe he fooled the seven-year-old kid attending his first minor league circus event, but no one else was buying his "Oops, I didn't get the shot off in time" act.

"What are you doing?" I yelled. "Why didn't you shoot it?" I knew the answer, but I wanted to hear it from him.

"I can't mess up my percentage, man," he said.

"It's a one-point game," I said disgusted. "Shoot the ball."

Your percentage?! You're barely shooting 33 percent from three. You don't have a percentage. Plus, they normally don't even count half-court heaves at the end of a quarter as an attempt. You already shoot as many threes as anyone on this team, so what's one more?

I guess it shouldn't surprise me that players were more concerned with themselves than with winning. My theory was that if you played hard, played your game, and focused on winning where you were, you'd get noticed for doing what you do well. Being *unselfish* could actually benefit players because it showed they could defer to team-mates, which was exactly what they'd have to do if they were called up.

Then again, I was the one who had been cut by the Jazz and not good enough to make it in China. So much for my theory.

* * *

We traveled to Albuquerque, New Mexico, in December to take on the Thunderbirds. They played in a rodeo ring. Literally. It smelled like animals and we walked across a dirt floor to get to the court. Maybe we were supposed to wrestle steer at halftime. In the minors, you never knew.

I was guarding their big guy in the first half. Jawad Williams, our leading scorer, wanted to guard him but I said no. I thought it was a better matchup for me to stay on their center, as Jawad was guarding a smaller and quicker guy. This brief conversation occurred as we were jogging back down court on defense.

About seven seconds later, their big guy (that Jawad *would* have been guarding had I not shaken him off) grabbed the ball and swung his monster elbows through and drilled me right in the face. It was a straight knockout blow. The elbow was unintentional, but I was down for the count nonetheless. I won't even pretend that I hopped up off the canvas and shook it off. His elbow caught me directly in my mouth and I was face down on the floor, hands covering my face. As I cautiously moved my tongue around inside my mouth to survey the damage, I knew it wasn't good.

I felt an upper tooth in a place where it shouldn't have been. My top front tooth had broken straight back on a severe angle inside my mouth. Blood was all over my mouth, hands, and the floor. My top lip was swollen with blood and had a massive cut from where the tooth sliced into it.

Amazingly, as I lay there, I could hear the big center arguing with the ref about him being called for an offensive foul. *You know what? You're right, I flopped. I throw myself on the floor and knock my own teeth out every game.* It's incredible how innocent many guys think they are on the court when it comes to fouls. A player could pull a gun out of his sock and shoot someone and he'd plead innocence. "I don't know who put that gun in my sock when I wasn't looking."

I eventually got up and walked off the court with our trainer to the locker room to analyze the damage. It was pretty clear that I would not be returning to action that night.

I sat through the rest of the game on the bench looking like a hockey player who picked the wrong fight. We were able to contact a dentist on call that evening. After the game, I went his office and they went to work on me. Following some X-rays, he said the words you don't ever like to hear in a doctor's office. "I'm afraid I have bad news … "

My tooth was broken beyond repair and I would need a new one. He didn't have the capability to do that at that time, but he did yank the tooth back into place, which felt every bit as pleasant as you might imagine. Even though the tooth was loose, it appeared normal to everyone else and I didn't look like a complete redneck yet. My mouth was very sore, but he molded a mouth guard for me to use, and I was able to play the next night.

Two weeks later I was back home in California. A new dentist checked me out and then sent me to an oral surgeon. I walked into the operating room to find straps on the padded table, designed to hold patients steady. Naturally, this comforted my already jangling nerves, as it looked like they were preparing for some kind of medieval ritual.

The surgeon numbed me with three shots of Novocain directly into my gums. Nothing like multiple sharp needles penetrating one of the most sensitive parts of your face. The one in the roof of my mouth was by far the worst. I then understood the rationale behind the straps. I wasn't expecting so much pain from the part that was supposed to "help" me. I'm not sure how I withheld the impulse to jump off of the table, stab the doctor with his own needle, and then throw him out the window.

Once my mouth was numb to the world, he spent about fifteen minutes with a pair of pliers, pushing and pulling every which way in order to rip out the tooth and its root. He inserted a screw where the root should have been and the process was a success. At least that is what he told me when it was all said and done. I took him at his word.

My eyes were closed the entire time as I wondered why anyone would ever think of taking up hockey or boxing.

I was stuck with a gaping hole in the front of my mouth that Santa could drive his sleigh through. Christmas pictures did look pretty sweet that year, featuring the giant who needed a new dental plan. And small children were easily scared.

The oral surgeon said I'd have to wait four months for the permanent replacement tooth to be inserted. In the meantime I looked like an NHL player. He gave me a temporary tooth to wear, connected to a retainer. But it was much too uncomfortable and gave me a killer lisp. On the bright side, I heard there were open casting calls for a *Deliverance* remake.

Jawad, you owe me a tooth. You're welcome.

* * *

The travel in the D-League wasn't bad overall. We only took the bus to two road opponents, the LA D-Fenders (owned by the Lakers) and the Bakersfield Jam. We flew to the remaining nine cities, all located west of the Mississippi. I quickly appreciated our situation in Southern California when we visited other teams. On one particular trip, we left North Dakota, where it was -20 degrees Fahrenheit. We arrived in Anaheim where it was 80. A 100-degree difference from departure to arrival.

We lost a game in Colorado and then got to mull it over in the hotel for two full days as we were snowed in. That's what you get when you go to Boulder in January.

I always liked playing away against the LA D-Fenders because they played in the Staples Center where the Lakers and Clippers played. The Clippers were one of the NBA teams that we were affiliated with, along with the Portland Trail Blazers (which made geographical sense) and the Orlando Magic (which made zero sense). Unlike the Lakers and their little brothers, the D-Fenders, the Clippers did not invite us to play in the Staples Center or practice in their practice facility. But when we took on the D-Fenders, we did get to play in front of 18,000 empty seats on Lakers game days. The Lakers would be scheduled to play at 7 p.m., and we'd play at 2 p.m. Your $500 Lakers ticket got you complimentary admission to the D-League game if you had nothing better to do on a warm sunny Tuesday afternoon in Los Angeles. Such a deal.

Our roster was constantly changing. Contracts were not guaranteed, and the players were at the mercy of the team and the league. They could be cut at any time with nothing more than a "good luck." Guys came in. Guys exited. Mid-season, it was determined that we needed more size, so a 7-foot-3 South Korean player showed up one day. I have never felt so small in my life with the exception of when I attempted to guard Yao Ming in the World University Games in 2001 before he went No. 1 in the NBA draft.

Our new Asian teammate was named Ha. That's all it said on the back of his jersey—HA. He could practically dunk without leaving his feet. Standing tall, I looked him right in the thigh. He had played for the Milwaukee Bucks for a while but was trying to get back in the league. The looks we got walking next to him in airports were priceless.

One player, Corsley Edwards, didn't show up to practice one day. His D-League contract had been bought out by a team in Turkey. The Turkish team paid the $30,000 league buyout, then paid Corsley a whole lot more. All of us minimum-wagers were happy for him but still envied his new pot of gold. After an NBA call-up, getting bought out for big money overseas was a respectable second.

James Augustine was actually sent down to play with us from the Orlando Magic. He wasn't seeing much NBA floor time after being a second-round pick, so he joined the Arsenal, where he played a lot more. James had played for the University of Illinois, who had lost in the NCAA Finals the year before to our teammate Jawad Williams's North Carolina Tar Heels. I'm not sure if Jawad ever showed James his ring.

Our head coach, Larry Smith, even got fired midway through the year. We weren't winning as much as management thought we should be, so he was released. Our assistant coach, Reggie Geary, took over and did a very nice job.

My road roommate, Greg Clausen, was traded to Albuquerque during one of our road trips, which I was disappointed about. Greg and I had become good friends, and he hooked me up with free Muscle Milk because he had a connection with a guy at BodyBuilding.com. I'd miss him and his supplements.

Thankfully, I was able to stay put for the entire season. However, there was one close call when the North Dakota coach tried to trade for me mid-season. Fortunately, Reggie turned him down and kept me in sunny Cali. North Dakota went on to win the D-League title that year, so I guess they didn't really need me. However, it was a gratifying moment to know that I was appreciated enough to be considered worth trading for, not to mention appreciated enough by my own team to be kept. Although maybe the North Dakotans wanted to get me for a cheerleader and three buckets of snow.

Either way, thanks, Reggie!

* * *

Guess who showed up in the D-League mid-January? Roger Powell. He played with the Jazz until the point in the season when contracts become guaranteed, and he was released. He played a few minutes here and there with Utah, and I was happy for him. I was even happier to see him again in person.

But by the end of the season I hated Roger. Well, "hate" is too strong. Let's say gently annoyed.

He stole my trophy.

There were various honors handed out at the end of the NBA D-League season. MVP, All D-League, etc. I wasn't going to get any of those. But there was one award at which I might have had an outside shot—the Sportsmanship Award. You didn't need to do outrageous things like score points or block shots—just show a little love. The award came with some bonus money, which didn't hurt.

Roger won.

So much for me being friendly. All year long … handshakes, smiles, "How's the family?" Nothing. Only a missing front tooth that put a serious damper on my offseason modeling tour. And I didn't even hold it against the guy who clocked me. But Roger hadn't even played the full season in the D-League.

He won it anyway—and that tells you what kind of person he is. Not only is he a tremendous player, but his character, which he openly attributes to his faith, is spectacular. Well done, Roger.

* * *

Our Arsenal team needed to win four games in a row at the end of the season in order to make the playoffs. Somehow, our final three games were all against the LA D-Fenders. The scheduling geniuses had probably run out of coffee at 3 a.m. when they made that decision.

We won our first game against the D-Fenders at home. In the second game, Jawad hit a buzzer-beating three-pointer from three steps behind the line to win and keep our playoffs hopes alive.

The third and final game of the season was away, and both teams sported NBA jerseys. We suited up in real Clippers jerseys and the D-Fenders wore Lakers yellow. Playing in the Staples Center, wearing authentic Clippers and Lakers uniforms, it was almost as if we were really living the dream. A dream within a very quiet stadium.

We jumped out to an early 11-point lead. I was making shots, and our other point guard, Davin White, was getting hot. But LA put a run together and ended up winning by more than 20. We missed the playoffs by just one game. And they didn't even let us keep our NBA jerseys. Rude.

* * *

In the offseason, I returned to the oral surgeon. He cleared me to have a new tooth installed. The root had grown up around the screw and the area had stabilized enough to allow for a fake tooth to join my real ones.

The dentist did the actual fitting and color-matching of my new tooth. When my new implant was screwed in tight, I asked how strong it was.

"Oh, that thing's not going anywhere," the dentist bragged. "You could take a brick to the face and it would hold steady."

About two hours later I bit into a piece of pizza and it came loose. A brick, huh?

I drove directly back to the dentist. *Hey, remember me? "Bricks" ring a bell?*

He screwed it in tighter and I was golden.

* * *

Many people will say, "Oh, the D-League is political. It's a waste of time." If you're not getting playing time, then yes, it could be a waste, because your stats will be awful, which will look bad for the next season, and you'll never get an NBA call-up.

I considered my year in the D-League a success. I was on a team for which I played a fair amount. I even managed to score almost ten points per game. A modest amount, to be sure, but enough that it would boost my résumé overseas for the following year. I hoped.

As Cara and I started the drive back to Pennsylvania, we couldn't help but be satisfied at having had the true southern California experience. Cara was in a movie (as an extra in a crowd scene). We went to Disneyland. And I had esthetic surgery.

* * *

Technically, I didn't see the Broadway musical, *Wicked*. But after driving across the country with the soundtrack on repeat and Cara describing each scene in detail, I'm pretty sure my mind has created the memory that says I was in fact there in the audience. Cara, my mom, and my sister all saw the show together in LA near the end of the basketball season when my family came for a visit. My sister, having given birth just a month earlier, even sneaked her baby, Elizabeth, into the show. She didn't make a peep.

As Cara and I headed back towards Pennsylvania, we decided to make a couple of detours in order to entertain ourselves. First stop: Vegas, baby.

A few weeks prior, I had received a random phone call after practice offering a three-day, two-night stay at a "luxurious" hotel in Las Vegas in exchange for a ninety-minute sit-through of a presentation. Yeah, we did one of those timeshare presentation deals.

Given our budget, there was no way I was interested in buying into any kind of vacation package. I just wanted the free hotel stay and some meal coupons. The company said that there was no obligation to purchase anything, but I knew they'd bring the full cavalry of sales sharks to try and brainwash us into "needing" eight more weeks of vacation every year from now until eternity.

The whole scenario was very well choreographed.

"Here's an amazing vacation package offer that 75 percent of vacationers choose. You can stay in any hotel in North America, South America, or the moon when we build there. Is a one-time payment of $14,000 and then $500 per year annual investment within your budget?"

No.

"OK, no problem. Let me see if I can work something out for you numbers-wise."

Be my guest. You have sixty-five minutes left until I leave.

"How about a $4,000 one-time payment and just $250 per year?"

Still no. Clock is ticking.

"Let's go see a suite where you'd be staying if you sign up." We went upstairs to the most amazing suite I'd ever stepped foot in. Straight out of Prince Charming's castle.

"Can you see yourselves being comfortable staying in a place like this?"

What a dumb question. No, I much prefer dirt floors, an outhouse, and lots of mosquitoes when possible.

"What if we waive the one-time fee and you just pay $99 per year? Would that fit in your budget?"

Oh, how quickly they come down in their offer. Cara and I looked at each other. It was a very good deal. But at this point it was a war of who could outlast the other that I had no intention of losing.

Still no.

"OK, look. Let's be honest here."

Yes, let's.

"You guys aren't going to buy anything today."

You're catching on.

"I'm supposed to stay with you for the full ninety minutes in order for you to get your free hotel and meal vouchers. But if it's okay with you, we can just finish this early. You'll get your vouchers and I'll move on to the next people."

Deal— ha ha— winner!

Cara and I had a great time in Vegas. We saw the Cirque du Soleil show *O*, which was spectacular. We walked the strip, played one dollar blackjack because that's how we roll, and Cara even talked me onto a roller coaster that did not end my life despite what the voices in my head were telling me.

At one point we were leaving a hotel's casino on foot and we weren't sure how far it was to our next destination.

I asked a woman working at the hotel. "Is it walking distance?"

"Oh no," she said convincingly. "You'll need to get a taxi."

I wasn't sold that we needed a ride. I looked at a map and it appeared to be within a reasonable distance, so we set out on foot. Twelve minutes later we arrived. Is this what America has come to? No one can walk more than thirty seconds before it's too far and they need a vehicle? Man, we have problems.

After Vegas, we were driving toward the Grand Canyon for one more brief sightseeing adventure. Along the way we passed a sign that read "Helicopter Rides $29." I slammed on the brakes and turned the car around.

Twenty-nine bucks to ride in a helicopter! I thought. *We are so doing this.* Cara had never been in a helicopter, and since we came out ahead by about $100 in Vegas thanks to her winnings covering my losses, what better way to enjoy a rest stop than to fly around for a little while?

Well, I got suckered in by the low rate, as twenty-nine dollars barely let us look at the helicopter. Any half-decent ride would be about twice that amount. Whatever, we were already there. We flew over the Hoover Dam and it was a beautiful ride.

We made it to the Grand Canyon with just enough sunlight left to take in the unbelievable view. Its size and beauty were breathtaking. I had visited there a few times before, but it never got old.

Visiting the Grand Canyon was much like my dunks. I don't get above the rim often, but when I do … it's glorious.

Chapter 12

BONUS? BABY? HOLLAND, TAKE TWO

"What the hell, Raul?" Dave said. "Do you want Tyler or not?"

Dave Gasman was working on a deal for me in Holland. I wanted health insurance for Cara as part of the contract, but the team wasn't budging. They said that they did want me, but they normally only gave health insurance to players.

"Well, then, you need to break your norm," Dave said.

Man, I loved agent Dave.

I met him during my second year in Italy when he came to visit his client and my teammate Jobey Thomas. Jobey had been very successful and gone on to play every season since then in Italy. I had … well, I had played every season since then. So there.

Dave and I had stayed in touch and he found me an offer in Holland. I really liked Dave for a number of reasons. He was honest, hardworking, and he typically placed players in mid- to high-level countries. Dave was very smart and understood the many sides of the international basketball world. When to push, when to be patient. When to say yes, and when to walk away. It wasn't a simple job trying to connect teams that sometimes barely spoke English with players who often believed they were God's gift to humanity and worth way more than anyone else in the world thought they were.

Dave had a great sense of humor, and we really clicked. He also became one of my first clients when I started a small company called Pro Player Video during the D-League season. The business was a website geared toward helping teams, agents, and players connect in one place. Agents and players would send us their game film and we would edit the videos and put them on our site. The person putting the game film online paid a fee, and then it was free for anyone to watch online.

I had grown tired of mailing out DVDs and figured that other players had as well. Since my computer skills consisted of being able to type, use a mouse, and open a Word document, I hired a guy to set up a website that simplified the whole video process. This way teams could search for players at a particular position and watch their game videos instantly instead of having to wait for DVDs in the mail that sometimes never arrived. Agents and players could then email their game links to as many teams as they wanted.

The site was already getting put to good use. "Do you have any game film of Tyler?" Raul, the general manager of the Dutch team, asked.

"Do you have your computer in front of you?" Dave replied.

"Yes," Raul said.

"Go to this website and you can watch him right now," Dave said.

It was August 2007, and I had two offers on the table, three if you counted the possibility of returning to Anaheim. I didn't. No NBA teams were calling during the summer, so I knew that it was time to move on. I really enjoyed my time in the D-League and was glad I played there. But it made much more sense to capitalize on that season by signing a better contract overseas than wishing my career away in the minors.

I had two options. The Matrixx Magixx in Holland. And a team in Japan.

Japan would be interesting. I had never been there but was pretty sure I wouldn't be able to read anything for seven months. Many athletes will tell you that reading is overrated anyway.

I had already played in Holland and liked it a lot. The Matrixx offer of $54,000 was well over twice what I'd made last time in Holland. Japan's offer had the slight edge in salary at $55,000. Was $1,000 enough to pull me away from that delicious cheese and stroopwaffles?

Holland had just adopted a new rule that allowed for unlimited Americans. The Matrixx already had signed five imports, and one had a Dutch passport. Four of them were Dave's players. If I signed, he would have an entire starting five on one team and we could change our name to the Matrixx Gasmen.

When they threw in health insurance for Cara, I said yes. Windmills and Heineken beat out samurai swords and sake. *We're going back to Holland.* Hand me my bike.

I verbally committed to the Dutch team but hadn't signed the contract yet. The next morning, I awoke to a text message from Dave. A new offer. Double the Dutch salary! From somewhere else. The catch: It was in Iran.

As Ben Sturgill, my fellow international basketball sojourner, said once, "For the right amount of money, I'll go live with Saddam [Hussein] in a little hole and only come out for practice and games."

I showed the Iranian text to Cara. Those of you who have wives, mothers, sisters, or even know a nun know that females have a "look" that only they can give. No words were needed.

Hey, I was just trying to be open-minded. Not like we're talking about Baghdad or something. Just their next-door neighbor.

Not one to be big on going back on my word or playing anywhere near a war zone, I stuck with Holland. And off we went.

* * *

Picture your high school gym. Now, shrink it down a little bit. A little more. Great. Now … name it "Horstacker." If you say it out loud, you get the full effect. It's pronounced just like it looks. None of the Dutch thought it sounded funny. But I did.

The Horstacker was the gym where I broke my nose during my first season with Zwolle, and it used to be the home of the Eiffel Towers. Since then, the Towers had moved to a different city and our Matrixx Magixx team had formed in my new town, Nijmegen (NI-may-gen).

Next, think of your high school colors. Maybe yours were tough, like black and silver. Possibly boring like red and white. Or just throw-up maroon and mustard yellow. The Matrixx Magixx were having none of that ordinariness. We rocked purple and shiny lime green. What board meeting was like, "So it's unanimous: lime green and purple"?

There was a perfectly logical explanation. Our major sponsor was the "Matrixx." I was waiting for Keanu Reeves to address the team and take us to an alternative reality. Instead, the Matrixx was a club. A dance club. All the European techno music you could handle.

But it wasn't just any dance club. It was the second-biggest dance club in Holland. And it was located just a five-minute bike ride from the Horstacker. During my first three weeks in Holland, I asked roughly nineteen people what the number one dance club was and no one had a clue. But they were all positive that the Matrixx was number two.

* * *

We had great team chemistry from day one. We didn't have a single selfish player, which was quite refreshing after the D-League. Our guys wanted to win and knew how to play together. Todd Abernethy was our point guard and a rookie right out of the University of Mississippi, where he had been second in the country in assist-to-turnover ratio. He always got the ball to the right guys at the right time, and he was a very good three-point shooter, too.

Another rookie, McHugh Mattis was a 6-foot-6 freak athlete from University of South Florida. His jump shot needed some help, but he could rebound and dunk over anyone. One day, he stood under the basket with a ball and jumped up and dunked it with two hands. He caught it as it came out of the net and jumped straight up and did it again. I lost track after fifteen consecutive flat-footed vertical two-handed dunks. Inspired, I walked out there to see how many I could do. My streak ended at one.

Antoine Jordan was a combo guard out of Siena who could do everything. He rebounded, played great defense, and could score. He never complained about not getting the ball enough or anything else, for that matter.

Gerrit Brigitha was a 6-foot-8 power forward with a game like mine except that he was a much better leaper. He was very physical inside and shot well from the perimeter. Gerrit played on the Dutch national team and had a Dutch passport because he was born in Curaçao, a small constituent country of the Netherlands located in the Caribbean off the coast of Venezuela. He didn't look or speak Dutch, which surprised a lot of people, but he was very talented.

Victor Thomas was our best player, and I don't even know how we signed him. At 6-foot-7, he could play the 3 or 4 position. Offensively, he scored any way you wanted, off dunks, from three, from anywhere. But the craziest thing about Vic was that he was so unselfish. I had never seen a guy score 20 points per game but never seem to need the ball to do it.

We were playing as though we had played together for six years, not six weeks. Everyone gelled on offense and transition was a breeze with our speed and athleticism. Our head coach, Mike Schuurs, was a young guy who let us play. He was very open to asking us our thoughts on the system and took our suggestions frequently. Before we arrived, he'd led the team to the finals, and our team looked like we could get there again when we got off to a fast start.

The Matrixx were very big on building a family atmosphere. All the players and families ate a weekly lunch together on Wednesdays at the gym. Families were even allowed to travel on the bus for road trips. All of the players' apartments were within a three-minute drive of the gym. My apartment building was actually next door to the gym, just a thirty-second walking commute to practice and games.

Feeding off of the family-friendly environment, Todd and I began hosting dinners for the team on Tuesday nights in our apartments. Todd was married to his college sweetheart, Micah, and they were both committed Christians who read the Bible daily and were trying to navigate their first year of marriage—out of college, away from family, and in a foreign land. We would all eat dinner and have a brief Bible discussion about topics such as sacrifices we make in our lives or finding peace in difficult times and how Jesus could relate to imperfect souls like us. Then we'd play card games or just hang out. The Dutch and American guys brought their girlfriends, wives, and kids. As cheesy as it sounds, it was great bonding time.

* * *

Cara came downstairs one morning and kind of giggled. I looked at her and she scooted out of sight into the kitchen. Something was up. I followed her and asked what was going on. She just smiled and kept giggling to herself. *What! Just tell me.*

"I think I'm pregnant," she said.

"Wow, are you serious?" I asked about eleven times. Sure enough. The test was positive. So was the second.

And the third. After she went to the doctor and it was confirmed yet again, I believed.

Part of the reason I was so shocked was that it happened so quickly. First try. If my jumper were that accurate, my foot speed wouldn't matter.

We were going to be a mom and dad, Lord willing. She was sick to her stomach for six straight weeks. It was pretty impressive how much was going on inside her belly. I could literally hear gurgling throughout the day. Signs of greatness for sure.

There was only one small issue. The due date.

May 21 fell right in the middle of playoffs. More specifically, during the finals. It was a long way off, but there was no escaping a baby's arrival. It would come when it wanted to come.

There were a hundred scenarios that Cara and I went through.

Would we even make the finals? *Possibly.*

What if there were complications? *Please, no.*

Maybe Cara could hold the baby inside an extra day or two while we finished the series? *Bad plan.*

I could fly home for the birth and then fly back to Holland for the last games. *Eh.*

We could have a doctor come to the gym and set up a "birthing station" in the extra locker room in case the baby came on game day. *A what?*

"Is there any chance you'd be willing to have the baby here in Holland?" I asked.

"No," she stated.

"You know," I reasoned, "lots of Dutch babies are born right here. I bet it even happens every day."

"Yes," she said. "Then the Dutch mothers go to their Dutch homes down the street. I'd like to be in my own home in America."

Point taken. Speaking of homes, we didn't have one. Everything was in storage or our parents' houses.

Note to self: buy a home.

"And you're sure you want me there for ..."

I didn't have a chance to finish because the *look* punched me in the throat.

"Kidding, I was kidding," I said laughing.

"No you weren't," she said. "That's not funny. You'd better be there."

"Of course I'll be there," I assured. "I wouldn't miss Baby Felipe's arrival."

"Your names stink," she said. "By the way, do you have any *good* names for a boy or girl?"

"I'm waiting to find out what it is before I go committing to a name," I replied. I wasn't big on her name choices and I didn't have any winners. Therefore, it seemed safer to me to wait until we knew the gender so we could narrow the arguing by 50 percent. Dads have to be efficient.

* * *

"Wow, congratulations!" Coach Mike said. "So when is the baby due?"

"May 21," I said.

Crickets.

"Oh," he said. "During finals."

"Yeah," I said as we both acknowledged what this could possibly mean.

"She could have the baby here," he suggested.

The odds of Michael Jordan showing up to play for the Magixx were better than Cara having the baby in Holland.

"Yeah, you know, I don't think she would be as comfortable with that," I said.

I surely didn't want to abandon my team at the most crucial time of the year—playoffs. The games that we had worked so hard all season to finally reach. That was why we played. For a shot at the title.

On the other hand, I *definitely* did not want to miss the birth of my child. My first child. You don't get do-overs on delivery day. It's one-and-done. And while I was fairly certain that Cara would forgive me if somehow I accidentally couldn't be there, I wasn't thrilled at the idea of it coming up every year at the kid's next sixty birthdays. "Too bad Daddy couldn't be there to witness your arrival into the world. He was in another country wearing lime green and purple shorts instead of holding you in his arms."

"But look at the shiny medal I won."

I don't think that would cut it.

No, my wife and baby had to come first. I loved my coach, my teammates, and the Matrixx fans. But their last names weren't Smith.

* * *

Six games into the season, Vic was dominating. He was averaging 23 points per game while shooting 64 percent from the field and 54 percent from three. Plus, he was grabbing eight rebounds per game, dishing out a few assists, and blocking shots on defense. He was playing better than anyone in the league and we were off to a terrific start, in large part thanks to him. The Horstacker was packed for every home game and we really believed that we should win each night.

The problem was that Vic had been playing *too well*, and the South Koreans had noticed. Samsung, a team in South Korea's KBL league, called our GM to try to buy out Vic's contract.

"You can't have him," Raul said.

"How much?" they insisted.

"He's not for sale," Raul said. With Vic we had a real shot at making it deep into the playoffs, and a championship wasn't out of the question. Without him, we were still very good but winning the title seemed a stretch.

"Give us a number," they said.

Raul gave them a number that he thought for sure would be out of range. Remarkably, the Koreans called his bluff and wired the money. Raul was shocked. Samsung had deep pockets. On top of the huge buyout, they were going to pay Vic a minimum $25,000 per month plus bonuses. His new monthly salary was more than all of our Matrixx Americans combined.

We were really happy for Vic that he had hit the jackpot. But we didn't want to see him leave. He was a terrific guy and was on his way to an MVP season. Samsung didn't just send Vic a plane ticket, they sent an official from their team to escort Vic all the way over to South Korea. For the money they paid for him, they wanted to guarantee that he got on the plane.

Vic, just stay away from the DMZ that borders North Korea. And if you see a 7-foot-4 dude named Ha, tell him I say, "What up, Shorty?"

* * *

As you are probably aware, pregnant ladies *love* to be awakened unexpectedly by loud music. Especially when they aren't sleeping well in the first place, which Cara wasn't.

One Saturday morning at 7 a.m., our apartment was rocking out to some weird album coming through the walls. I was forced out of bed with bad breath and boxers to ring the neighbor's bell and explain to our single friend next door that some people like to sleep in on weekends. Seeing as we hadn't even formally met before, she was actually pretty pleasant about it, so that was nice.

Next morning, same thing. *Are you serious? Who repeats Shania Twain's "From This Moment On"?* I was pretty sure she must be having man issues. I got out of bed *again* and repeated my request for her to turn down her DJ skills. She was all dressed up with makeup and everything, practically cementing my man-problems theory. Again, she was friendly about it. But I don't think we'd be vacationing together.

I found the Dutch to be wonderful people. They were friendly, but not in such a lively, outgoing way as the Uruguayans or Argentineans. The Dutch were usually very direct and said what was on their mind. Sometimes it could come across as rude, but they were just very matter-of-fact at times.

They knew how to have a good time, though. The standard vacation allotment for a typical job in Holland is six weeks. Their unemployment benefits are unreal. Our other next-door neighbor had been out of a job for about a year and still collected about 60 percent of his salary. He would continue to do so for another year until he found a job. These perks come with a price, though, as the Dutch pay almost 50 percent of their salary in taxes.

* * *

The Eiffel Towers moved to a different city about thirty minutes away and became the Magixx's biggest rival. We played them at home early in the season and the Horstacker was rockin'. I fouled out in the fourth quarter, as the refs hadn't improved since the last time I was in

Holland. A couple of my fouls were real, but two or three were flat-out bad calls.

Eiffel had the biggest budget in the league, and they had a ton of talent. One player was rumored to be making $17,000 per month. Another player was Greg Stevenson, who played at Penn State for two years before transferring to Richmond. They also had a couple of the best Dutch players, who played for the national team.

We needed a small miracle to beat Eiffel when we were down by four with ten seconds to go. We came down and scored, cutting it to just two with about six seconds remaining. We fouled Greg Stevenson after the basket and sent him to the line.

He missed the first free throw. *We've got a chance to tie it.* Then he missed the second. *Should we go for the tie or the win? Down two. Here we go.*

Our Dutch big guy Sjors (Shores) grabbed the rebound and gave it to Todd, who pushed it down the floor. Antoine spotted up in front of our bench and Todd hit him with a pass with two seconds left. Antoine launched a three and drained it. We won by one. The crowd went berserk and we mauled Antoine. Wins against Eiffel meant even more because of the rivalry. And with Antoine hitting a last-second shot, it was even sweeter. I was so happy, I almost hugged a ref.

* * *

With Vic gone, we had to bring in a new player. Gerrit hurt his back in the second game and looked like he might be out for a while. We really needed a bigger forward who could score and still fit in well with our team. We had such good chemistry and no one wanted to mess that up.

GM Raul found Chris Copeland, who had been playing in Spain. He was a strong, talented perimeter 4-man who could also score inside. Chris was the only guy I had ever seen who seemed to shoot better with a hand in his face. In practice, I'd be as close as possible without fouling him or actually blocking his shot and he probably made it 80 or 90 percent of the time. It made more sense for me to leave him wide open. He was a very good three-point shooter and was aggressive offensively, driving to the basket and drawing contact. For our team, he was a great addition and he fit right in from day one.

We continued playing well but weren't quite as strong as we had been to start the year. It wasn't any one reason that I saw, but Coach Mike and Raul felt like we needed another guard as a perimeter scoring threat. Todd was more of a set-up man in our offense, and Antoine was playing well doing everything, but we didn't have a great slasher and scorer. Our Dutch guys, "Quick" Nick Domhof and Thijs Vermeulen (TICE ver-MOO-len), were solid also but they were stronger shooters than drivers.

Alhaji "Mo" Mohammed's name came up. He'd played for the Magixx last season and had led the league in scoring. Mo was a super-talented 6-foot-4 guard who could drive and finish better than anyone in the league. The only question mark was whether he would gel with the guys we already had.

"Sometimes he looks into the crowd too much," Coach Mike told me. So he had a little Tim Jones in him. Let's just hope he didn't try to fight anyone in the stands.

Mo arrived in December from Germany, where he had begun the season. It didn't take long for him to get acclimated, since he had played with the Magixx last year. We were the ones who needed to adjust, as Mo liked to have the ball in his hands. There were times when he would come down and hit four three-pointers in a row. And then there were possessions where he'd take on three defenders and force a shot. He could drive you nuts, but he often got you twenty-five points per game.

* * *

Cara and I flew back to Pennsylvania for Christmas, which was a refreshing midway point in the season. Going home felt so good, but it was also a tease, because it was only for five days. And we had to use the days wisely because we were on a mission. We had to buy a house.

We scheduled an appointment with a real estate agent in State College. We had one day to find the house of our dreams. Or at least something with four walls and a dishwasher. We were tired of washing dishes by hand everywhere we went. If I was going to spend all that money on a house, at the very least I wanted a machine to clean my dishes.

We looked at eight houses and weren't crazy about any of them. Then, we could see ourselves in the ninth. But number ten was the winner. It was in a new development and was only the second house on the street. There was dirt surrounding the entire house, which was fine by me, as I wouldn't have to cut grass for a while.

Naturally, it was the most expensive house we saw. But it had nine-foot ceilings downstairs and double sinks in the master bath, and we were sold. The asking price was a little beyond what we had budgeted for, but the negotiations went better than we expected and it came down into our price range. They even threw in stainless steel appliances. Baby Smith would have a home after all. And she'd never have to worry about hitting her head on the ceiling.

Yes, it's going to be a girl! We found out right before the house hunt. We were initially hoping for a boy. You know, the whole sports and following-dad-in-basketball thing. Cara was never a girly girl, either. But the minute I found out it was a girl, I was thrilled. Cara had to warm up to the idea at first, but it didn't take long. Now that at least the boy names were off the table; let the girl-name rumbles begin.

* * *

I flew back to Holland first because we had to prepare for our next games. Cara stayed behind for an extra week to finalize the house negotiations and paperwork. We wouldn't close on the house until April.

By January, team management was looking for a true center. Gerrit's back continued to sideline him, and adding a big body couldn't hurt against a couple of teams with strong post players like Amsterdam and Eiffel.

Who showed up? None other than my fellow Utah Jazz co-reject, Frans Steyn. All 7-foot-2 of him. He only got bigger each time I saw him.

We were on the bus headed to Rotterdam to play an away game. Cara had returned from the United States and sat next to me on the bus as usual. On the first road trip we took, back in October, she played cards with the Dutch guys and took all of their money in Texas Hold'em. I don't think they let her play again. But that didn't stop her from having fun with the guys.

"Hey, McHugh," Cara said to one of the American rookies. "Do you see all those cows out there?" We were passing by never-ending farmland alongside the highway.

"Yeah," he said. "I didn't know Holland had so many cows."

"I know," Cara said. "You heard about the Dutch cows, right? Why some are white and some are brown?"

McHugh was really curious. "No, why?" he said.

"Well, the white ones make regular milk and the dark ones make chocolate milk," she said.

McHugh looked at Cara. His eyes got big.

"For real?" he asked. He didn't know what to think.

There was a pause as everyone was listening. Then we all burst out laughing.

"Man, you were all serious, I didn't know," McHugh tried to explain. "I don't know what the Dutch people are doing to those cows."

When it's your first experience overseas, so many things are different, and who's to say foreign cows don't make milk with a little cocoa. After all, at Dutch McDonald's they sell beer and you have to pay for ketchup packets. Madness was everywhere.

* * *

Rotterdam was usually one of the weaker teams in Holland. But we were having an off night and everything seemed to be going their way. Late in the fourth quarter, we were tied, 84–84, and held the ball with the last possession. We missed the shot, and after a chaotic scramble the ball went out-of-bounds and the horn sounded. But somehow the official working the game clock thought he had messed up, and insisted that there was still 0.2 seconds remaining. It should not have been our ball, but one of the refs gave us possession under our basket, where the ball had gone out-of-bounds.

We couldn't believe what was happening, but we didn't complain. Rotterdam and all forty-six of their fans were up in arms. Their head coach was on the floor pleading his case, but the ref's mind was made up. It was our ball, under our basket, with less than one second remaining.

Coach Mike called timeout and drew up a simple play. Todd took the ball out-of-bounds and giant Frans parked himself under the rim. The other team saw what was coming, but they couldn't budge Frans off of his spot.

Rotterdam's biggest guy was 6-foot-7 in heels, and our secret weapon was like an oak tree. Todd lobbed the ball high over the backboard so it came down just in front of the rim. Perfect. Frans jumped straight up, with his smaller defender hopelessly trying to climb Frans like a tree. Frans gave it a gentle tap with both hands, just enough to control it. It bounced around the rim and fell right through the basket. Game over.

We rushed the court and attempted to tackle Frans, but since he is about as big as a pickup truck, we ended up just jumping on his back and riding him around the court. Game-winners against last-place teams are still exciting.

* * *

A week later, the Matrixx received an official notice from the Dutch government. Frans's work visa had been denied. He had to leave the country immediately or face deportation. It made no sense whatsoever, since six other Americans on the team didn't have any problems getting our work visas. It may have had to do with the fact that Frans was technically from South Africa and didn't have an American passport yet. Frans had been in Holland less than one month and they were forcing him out of the country. The team hired some lawyers and tried to fight it, but the rejection by Dutch authorities was final. Personally, I thought that Frans should have stayed until they sent the police to the gym. I'd have loved to see them try to wrestle him into a plane.

* * *

In February, Raul and Mike called me into the office. They wanted me to stay another year with the Magixx and sign a contract extension during the season. I was completely caught off guard, because usually those mid-season meetings with a coach and GM meant you were getting fired, not rehired. I had never been asked to return to a team during the season. It was an honor to be asked, as they had not done this for any other players.

I loved so many things about the situation there with the team. Lots of Americans, great coach, family atmosphere. It was arguably my favorite place to play. But who knew if the team would sign back the same players next year? I liked our group and wanted to see it stick together. It was the first time I'd ever had even the slightest possibility of job security for the next eighteen months, and it was really tempting. Especially with a baby on the way now and a mortgage to pay.

But anything could happen during the summer, and I wanted to see what types of offers would be out there. The Matrixx offer was only for a few thousand more than what I was currently making. How much more in salary would it take to lure me away from an outstanding situation? I didn't know. So I told them that I needed some time to think about it.

While I was thinking about it, an agent named Lee Cohen contacted me. I had met Lee in Anaheim the year before, when he came to one of my D-League games with the Arsenal. He was nice, but I couldn't get a read on him. He seemed a little strange at first. His voice sounded funny on the phone, and I didn't know if he was a legit agent or not. He called me a number of times when I was in California, and at the time I wasn't sure what to make of him.

Now Lee was back, getting in touch with me on Skype in Holland. He had been talking to a Japanese team in the JBL (Japan Basketball League) about me.

"I want to try and get you a deal with a team here for 125,000," he wrote.

Dollars? Cuz that would be ridiculous.

That would be more than twice what I was making then with the Magixx. I'm not a big sushi guy, but that amount would turn me into one in a hurry. I couldn't get my hopes up, though. Agents say things to get players' attention and this could be just that. A whole lot of talk.

* * *

By March, Cara was seven months pregnant and headed back to the United States with her growing baby-belly. She had stayed as long as she could in Holland before she was too far along in her pregnancy to be allowed to fly. The baby was breech, and unless she could flip back around the correct way, Cara was going to have a C-section. This would make things even more uncertain as we neared the playoffs. I was struggling to find a way to win games in Holland and help deliver babies in America.

To make matters more stressful, our team was slipping. McHugh was homesick and had hurt his hand, so he couldn't practice or play. He went from being one of the most social guys on the team to the quietest.

Gerrit didn't look like he'd be back at all this season. As soon as he made some progress with his physical therapy, he would have a set-back. We all felt really bad for him, because he was asked every single day by someone "So how's your back?"

"The same."

"And why don't you speak Dutch?"

"Because I was raised in America, for the 9,000th time."

Since Gerrit had his Dutch passport, everyone thought he'd be fluent in their language. It drove him and his wife, Andrea, crazy sometimes. I advised Andrea to remove all sharp objects from their apartment.

We were losing games. More than we should have been.

One Magixx fan told me that the players' wives should stop sleeping with us so that we could regain our focus. *Oh so that's the problem. See I thought it was because we were playing crappy defense and not scoring more than the other team. But you've had the secret all along.*

Raul called me one night asking me what the problem was. "What's wrong?" *We're out of sync.* "Why can't Mo make free throws?" *I don't know. Ask Mo.* "What are you going to do about the baby being born?" *Hopefully not pass out.*

* * *

We finished fourth in the league and would take on Gröningen in the quarterfinals. They were the fifth seed, but very dangerous. Gröningen played at a maddening pace and relied on an aggressive style to take opponents out of their game. We had the home-court advantage in a best-of-three series, but the Dutch league structured the playoffs in a very unorthodox way. Game One was away and Games Two and Three would be played at home. Evidently they missed the playoff format memo sent out to the rest of the world, which is home-away-home for the higher seed.

The day before Game One, I got an email from Max in Italy. He had been speaking with a South Korean team about me, and they were going to come to the game. Max stressed how important it was that I play well, because the team was very interested in me. Seeing Vic depart for $25,000 a month in South Korea had me ready to play the game of my life.

More like worst game of my life. I was bad. Gröningen played fantastic at their place and beat us convincingly. We were down, 0–1, and I didn't know how we were going to beat them twice in a row, even at our place. They played with much more energy and were way more aggressive. I never did see any Koreans in the stands, but if they were there, they might as well have left after warmups, because I didn't show them anything worth remembering.

Coach Mike gave us some adjustments for Game Two. We used their aggressiveness against them since we knew they wouldn't change the way they played. They always trapped and rotated hard on pick-and-rolls. In the first game, I had popped out, and it didn't work. In the second game, I rolled to the basket and they couldn't stop it. Our Horstacker fans were on fire and we turned into the aggressors. We won and swung the momentum back our way.

In Game Three, we figured out their press and didn't turn the ball over nearly as much. They were getting tired as their hectic defense was losing its effectiveness against us. We kept things very simple and didn't try to run any plays, because it was impossible against their chaos. In the fourth quarter, we increased the lead to double digits and finished them off.

We advanced to the semifinals versus Amsterdam. Things were about to get very interesting.

Cara had mixed emotions about us pulling out the big Game Three win. She was happy that we won and advanced to the semis. But she was also getting anxious for me to get home. It was May and she was ready to get the baby out of her. She was full-term and was at thirty-eight weeks. If she went into labor, it wasn't like I could hop on a plane and be there in two hours. Having a C-section meant that she might have to have the baby earlier than her May 21 due date. So she tried to get the baby to turn any way she could.

Cara visited an acupuncturist who claimed that he could turn nine out of ten babies. I had no idea that flipping babies was a big business. The baby tossed and turned all right, but refused to rotate the correct way, head down. We were the one out of ten. Fabulous.

Meanwhile, Lee wrote me again to tell me that Hitachi was sending their head coach and translator from Japan to Holland to watch me during the playoffs. Their season had finished and they wanted to sign new players. I'd already messed up my chances with one Asian country, and I didn't want to let it happen again.

* * *

The semifinals were a best-of-five series, and Amsterdam had the home-court advantage as the number-one seed. The first game was at their gym. Despite being in Amsterdam and playing in a nice facility, they didn't draw large crowds. It turned out that they didn't need much help from the crowd, as they beat us with their abundant size and talent. They had a couple of terrific guards and one of the best big men in the league, who was also the Dutch national team's center.

Game Two was back at our place, and we were ready for a fight. The game was back and forth, and I took a charge in the second half that knocked the wind out of me. I had to come out of the game and catch my breath. I hadn't played very well up until that point and was frustrated with myself. When I returned to the court my back was really hurting and I couldn't move that well. It proved beneficial, though, as I didn't try to do too much. It forced me to play smarter and simpler. I hit a pair of threes in the fourth quarter that were big for us, but it wasn't enough, as we lost by only a few points. In danger of being swept, we were down, 0–2, and headed back to Amsterdam.

I was not happy about the loss, but I recovered quickly when I met the two guys from Hitachi after the game. We ate dinner together at a restaurant and talked about basketball and my family. They even brought some presents for my unborn baby girl. They could not have been nicer. Fortunately, I played much better in front of them (21 points, six rebounds, three steals) than I had before the South Korean coach (five fouls, three turnovers). I never did notice them in the crowd, even though they weren't exactly camouflaged next to their long-lost giant Dutch cousins. It didn't matter, though. The important thing was that they saw me defend and score well against Amsterdam, the top team.

I remembered Lee mentioning that he was shooting for a salary of $125,000, and I was dying to know how much Hitachi typically paid their players and if they wanted to turn me into a samurai. I had no plans to tell them how much I was currently making for the Magixx, because that would not help my negotiating power.

It always seemed funny to me that I would earn different salaries in different countries even though I did the exact same thing everywhere I played. My game didn't suddenly get 40 percent better if my salary increased as much. I still set screens, waved towels, and made jumpers. Paying me more wouldn't make me play any better. Paying me less wouldn't make me play worse or care less. But, hey, if teams wanted to throw a little extra my way, who was I to say no? That's the marketplace.

The dinner with the two guys from Hitachi went very well, and I thought the three of us hit it off, even though the head coach didn't speak a word of English. Smiles and quirky hand gestures go a long way. After dinner, I took them to my favorite dessert place. There I was in Holland, making idiotic sign language with two Japanese men and eating Italian gelati. The night finished, appropriately, with a photo op of me towering about two feet above the head coach.

They didn't hand me a contract, but I was hopeful I'd bowed deep enough and hadn't said anything too offensive for them to consider me for next season.

* * *

Cara was getting anxious. We were one game from elimination and she was one day closer to giving birth. If we lost on Thursday at Amsterdam, our season would be over and I'd be on the next plane home. Cara couldn't wait for me to return. I wanted to be there with her very badly, too. I missed her and didn't want her to be by herself as she went through the difficult final days of pregnancy.

I struggled with the thought of departing from my Matrixx team at such a crucial moment and, conversely, the risk of pushing the limits of my stay in Holland and potentially missing my daughter's birth. The odds of us beating Amsterdam on the road and winning three consecutive games against them to advance to the finals were not in our favor. But anything could happen.

And it did. We played out of our minds and pulled out a big road win in Amsterdam. They seemed a little tired and unmotivated, which was highly unusual for them. Their coach never let them remain satisfied, yet this time they didn't play their typical game. Now we were headed back to our home court with a huge boost of confidence. We'd play in our house this time. In front of our fans. And with a chance to tie the series at 2–2. It is amazing what hope can do.

While we were celebrating in Holland, Cara was groaning in the States. *"How much longer was this going to drag on? Get my husband home and get this baby out of me."*

She had already moved into our new house by herself at eight months pregnant. My parents and some friends had assisted with the move, but I was nowhere to be seen.

Then, on Friday, she got some serious news at her doctor's visit.

"I'm already two centimeters dilated," Cara told me.

"Wait, I thought your C-section was scheduled for Monday," I said, confused. "The baby should be coming on Monday."

The baby couldn't come yet. It was still Friday.

I had it all planned. We win Saturday. I fly home Sunday. I catch the baby as she pops out on Monday. Maybe I fly back for Game Five. We win and advance to the Finals. Bonus money. New baby gets designer sheets.

"The baby will come whenever she wants to come," Cara informed me. "The doctors said she could be getting ready to arrive early."

Uh-oh. Not good. That would mean an emergency C-section rather than a planned one. I'm no doctor, but a "C-section" is much better without "emergency" in front of it.

It was decision time.

Our biggest game of the year was the next day, Saturday. I could play in the game and fly home first thing on Sunday. If we lost, then the season was over and I was home for good. If we won, then I would have helped the team make it to Game Five of the semis. But I'd still have to fly home on Sunday, because the baby would be coming on Monday. Maybe I could get back for Game Five after the baby arrived. Or maybe that would be too much and the team would have to understand that I had to stay with my wife and newborn.

This was driving me crazy.

It was a gamble. Cara could literally go into labor at any moment, resulting in an emergency C-section. If I stayed just twenty-four hours too long in Holland, I would risk missing the birth of my child and being by my wife's side for the biggest event in both of our lives. It's not a good idea to mess up on something big like that with the person you will be sleeping beside for decades to come.

I prayed about it and knew what I had to do. *Lord, give me guidance. Help me to make a wise decision and one that honors You.* Someone would have to be let down. My team, coach, management, and fans. Or my wife.

I choose my life. I mean wife. I choose my wife.

I walked into practice Friday afternoon and gathered the team at half-court. I told them I'd be leaving the next day. Instead of playing with them in the biggest game of our season on Saturday, I'd be getting on a plane to fly home. I felt terrible saying goodbye before we had finished the season. As the team captain, I didn't want them to think I was abandoning them, but I understood that they could possibly feel that way.

Then, a funny thing happened. Every single guy there supported my decision.

"We completely understand."

"You're doing the right thing."

"Go be with your family."

I don't know what I was expecting. Maybe I thought a few guys would be encouraging and a few wouldn't. I feared being a hypocrite as the leader of the team who left them at the most crucial time.

But I underestimated them. Thankfully, none of those fears came to fruition. We had a tremendous group of guys. I knew I was doing the right thing before I walked into the gym, but after the team's response and support, I had much greater peace about the decision.

* * *

I landed in the States with the baby still secure in Cara's belly. I checked the Internet for the box score of our game. The Magixx lost by 20. The season was over.

I felt bad that I couldn't be there to help them fight against Amsterdam. But let's be honest. I wasn't a 20-point difference-maker.

Cara and I both relaxed now that we were both in the same time zone and continent. Maybe that calming presence helped prevent an early labor. The C-section was pushed back a day and everything went smoothly. Cara delivered our precious baby girl.

Hannah Willard Smith.

Lord, please let her look like her mom.

Chapter 13

NOMO, TODO, ONO, AND AONO: JAPAN

About two weeks after arriving home, I received an offer from a team in Belgium. They were one of the weaker teams in the league because they had only been in the first division for a year or two. But Belgium was a stronger basketball country than Holland and it would be a very good step-up. Their offer was my best one yet—$90,000. I was psyched. Ninety typically had only one or two zeros after it in my contracts, never three.

My only concern was that the team might not be very good. They were young and they even included a bonus in my contract for not finishing last. On one hand, "Great, we should be able to get that bonus." Then again, "What kind of goal is that?" It was only May, but they wanted my answer quickly.

I had two offers—the Matrixx and the Belgium team. Plus, Lee kept calling me about Hitachi.

"They're going to offer you," Lee kept saying.

"Lee, I have an offer for $90,000 on the table in a good league and they need an answer," I said.

"I'm trying for $125,000 with Hitachi," he said. "You're their number-one guy. We just need to wait a little longer. I'm telling you, *they're going to make you an offer.*"

I'd heard that before. "You'll get an offer." If there was one thing I'd learned about overseas basketball it was: until you sign the contract and are getting on the plane to fly overseas, nothing is certain. When the money arrives in your bank account, then you're officially employed.

How do I turn down $90K on the table? Especially for a "better" offer that was nothing but a "possible" at this point?

Still, there was something about the interest from Hitachi and the vibe I got from their coach and translator when we met in Holland.

The Belgium team needed an answer.

"No," I said to Dave over the phone. "I'm going to wait. Sorry."

I hung up and looked at Cara, holding our newborn in her arms.

"I can't believe I just turned down a $90,000 job," I said. "Who does that? Am I an idiot?"

"We will see, won't we?" she said and gave me a smile.

The next few days dragged by as I anxiously awaited an offer from Hitachi. Getting about four hours of sleep at night in one- to two-hour shifts with the new baby wasn't helping my sanity.

Then I got an email from Lee. Hitachi made an offer—$105,000. I was a little annoyed. I shouldn't have been, but I had $125,000 stuck in my head as the number it would take for me to go to Japan. Hitachi's offer of $15,000 more than Belgium made me want to stay in Europe, where they had forks and good chocolate. If I was going to take my family to Japan, where we couldn't read anything or communicate with anyone, I wanted to feel really good about it. And I didn't.

We negotiated with them and they came up to $110,000. Getting closer.

I was forced to adjust my expectations and accept that $125K wasn't going to happen. And truthfully, with talks reaching past the $100K mark, I was already pleased.

Negotiations were interesting to say the least. The communication line was like playing "telephone" as a kid. I talked to Lee. He talked to Masa, the Hitachi translator. Masa spoke with Takakura, the team's general manager. And then their response came back down the chain again. Things had to be made very clear, as the GM didn't speak English, nor did I speak Japanese. Lee and Masa were instrumental in communicating expectations between me and the team. Fortunately, they had a good relationship, and the negotiations went rather smoothly.

A couple days later we reached the sweet spot for both parties—$115,000.

I signed the contract and sent it back before they could change their minds. They even threw in a rice cooker in the fine print without me asking. I assumed it was standard procedure with all Japanese basketball contracts. Salary, shoes, rice cooker. At twenty-eight years old, I was about to own my first rice cooker. Bucket list almost complete.

As much as I wanted to consider going back to the Matrixx, where the living and basketball situations were terrific, Hitachi's offer was too good to pass up. It was more than double what I had made the previous season in Holland. Forget last year—it was more than I made in my first five seasons of pro basketball combined. Bring on the rice balls.

* * *

Hannah was just two months old when Cara and I figured she had lived long enough in America and needed to experience the world. On August 1, 2008, we began our journey to Japan with a 6 a.m. flight out of State College. There's nothing like waking your sleeping infant at 3:30 a.m. to begin a twenty-four-hour journey. I never went to sleep the night before our flight, as we discovered that going overseas is slightly more complicated when trying to close a house and bring a small eleven-pound person with you.

When we checked in for our flight, we heard those magical words that every parent loves to hear before dawn, after dragging 500 pounds of luggage to the counter.

"You're not getting on the plane."

Very funny. Just give me an aisle seat and we'll be on our way.

"You're not going anywhere," an angry United worker said. "Your tickets have return dates for nine months from now and you don't have visas to stay that long in Japan."

Would choking you make this move along faster? I wasn't my friendliest self before the sun came up. And this lady's rude demeanor was not helping things.

I couldn't call Lee because it was 2 a.m. in California. I didn't have Hitachi's number, but I wished I did so I could yell at someone who didn't understand me. Cara and I were furious. After all the preparation to leave the country for the next nine months, we were grounded.

So we did the only thing we could do. We went home and went back to bed.

* * *

Four days later, things were sorted out with the plane tickets and we headed to Japan. Hitachi gave us business class seats, a first for us, and it made the fourteen-hour flight from Washington Dulles to Tokyo a lot more comfortable. Hannah did very well on the trip and got her first passport stamp in the Narita airport.

Masa met us at the airport, and a van drove us to Kashiwa (KAH-shee-wah), our new city. When we pulled up to our apartment, someone was standing outside our building with a towel around his neck.

"That's the assistant coach, Todo," Masa said.

Coach? He looked like he was fourteen. He was small and appeared so young that he could have been the ballboy for a high school team. But I was too exhausted at that point to care.

* * *

The moment of truth in any new country is the first visit to the apartment. When we walked in, I wanted to turn around and walk right out. The apartment was tiny and felt like a glorified prison cell. While it was clean and organized, I hadn't felt so cramped since freshman year of college, when I roomed with another 6-foot-9 guy in the dorms. My shoulder hit the top of the bedroom doorway and the bathroom sink came up to my knees. In fact, Hannah was the only one who could navigate the apartment without hitting her head.

Cara gave me a look like, *Are we really going to live here?*

Not only were we going to, but I had to leave for training camp in thirty-six hours. *Here's some Japanese yen and the grocery store is over there. Good luck reading labels. See you in a week.*

I just prayed that they'd both be there when I returned.

* * *

Japan was the biggest culture shock we'd experienced. So many little things seemed to add up to big things that eventually made everyday life a challenge. We had to take our shoes off any time we walked into a building or a house. There was a list of about a hundred items that could only be recycled on certain days in certain color-coated trash bags. Food was hard to identify and locate in the grocery store. And everything was expensive.

An apple was five dollars. My teammate ordered a pizza from Pizza Hut. Twenty-six dollars. For a medium! I love pizza and was initially thrilled to see a familiar franchise. But my conscience wouldn't allow me to pay that much for a measly pizza if they weren't going to throw in a massage or clean my apartment.

Sandwich bread barely lasted twenty-four hours before it turned into concrete. The bread came in bags with three slices. What was I going to do with three slices? There weren't any seagulls around.

Everyone was in a hurry. It was New York City on crack. People sprinted to get on trains even though trains came every four minutes. I was shoved more than once by little old ladies in the train station. At practice, my team manager sprinted to fill up water bottles. My assistant coach raced to hook up the scouting video. I'd never seen anything like it. I sprinted to get out of the way.

One time at a restaurant, Cara was just a few steps away from an open table where she and Hannah were about to sit down for lunch.

A lady saw Cara was headed for the last open table. The woman ran in front of Cara, stealing it right out from under her. Holding Hannah in her arms, Cara just looked at the woman in disbelief. Fittingly, the next table opened up about sixty seconds later, two feet from the table thief. *Fancy seeing you here.*

If people weren't sprinting, they were sleeping. I took the city bus to practice every day. Everyone was knocked out, with eyes closed and heads hanging limp. I also rode the train frequently and had never seen such exhausted people in my life. People dropped things on the floor while they were dreaming on the trains and they didn't wake up. Some even slept standing up. How they didn't miss their stop, I'll never know.

One of the other interesting things about the buses and trains was that it was highly frowned upon to talk on your cell phone. We're talking big signs with X's through cell phones. Stern reminders were made in Japanese and English: talk, and suffer the consequences. There wasn't any punishment other than dirty looks, but it felt like you'd be thrown out onto the tracks.

Japanese technology was awesome. Almost every car I rode in had a GPS, an MP3 player, a TV, and some sort of hard drive for music and movies. Their cell phones could do video calls already. I know that kind of thing is not so unique now, but in 2008 it was cutting-edge. Our washer and dryer was one unit. Granted, it took about three hours to complete a cycle, but it was still impressive not to have to transfer damp laundry. There were even TVs in Coke machines, which begged the question: did we really need to watch some sort of Coke commercial for the three seconds after we bought our drink? Absolutely.

Most of the Japanese were very friendly and incredibly polite. They bowed all over the place. Nice to meet you. Bow. Sorry, I just closed the elevator on your small child. Bow, bow. I tried to bow a lot, too, and I'm sure I looked ridiculous.

Everything was so organized and neat. The streets were spotless and no one littered. Having been to Uruguay, where the sidewalks and streets were sometimes filled with trash, it was interesting to see the opposite end of the spectrum. What made Japan's cleanliness even more amazing was that there were so few trashcans.

* * *

Our preseason was like nothing I'd ever experienced. First off, the heat and humidity were off the charts. It never took long to get loose at practice because we didn't have air-conditioning. I was already in a full sweat by the time I walked into the locker room to get changed.

About a month into our preseason, we went away for another training camp. I'd never heard of a team having two training camps, but when you have two months of full practice to kill before your first game, you have to be creative. "Let's just go to training camp again. The guys will love that."

One thing I noticed early on was that there was very little complaining. In fact, I couldn't recall any players griping about the heat, multiple training camps, or anything for that matter. They showed up, worked hard, stayed late, and went home. The next day they would do it all over again, starting with a 6 a.m. wake-up.

Half of our team worked for Hitachi as regular employees and went to the office in the morning every day, wearing a suit and tie. They'd work a desk job in downtown Tokyo until lunch, then take a one-hour train ride to practice in Kashiwa. Their basketball offseason lasted only about two weeks, during which they'd put in full days at the office instead of splitting their time between practice and work. After this short break from basketball, they'd get back to practicing. So while I was whining about two months of training camp, these guys had been going at it since May. I kept my mouth shut.

One thing I did like about basketball in Japan was that we practiced only once per day, in the afternoon. It was much better than going twice per day in a lot of other countries, like Holland and Argentina. Even after the Japanese players' long days, I was never the last guy in the gym. They would hang around and shoot and continue working out. I'd never seen players put in as much time and effort as the Japanese. Their relentless work ethic was impressive and ingrained in their culture.

And they were so unselfish on the court that I'd have to tell them to shoot the ball. We would milk the shot clock until the last five seconds on almost every possession. Our guards would drive to the basket and have a wide-open layup only to make a jump pass to a three point shooter. Everyone was waiting for someone else to shoot.

* * *

We played our first exhibition game at our practice gym against a college team. When we walked out of the locker room for warmups, I thought we were playing a small army. There were at least thirty players on their team. Not one was over 6-foot-4. Many Japanese universities had a "no-cut" policy. If you could hang with their grueling practice regimen, you could stay. But playing time was pretty limited when you have as many players as a football team.

They were yelling and chanting at the top of their lungs during stretching and pregame drills. Our practice gym didn't have any stands, so they weren't trying to impress any girls. Maybe they were trying to intimidate us.

Initially, I gave them some serious respect before the game started, as they sounded fearless and ready for a war. They weren't big, but they were much more disciplined and intense than we were, especially for a closed preseason practice game.

Then I looked closer at the name on their uniforms. It was something in English, but I couldn't make it out. I walked over to their side of the court where I could read it and started laughing.

Sleeping Sheeps.

There has never been a more intimidating mascot in the history of sports. Sheep. Who were sleeping. And grammatically incorrect. Was Japan known for its wool and I was ignorant of this fact?

A mascot should be something that embodies a fighting spirit. It needs to be representative of a team that competes to win. Something powerful, clever, or unique. The Sleeping Sheeps might as well have been the Little Goldfish or the Fluffy Pillows.

We didn't have the hippest name in the world, either—the Hitachi SunRockers. It sounded like a cheesy '80s band. The sun is symbolically powerful in Japan, so I got that. But "Rockers"?

And it wasn't like the other mascots in our league were any better. We had teams named the Diamond Dolphins, the Brave Thunders, and the Seahorses. Dolphins are loveable. I was unaware multiple thunder could be brave. And who was scared of a seahorse? Nike really needed to send some of their marketing and branding people our way.

Well, either the Sleeping Sheeps were horrible or we were the Lakers. We destroyed them by more than 40 and played our second- and third-string guys most of the game. Following the game, their entire team lined up and bowed in our direction. *Thank you for destroying us and our confidence today. We are humbled at the opportunity to be beaten so badly. Maybe if we play all thirty players at once next time we will only lose by twenty. It was an honor.*

I made sure to grab one of the college players after the game and get a picture with him. I had to bend down to fit in the picture with their 5-foot-2 power forward. It's not every day you get a photo opportunity with a Japanese Sleeping Sheep.

* * *

After two months of hot and humid practice, it was finally almost game time. Two days before our first regular-season home game, I picked up my first English newspaper. How nice to be able to read my native language and left-to-right instead of up, down, crisscrossed, slashy lines that looked like my poor art skills.

"The U.S. Loses 9 Billion New Jobs." "Iran Still Hates Us." Blah blah blah.

Then, the real news.

A man in Tokyo was arrested after they found his dead wife in a suitcase in his hotel room. Read that again if you need to. In a suitcase.

Apparently, she had been dead for over a month, but he was having a hard time saying goodbye so he carried her corpse around with him in a suitcase. I guess this seemed like a good idea to him until there was an awful smell coming from his room. He was then apprehended. If that's not news, I don't know what is.

The tiny fact in the article that jumped out at me was the location where this all went down—Washington Hotel, downtown Tokyo. The very same Washington Hotel where our team would be staying for home games. Oh, joy.

Now, of course the hotel wasn't going to divulge exactly which room it was where the late Mrs. Suitcase was discovered. But you can't help but wonder in the back of your mind, *Was it my floor? My room?*

As I approached the hotel to check in that Friday, wheeling my athletic bag behind me, I nervously looked up to see which windows were open and might be "airing out." And there was indeed a distinct odor in the air of my room that weekend. Turns out it was just my shoes.

* * *

We played our home games one hour away from our practice gym in downtown Tokyo at a small stadium called Yoyogi (yo-YO-ghee) that seated 3,200 people. Even though this was our home gym, we stayed in a hotel before each game. Since we played games every Saturday and Sunday, it meant that every game would be an away trip. I'd have to leave on Friday morning and not return until late Sunday night. I was not a fan of staying in a hotel before games when we didn't need to, especially home games. It seemed like a waste. I slept much better in my own bed than in a small Japanese hotel room. Plus, it was time away from Cara and Hannah that seemed unnecessary. But Coach Ono felt it was important for us to be sequestered and focused on the game.

* * *

We were playing the Toyota Alvark, yet another mascot dreamed up out of thin air. Maybe they were thinking "aardvark," but aardvarks aren't native to Japan. Nor do they have massive shoulders and fore-arms like the creepy Toyota mascot.

Toyota was the two-time defending champion, and Hitachi had missed the playoffs the year before. None of that mattered now, though, as it was almost game time. When I walked into the locker room for our pregame meeting, the entire white board was covered in perfect English.

"Who wrote this?" I asked Todo, our assistant coach. All the team's English speakers were out on the floor during warmups, and only Coach Ono had been in the locker room.

"Coach Ono," Todo answered.

"I thought he couldn't speak English," I said.

"He can't," said Todo. "But he can read it and write it."

Tricky old guy. His English and handwriting were better than my college coach's. I'd better watch what I said.

All hyped up on adrenaline from the first game of the season, our Japanese guys played like rock stars and we won by 20. Our point guard, Kei (KAY), showed off one of his fancy shots that I'd never seen before in a real game—the underhanded running scoop. He was already short enough as it was, at 5-foot-10. So the fact that he was able to shoot an underhanded shot without getting it tossed into the stands was pretty impressive.

Kei had a little flash to his game and was as fast in the open floor as any point guard I'd ever played with. He was also the Justin Tim-berlake of our league, as the women loved him. Over 80 percent of our fans were female, thanks in large part to Kei's popularity. After every game, they would line up to give him gifts. He would get on the team bus with grocery bags full of presents from the fans, everything from chocolates to lotions to boxers. Each gift was intricately wrapped and presented as if his fan were giving the most important offering of her life to the emperor.

* * *

After the game, I was in a great mood. I hadn't played that well, but was happy that we had beaten Toyota. I was anxious to see Cara and Hannah and share in the excitement of the win.

Instead, I found Cara holding Hannah underneath the stands almost in tears. When the game had started and the music and crowd noise erupted after each big play, it scared Hannah so badly that she wouldn't stop screaming. Cara tried to step outside, but the person working the door didn't understand Cara and wouldn't let her leave. Finally, with a crying baby in her arms, Cara pushed past the gate-keeper and found some quiet outside the gym doors. But just as Hannah began to relax and stop crying, a huge gust of wind knocked over an advertising tent and barely missed collapsing on top of them.

Cara went back inside the gym where the blaring noise had only increased, and Hannah started screaming again. They had travelled by themselves over an hour by train to get to the gym in downtown Tokyo and now Cara couldn't even watch the game. Desperate for a quiet place, she went into the bathroom and sat down in one of the stalls to ease the pain in her back from holding Hannah.

"This might be the last game we come to," Cara said to me afterwards, frustrated. "The noise scared Hannah and hurt her ears."

I felt terrible. But I wasn't about to let a loud arena keep Cara and Hannah from seeing us play. The games were one of the best parts about being overseas.

I searched online and discovered a company in Australia that made baby earmuffs that drowned out loud noise and bought a pair immediately. Understandably, Cara had her doubts about the earmuffs. Would they work? Would Hannah even keep them on? A couple weeks later, Cara brought Hannah to another game, rocking her new bulky Hooked-on-Phonics-style headphones. When the music started blasting, Hannah never made a peep. She looked like a chubby chipmunk ready for the shotgun range. I should have ordered orange ones to make it complete. She even fell asleep in her stroller wearing them. I love Australia.

* * *

We beat Toyota again the second night by just two points. We were off to a great start at 2–0. Our SunRockers squad continued winning with our methodical and deliberate style. We played a slower tempo and were best in the half-court. Our final scores were usually in the 50s and 60s. Not super exciting, but very effective. The JBL had implemented a rule that allowed for two import players on each team, but only one could be on the court at a time. They were trying to give the Japanese big men more opportunity to play, because so many teams had been bringing in two American big guys and it didn't leave much playing time for the Japanese bigs.

Lamar Rice was my American teammate. He was 6-foot-8 and was a very versatile player. He scored well from the post and had a nice outside shot as well. Lamar was athletic, and his exciting dunks made up for my uneventful style of play.

Lamar had journeyed to some unusual countries for basketball, like Costa Rica and Angola. In Angola, he played in a gym that didn't have a roof and on one of their road trips, they took a military plane that didn't have seats. At least they didn't make him jump out from 10,000 feet.

Because of the one-American-on-the-court rule, I split time with Lamar, and I always knew who I was subbing in for when Coach Ono called my name. Whoever was playing well would usually get more of the minutes. It was difficult to get adjusted to our limited roles, as we were both used to playing 30 to 35 minutes per game in other leagues. Now I was playing just 15, sometimes 20 minutes per game. Often it took a few minutes to get into the flow of the game. In the past, if I missed a couple of shots, I could play through it. In Japan, I'd get taken out and then have to sit around being angry at myself until the second half before I'd get another chance.

Lamar was playing well and averaging twice as many points as I was and almost twice the rebounds. He was getting more minutes than I was, but I wasn't being as productive as I should have been.

Todo, the assistant coach, pulled me aside one day in November.

"You need to really start being more productive," he said. I could tell he didn't want to be having this conversation, but he knew it was necessary. "You started out having a great preseason. Your first practice here was the best I've ever seen by an American on his first day. You need to relax and just play with confidence."

He was right. I knew I should have been shooting better. I was trying to be aggressive, but I was forcing things sometimes. And when I did have better shot selection, the ball seemed like it wouldn't go in the basket. Fortunately, we were winning, so I had a little more leeway. When a team was losing, the Americans were always the first to go. Even though we were winning, I didn't feel very secure in my current job.

"Is Coach Ono thinking about making a change?" I asked nervously. I wasn't sure I wanted to know the answer, but I figured it was better to know the situation instead of worrying about "what ifs."

"Well, I don't know what he is going to do," Todo said. He wasn't very convincing. "But I do know that you just need to focus on playing the best you can. Let's start by putting in some extra work before practice."

"OK, sounds good," I said.

For the next few weeks, Todo and I did extra pre-practice workouts. I worked on inside moves and finishing near the basket. It definitely helped get me ready for practice each day and, as a result, my performance and confidence began to improve.

One day, I was doing a drill Todo called "Hanging Tiger." I didn't have to growl or hang from any trees, so I don't have a clue where he got the name. I think he just made up names to make drills sound fun when they really weren't. In the drill, I picked the ball up from the low block, drop-stepped, and dunked. Or in my case, 99 percent of the time, I laid it in. The idea was to take the ball up strong and finish with power at the rim. While bending over to pick up ball after ball and explode up from the ground, I felt a sharp pain in my lower back.

It locked up, and I couldn't walk or stand without pain. So much for my pre-practice workouts.

Fortunately, I was only out for one week. We had a bye that weekend, and I didn't miss any games. I don't like missing practices due to an injury because I don't want the coach or team to think that I'm just being lazy or to question my toughness. There is no way for them to tell how much pain I'm in. Every player is expected to play through a certain amount of pain. That comes with the job description. So when I was watching from the sidelines while everyone else was working hard, I couldn't help but feel a little guilty even though there was nothing I could do. Going out there would only make my injury worse and prolong my recovery.

It's funny, I don't love to practice. I love games. Practice is like paperwork. Nobody is foaming at the mouth to practice, but it's a necessity. And as soon as I'm injured and can't practice, I miss it and want to be out there again. OK, maybe not the first day. Sometimes a short break is welcome. But shortly after that I'm itching to go.

* * *

"Man, I miss Taco Bell," Nomo said.

I was in the training room before practice. Nomo was our trainer, and he'd gone to college in the United States and then worked for the Boston Celtics. His real name was Koide Atsuya (KOY-day AHT-su-ya), but when he got to America he told people to call him "Nomo," after the famous Japanese baseball player, Hideo Nomo, who pitched with a crazy corkscrew windup for the Los Angeles Dodgers. Our Nomo didn't play baseball, but he needed a nickname that Americans could pronounce and, according to him, it was better than Godzilla.

Nomo was a very disciplined and intelligent trainer, but there was an eccentric side of him that we rarely saw. In college, he took acting classes and wanted to pursue theatre. He became the school mascot and would surf down the bleachers from the top row on a sled—crashing onto the basketball floor. He also had a full-body bunny suit that he took with him wherever he went, and he had pictures to confirm it. He wore it throughout the country at places like the Grand Canyon and Niagara Falls.

But when Nomo called home one day to tell his father of his major, his father's response was simple and direct. "Pick a new major."

Nomo was furious. But, later on, he admitted that his dad was right.

Nomo loved America and we often spoke of the things we missed about living there—free refills, Walmart, and not having to take your shoes off everywhere.

"I miss Krispy Kreme," I said gazing off into the heavens.

Nomo looked at me confused. "We have Krispy Kreme here."

"What! Where?" I asked. I hadn't thought for a second that Japan would have a Krispy Kreme. The Japanese ate far too healthy of a diet to allow something like Original Glazed into their country. Plus, Japanese sweets just weren't all that sweet. Compared to America, where cheesecake is ultra-rich, thick, and creamy, and high-fructose corn syrup invades everything, Japan's desserts were a big letdown. That was OK. I'd seen all of two overweight people in my first four months in Japan.

"In Tokyo there are a few of them," Nomo said. "One is not too far from the hotel where we stay for home games."

"I need a map," I said desperately.

When we arrived in Tokyo that weekend for games, I headed straight for the land of wonder. Just a fifteen-minute walk from our hotel was sweet glory. The line out the door was a hundred deep. I counted while waiting. It was like standing in line at Disney. There were even signs that read "1 Hour Wait From This Point." I happily waited with a smile on my face. I knew the ride at the end would be worth it.

Glazed cake professionals brought out trays with dozens of donuts for the salivating customers to sample while standing in line. *Since I am twice as large as some of these people, doesn't it make sense that I should be allowed two donuts? After all, I come from the kingdom that started this beautiful experience.*

After standing in line for an hour, I made it to the register and my smile only widened. I was almost there. One dozen donuts—twenty-two dollars. Maybe they were layered in frosty gold. It could have said $122 and I wouldn't have blinked. I walked out with three dozen so my teammates could share in the love.

* * *

We stayed in Japan over the Christmas break because we only had three days off, not nearly enough time to go home. In Japan, the emperor's birthday is celebrated on December 23 every year. It's a national holiday and everything is closed. Two days later is Christmas, Jesus's birthday. Everything is open. Japan's main religion is Buddhism and many people will go to the gravesites of family members and pray to their ancestors. Christians make up roughly one percent of the population. I found this stat very interesting because the Japanese and their culture already share many similar values of Christianity. They are humble, giving, and very service-oriented. They respect other people, especially their elders, and honesty and hard work are pillars of their society. As a result, it's a very clean and safe country. They just don't happen to believe in Christ.

* * *

During the holiday break, my family had an entertaining day trip planned to Asakusa (ah-sah-KOO-sah) to do some sightseeing. I accidentally left our diaper bag on the train, containing every necessity for Hannah, who was seven months old. If you don't have kids, just know that they need something about every ninety seconds. So going anywhere for a full day without the bag of glory is like trying to walk somewhere without your feet and lungs.

The look I got from my wife was priceless. You'd have thought I left the baby on the train. Do you know how many trains there are in Japan? I had a better chance of finding a unicorn than that baby bag.

But about four hours later, I got a call. The baby bag was safe and resting comfortably in a Japanese train station not far from our apartment. Unreal.

About one month later I left something else on the train. My laptop. Arguably a hundred times more valuable than that diaper bag. I'm officially an idiot. Some humans apparently do not evolve.

This time I wasn't that worried, though. Given my previous case study of losing the diaper bag, I rested in the confidence of the Japanese Lost Bag Special Forces. They were even faster this time. Ninety minutes later, my Mac and I embraced. Tears of joy.

The Japanese continued to amaze me with their organization, honesty, work ethic, and planning. I've even heard stories where people lost their wallet and someone personally delivered it to their home two hours away with nothing missing. Think that's going to happen in the New York City subway system? Probably, um, never.

I'm sure I'll forget something again on a train. Let's just hope Hannah's wearing a coat with her name written inside.

* * *

Basketball continued to be surprising. We had a one-month break from regular-season games after Christmas. During the break, we played in the All-Japan Tournament. And when I say *ALL-Japan* I literally mean every pro, college, high school, and probably old-guys-playing-on-their-lunch-break team included. The tournament is meant to crown the best overall basketball team in the country, be it amateur, pro, or some other unknown category. I thought our league was professional and that we'd already narrowed things down. But this was something unique: every team in Japan got a shot at the title. If nothing else, it was amazing to me that every team at basically every level in the entire country could compete to determine a champion *in two weeks*. In the

United States it would take two decades. If the NCAA were involved, which of course it would have to be, it either would never get played or Armageddon would happen before the tournament ever finished.

In the weeks leading up to the tournament, everyone around Hitachi was talking about it. This tournament was a huge deal, arguably even bigger in importance than the regular-season title. It was like *Hoosiers*, with everyone dreaming big, only without tight shiny maroon-and-mustard jerseys. Oddly enough, the other pro league in Japan, the BJ League, was banned from participating because of basketball politics.

We played a college team in the first round, which was kind of a joke. This was not UNC or Kentucky warming up at the other end. I don't recall a player over six feet tall besides a skinny dude from Africa. We were about as motivated as LeBron would be playing against a chair. We were barely ahead at halftime, though, and Coach Ono unleashed more wrath on us than he had all season long. He wasn't a screamer by nature, but his full fury came out as we sat on some hallway stairs taking his verbal thrashing. In the second half, we rallied for an unenthusiastic victory.

We won our next two games versus JBL teams, and I was playing much better. I was making shots and being more aggressive and effective on offense. Our big Japanese forward, Joji Takeuchi (JO-jee tahk-ay-OO-chee), also played great. He was 6-foot-9, 225 pounds, and very skilled. He could score inside and outside and he was athletic. Joji was a very good defender, and he competed for the league rebounding title every year with his twin brother Kosuke (KO-skay) on Aisin (I-shin). I loved playing with Joji, but he often stole rebounds away from me because of his length and leaping ability. *Joji, you already get fifteen rebounds a night, let a slow white brother have one or two.* In his second pro year, he was already one of the best three or four players in Japan.

We ended up making the finals of the All-Japan tournament, but lost to the defending champs, Aisin. It was the farthest that our Hitachi team had ever been in the eighty-five years of the tourney. The previous year they'd lost in the semifinals, and the coach told me that they had finished third.

"Oh, do they play a third-place game for the losers in the semis?" I asked, assuming that there was one.

"No," he said.

Right. I loved the confidence. Hitachi designated themselves the third-place winner on their own.

While I was happy that we'd made it to the championship game, I was frustrated with not winning it all. Finishing second never leaves you with a great taste in your mouth. Like Jerry Seinfeld says about the silver medal, "Congratulations. You almost won. Of all the losers, you were the best. No one lost ahead of you."

* * *

Along with our Hitachi rice cooker, which got used as much as the aerobic fitness equipment in your basement, we also received about eight manuals for what to do during an earthquake. I grew up in Illinois, so the closest I ever came to an earthquake was watching the end of *Indiana Jones and the Last Crusade*, when the whole temple floor shakes and cracks and the entire place collapses. But earthquakes in Japan are as real and unavoidable as my receding hairline.

The first earthquake we experienced in the fall felt like the washer and dryer were overheating. Over the next few months we had numerous small earthquakes. A little shaking. Side to side, back and forth. Ooo, ahh. They were kind of fun. That is, until you realized that if the ground decided to shake a lot, the building could collapse on top of you. What could you really do? You couldn't prepare for it as you would a hurricane or outrun it like a tornado. Should we jump out the window? Tear our clothes off and run through the streets screaming? The manual says to get under a mattress. Who has time to run into the other room, yank a heavy mattress off the bed frame, and place it comfortably on top of you? Not to mention that earthquakes happened in Japan sometimes multiple times per week. Wouldn't you feel kind of funny if you sprinted for a mattress cover at every little shake? I considered carrying a queen-size around town with me while shopping. I'm sure no one at practice would think it odd if I showed up carrying one. *You never know, guys. Just in case.*

* * *

By the end of our season, Hannah Japanah had spent more time in Asia than she had in the United States. She had pretty much become a baby celebrity just by smiling at everyone when we took her out for walks. People would stop and stare at the curious Western baby. It was hilarious—like if you rubbed her belly, she'd give you three wishes. I saw people grab the person next to them to show them Hannah. Others sometimes tripped or ran into people because they were too busy checking out the little pink-jacketed foreign baby who, *hmmmmm*, didn't look like the other babies around there. Occasionally moms ignored their own kids standing next to them to gawk at ours. While Hannah was best friends with them from a distance, she did not like it when others invaded her personal space. A few too many came up to her and touched her face. Hello, do I know you? It made Hannah flip from smiling to screaming in an instant. *Great, she's only ten months old and already is somehow prejudiced against the nicest people in the world.* Clearly her parents needed a visit from Social Services.

* * *

We finished the season in second place, just one game behind Aisin. If they had lost their last game, we would have been first because despite identical records we owned the tie-breaker. With only four teams making the playoffs, we played Panasonic in the semifinals. It was a best-of-three series and we had our hands full.

Panasonic had two outstanding veteran Americans, Jerald Honeycutt and Ace Custis. At 6-foot-9, 280 pounds, Jerald still had the game of a perimeter player who could pass and direct the offense better than many point guards. He was originally drafted by the Milwaukee Bucks and played two years in the NBA as a wing. Eleven years before, I had visited Marquette on a recruiting visit and saw Jerald, playing for visiting Tulane, hit a game-winning three to beat them. Eleven years later, I prayed he didn't do the same to us.

Ace played at Virginia Tech and had his jersey retired there. Like Jerald, he'd played in Japan for many years. He was so smart on defense and stripped the ball from me more times than I care to remember. He and 'Cutt were a tough duo to stop.

Panasonic's biggest player was Aono. He was a 7-foot, 290-pound giant. Everything about him was huge—his hands, his feet, and especially his head. With his crazy hair, he could have been a cartoon character. Maybe he appeared even larger than life because of his tiny surroundings—the Japanese people and players—but he was still ginormous no matter what country he was from. In one game during the season, I was trying to defend him in the post and he picked me up off the ground and shoved me to the side—with one arm. Big as he was, I swear he complained more than anybody in the league. How does the biggest guy, who dishes out monstrous elbows on every possession, complain the most? Every time we played them, I said an extra prayer that I'd finish the game with all my teeth and facial bones intact.

* * *

Our semifinal series versus Panasonic was played at a neutral site in northern Japan. *Hey, I know. Let's play the biggest games of the year in a location where neither team has any fans.* Yet another overseas oddity.

In Game One, we were ahead by one point with under 60 seconds remaining. I received a pass on the wing and knocked down a three. Panasonic had to foul to try to extend the game, and I went to the foul line multiple times. Usually I'm a good free-throw shooter, but I went just 2-for-8 that night, which let them hang around longer than necessary. We held on to win by three and were just one game from the finals.

The next day we played again but lost. I played my best game of the year, with 22 points, and only missed one shot. But as a team we shot a miserable 20 percent from three. It was frustrating to be so close to advancing to the finals and miss this chance. Of course, we still had another opportunity with Game Three, but with Panasonic winning the second game to tie the series, it felt like they had the momentum and confidence going into the final game.

Game Three was played without rest on the third consecutive day because some scheduling genius in the JBL never played basketball before. Thankfully, our guards found their three-point stroke again and we never allowed them to make a big run. We had four players in double figures, pulled it out, and were headed to the finals. I had played a strong series against Panasonic and couldn't wait to take on Aisin in the championship.

* * *

It's a little sad to say—and maybe strange —but I had never played for a championship in my life before this. My Penn State team made the NCAA Sweet 16 during my junior year, which was huge for us, but it wasn't a title game. None of my pro teams had made the finals either. There seemed to be a common factor here. Maybe I was the problem.

Lamar had played in three championships, one in college for the junior college national championship and two overseas. He had lost every one. But at least he'd been there. Now we were both eager to have a chance to call ourselves Japanese World Champions. It's no NBA trophy, but after nine months of eating rice, we wanted to go home with something.

Aisin had the X-factor in the league, J. R. Henderson, now known as J. R. Sakuragi. He scored a Japanese passport a few years ago and didn't count as an American player. No one knew exactly how he got his passport, because he didn't speak much Japanese and, as a 6-foot-9, 240-pound African-American, he definitely didn't look Japanese. He was, however, a dominant player in the league and his coach at Aisin was also the national team coach. The word around the league was that it was very convenient for J. R. to get his Japanese citizenship so he could play for Japan's national team and they could be more competitive internationally. Other Americans who had been in Japan as long as him had tried to get nationalized, but were denied.

With J. R. now Japanese, Aisin could play two Americans on the court instead of one. They also had Joji's twin, Kosuke, and a few very talented guards. They were a big, strong, and experienced team who played with a lot of confidence. Their offense ran through J. R. in the post, where he was very difficult to stop. He was strong and could score and rebound extremely well. He also knew how to work the refs and got more than his share of calls.

Our SunRockers, on the other hand, were scrappers. We played slow and we played hard-nosed team defense. While we weren't super-talented, we had just enough firepower to win games, and we had even won the regular season series, 4–2, against Aisin. But Aisin always seemed to show up for big games, like the All-Japan Tournament, where they beat us pretty handily. The playoff finals series was best-of-five and none of the earlier games mattered now.

* * *

In Game One of the Finals, we were up by seven heading into the fourth quarter. But it wasn't enough to hold them off. We only scored eight fourth-quarter points, and despite it being a one-point game with 90 seconds left, we couldn't finish it and ended up losing by four. I played one of my best games—17 points and 12 rebounds. But, of course, all I could remember were my missed shots and two turnovers.

In Game Two, we were down seven points with four minutes to go and went on a run to tie it. Then Joji hit some key free throws at the end and we won by three, tying the series at 1–1. Joji and Lamar had great games and led us to the crucial win.

I was hoping that J. R. would be running out of steam by Game Three, as he had played all but two minutes total in both games combined. But he responded with 20 points and 10 rebounds in 39 minutes and led Aisin to a ten-point win and a 2–1 lead. Again, Joji and Lamar played very well, but Aisin had too many weapons and we couldn't stop everything, as they shot 41 percent from three and 53 percent from two. OK, we couldn't really stop anything. I thought we should have gone with a zone defense, as they played such a big and athletic lineup and their offense went inside-out. Maybe it would have mixed things up a bit and disrupted their rhythm. But Coach Ono preferred man-to-man defense, so we kept grinding it out.

Coach Ono called a team meeting before Game Four.

"I believe whoever wins this next game will win the championship," he said.

Interesting statement. If Aisin won, then it would be over. So yes, they would be champions. If we were to win, then we'd still have to play Game Five, and Coach Ono believed that we would win that, too. It was a strange way to phrase it, but I think he was trying to prepare us to think big.

Unfortunately, Game Four was over early. Freakin' David Young, an American who had hit all of one three-pointer in the first three games for Aisin, decided to have the game of his life and hit five threes and lead them in scoring with 20 points. I only played nine minutes, as Lamar was playing very well and finished with 20 points and 11 rebounds. So much for our championship bonus.

It was very disappointing to lose in the Finals. We were the underdogs and fought hard. But Aisin was too talented.

In our exit meeting before heading back to the United States, our GM asked Lamar to return for the next season. I was happy for him. He had a terrific season and he deserved it.

They didn't ask me. It didn't necessarily completely close the door for me to return, but the message was clear that I wasn't a top priority. My pride took a hit. I didn't know if I wanted to come back, but I wanted to be asked. It would have been nice to at least have the option. After all, we made the Finals of All-Japan and the Finals of the playoffs, both being the farthest the team had ever advanced. My first half of the season had been slow, but I finished strong. Plus, I felt I fit in nicely with the team and Ono's system.

It had been a long and challenging season, with the tiny apartment, a baby who cried for up to three hours each night before falling asleep, and away trips every weekend. The twenty-four-hour journey back to the US felt like we were on a chariot to heaven. Well, *after* Hannah's vomiting at 7 a.m. on the ride to the Tokyo airport. Then, it was glorious. Cara was looking forward to having friends again. And I was back in the unemployment line.

* * *

When we returned to Pennsylvania in April, everything seemed huge. People were taller and wider. My car felt like a tank. Not having driven in nine months was strange, and we were back on the right side of the road again. When we walked into our house, it felt like a mansion. *Space! Oh, how we missed you.*

The minute Hannah had her own room, she was sleeping thirteen hours a night. She barely cried at night anymore. Even she seemed thankful for a change.

I was ready to head back to Europe. Japan had been so different than anywhere I'd been. The money was very good and I never had to worry about getting paid. It was in my account on the exact day it should be or even early during some months. But it had been a hard year with a new baby, and we didn't want a repeat.

Cara, especially, was ready to go anywhere but Japan. The season might have taken a couple of years off her life.

But Europe was silent. South America acted like they had never heard of me. The world economy was in shambles in the summer of 2009, and it was having a major effect on international basketball. Team sponsors stopped paying. Clubs were offering players half of what they made before, and even that money wasn't guaranteed. Some teams simply folded altogether.

And then Hitachi called.

Their offer was $80,000.

I thought Lee was joking. *We did just make a run at a championship a couple months ago—did they forget that? Since when do teams offer less money after they are successful?* I wasn't insulted as much as I was shocked. I knew that the recession had hit Japan also, but the offer still caught me off guard.

I said, no. I wasn't dying to go back to living like the Smurfs.

Then, they came up to $90,000. It was better, but I was having a hard time rationalizing a $25,000 pay cut after we'd gone to the Finals of the All-Japan Tournament and the JBL Playoffs. If we had actually won one of them, maybe their offer would have been $60,000. It was like some odd reverse-reward sliding scale.

"The only way I'll go back is if they get us a bigger apartment," I told Lee.

The highest they'd go was $92,000 and they said yes to a bigger apartment. With no other offers on the table, I talked it over with Cara. It wasn't our first choice, but it was still a good contract.

It's funny how relative things can be. Compared to last year's deal, it wasn't that great. Compared with any other contract I'd had in the past, it was terrific. We had to readjust our expectations, because the truth was, no matter what I thought my value was, I wasn't the one who determined it. It was up to the team.

I said, yes. And Cara cried.

Chapter 14

NEW FRIENDS, OLD OUTCOMES: JAPAN AGAIN

I headed back to Japan by myself this time. No, we didn't get divorced. Cara and Hannah stayed behind for a few perfectly logical reasons. First, it was insanely hot and humid in August in Tokyo. It didn't make sense for them to come and just sit around inside for a month while I went to lots of training camps. After having two camps last year and making the Finals, maybe Coach Ono would think we should do three this year. Surely that would push us over the top.

Second, I didn't know what our new apartment would be like, and if it would be something comfortable for Cara and Hannah.

And third, Cara wasn't all that enthused to return to the place that had been so difficult the year before. Some extra time at home would be welcome.

So I got on the plane. Business class again. (On the team's dime.) And business class just cracks me up. It's like your own special club. "Here's your favorite drink, Mr. Smith." Your own secret society. "Let's massage those tired feet for you, Mr. Smith." *Excuse me? Do we know each other?*

The weird thing is that everyone else apparently knows the handshake but you. But you can't *show* that you don't know the handshake, because you fear they'll find out and send you back to the dark depths of Economy. So you totally fake it and pretend like this happens every minute of your life.

I swear they know everything about you in business class. *"Welcome aboard, Mr. Smith,"* says super-happy flight attendant. Big smile. *"How is your brother-in-law's new puppy? You know, the pilot ran into your middle school gym teacher, Mr. Dieden, and he sends his best. I hope you're not still pushing girls on the playground and blaming Steven. Your daughter has a new word now. Do you know what it is? While you're gone, don't worry about cutting your grass this week. We've already taken care of that."*

Who *are* these people? I felt like I was in *Enemy of the State* with Will Smith.

In economy—they might as well just say it: the "loser" class—it's every man, woman, child, and kangaroo for himself. Not in business class. Each person gets a king-size bed in business. And when you fall asleep, they come and whisper in your ear … *"You're so much better than those people back there. That's why we give you twenty extra pounds of room in your luggage and a personal placemat for your caviar. You don't even have to walk through the regular tunnel with those ordinary people. You get your own tunnel. You're special. Shhhhhhh."* It's creepy.

I landed in Tokyo. As I walked casually to the final customs check with my bags, I had to pass one final test. Why is it that they always try to make you feel guilty in customs even if you aren't doing anything wrong? It's like they're evening out the score after all the scary niceness on the plane.

A Japanese woman wearing a white dentist mask took my papers and asked me what was the purpose of my stay. I had to say that I was only "traveling as a tourist," because my team had not set up my long-term visa yet. If I said I was there for business but did not have a work visa, there would be beatings and ransom demands. You know how it goes with customs.

She looked at me through her little mask and said, "That's a lot of stuff for only vacation."

Oh, here we go. I looked down at my 200-plus pounds of luggage. Six bags total, including carry-ons. I was packing two months' worth of protein powder in unmarked plastic bags (hmmm), a video camera, and women's underwear. (Disclaimer: packed by Cara for Cara. Not sure why that needed to happen.) All of a sudden I got a little sweaty.

Dental-hygienist lady looked at me waiting for my answer.

I looked her square in the eyes and said, "I'm a big guy and wear big clothes. They take up a lot of room."

Listen, it's the best I could come up with. If you hesitate, they cuff you—end of story. I'd woken up at 3:45 a.m. and had been traveling for twenty-three hours straight without sleeping. If you had a better line, help a brother out for next time. The CIA wouldn't be sending me to infiltrate Al-Qaeda's camp anytime soon.

I held my breath nervously.

"Enjoy your stay in Japan," she said and gave a little laugh.

Get me outta here. I picked up my massive dead-body bags and sprinted out the door to freedom.

* * *

I was back in Japan. I'd missed many of its nuances. Like using chopsticks and not being able to read anything. Fake-laughing as I pretended to understand a locker room joke in an unknown language. Hitting my head on doorways designed for people three feet shorter. An apartment that felt like a Mini Cooper. A gym that had no AC in the blazing summer nor heat in the freezing winter, even though the team sponsor made air conditioners and heaters.

We had a new assistant coach, Sassa (SAH-suh), who picked me up from the airport, and naturally within our first twenty minutes of conversation, the life-changing topic of Krispy Kreme came up. He laughed and said, "But it's *just a donut!*" I told him that if we were going to have a chance at any kind of healthy relationship this season, he had better take that back and rethink his priorities.

The team wasn't lying—my apartment *was* bigger that year. We could fit four people inside now instead of two and a half. It was actually quite nice, and I thought it would make things much more comfortable for all parties involved. Hitachi transferred literally everything from our old apartment to this new one. Even our fourteen dollar lint roller made the move. And the rice cooker. Which, by the way, I was committed to learning how to use this year.

Everything was still expensive. I had to shell out five dollars for ChapStick. Five dollars! But you ChapStickers know where I'm coming from. You'll spend anything for that high.

The prices just killed me. It was like every store was Tiffany's and each restaurant was Ruth's Chris Steak House.

"I'd like a salad and glass of water."

"Hai, Tyler-san, hai. How you say … twenty-six dollars." Bow. Bow.

They had less expensive things to eat. But I had no clue what they were. Even when I actually saw the dishes, I didn't recognize many of them. Plus, no one there ate as much as I did. A tiny bowl of soup was a sufficient meal for the locals. But for me it's the equivalent of a third of a Tic Tac. *Yes, hi. I'll take the first two pages of the menu.*

* * *

You might be curious how much attention pro basketball players get overseas.

Q: Did they recognize you out in public?
A: Let's just say I blended in quite nicely in Japan in all my 6-foot-8 whiteness. I got a lot of looks. Not the looks of "*Wow*, it's a pro athlete." More the looks like, "Please don't hurt me, you strange foreign creature" as the mother shifts her child behind her.
Q: Did you sign autographs?

A: Yes. But only for women. They are the strong majority of our fan base.

Q: Did you eat free meals at restaurants because of your rock-star status?

A: Yes, Hotel Smith has a delicious corn flakes-and-granola breakfast dish.

In all honesty, it did feel good to be back in a place where things were familiar. As familiar as Japan could be for me at the time. I knew where the grocery store was on my first try. *Check*. I knew to stand to the left on escalators so that little old ladies could burst by me on the right. *Check*.

When you move from country to country each year, any kind of consistency goes a long way. This was the first year I'd returned to a team. I'd played in Holland and Uruguay multiple years, but never on the same team. Now I had my samurai sword. Hannah had her kimono. Cara had chocolate-covered peanuts. We were good to go, I thought.

* * *

Lamar had re-signed with Hitachi too, which was great. But we lost a Japanese starter named Kan who retired from playing to work full-time for Hitachi. He had turned the magical age of thirty. Supposedly, at age thirty, the company turned the heat up on the Japanese players and expected them to stop playing basketball and commit to full-time office work. Not the nicest thing to do to an athlete who may still have some good years left on the court. Kan was a very reliable player for us and a good leader. He must have weighed 150 pounds holding two typewriters, but the guy was tough and could really play.

The other departure was our Japanese Justin Timberlake, Kei. He signed with Toyota. After he played his first few years for Coach Ono, I think they both needed a break. There had been some tension last year and it all came to a head one day.

At the start of last season, Kei was upbeat and had a great attitude. Midway through, he wasn't his usual cheerful self. He was very private about it, and my attempts to get him to open up went nowhere. Then one day during practice, our manager and practice referee, Sakamoto, made a call that Kei didn't like. Kei stopped, smacked Sakamoto upside the head, and yelled at him.

We were all stunned. Sakamoto got my vote for the nicest and hardest working guy in Japan, possibly in the world. Lamar and I believed that he must have had nine twin brothers, in order to finish all the stuff he was responsible for. He was also the smallest guy in the gym, and two of him could likely fit in most high school lockers. Everyone on the team loved Sakamoto, even though his poor refereeing skills drove each of us crazy at times.

Kei's inner turmoil erupted onto Sakamoto because he was an easy target. He was a gentle soul and wouldn't fight back. Plus, Kei was older than him. And in Japan, you didn't ever disrespect your elders.

We told Kei to chill out and practice resumed as normal. At the end of practice, we huddled around Coach Ono as we did every day for his departing words. Todo was in the midst of translating, "Play better defense. Cut down on turnovers…" when coach Ono turned to Kei and, without warning, unleashed a verbal thrashing. It scared me at first because Coach's voice had been so controlled. *Normal. Normal. YELLING!!!*

Coach must have gone on for a solid seven or eight minutes. Kei just stood there and took it. We did, too. Unfortunately, Todo stopped translating. He obviously didn't need to relate word-for-word what was happening, but it was one of the many times I wished I'd shelled out money for language lessons.

Eventually, Coach's rage subsided and practice was over. Poor Sakamoto was unsuccessfully trying to hold in the tears. He looked up to guys like Kei and others on the team. There was a joy he had in doing his part to serve the team and help us be our best. The incident with Kei really hurt him emotionally.

I took him aside.

"Sakamoto, are you okay?" I asked.

He nodded, trying to keep his emotions under control.

"Listen," I said. "You are incredibly important to this team. I appreciate everything you do for us. You work harder than everybody and you never complain. You need to know that you are loved and appreciated by every player and person here at Hitachi, starting with me. Got it?"

He nodded again and smiled. "Thanks, Ty," he said as he wiped his red eyes.

Kei wasn't a bad guy, and I liked him a lot. He had simply let too much frustration build up and it exploded in the wrong way toward the wrong person.

* * *

In God's providence, a Costco had just opened forty minutes from our apartment in Kashiwa. Thank you, Lord, for bulk items. I love a place where I can purchase a life-size Santa in August, ten pounds of oatmeal, and a Roomba all while eating a hot dog the size of my arm while pushing a cart that's bigger than many Japanese cars. Year Two in Japan just got a little bit sweeter.

To make the transition smoother and more comfortable, I picked up a couple of key things. I bought a rather large kids playhouse for Hannah. I wasn't entirely sure that it would fit in the living room, but I figured I'd find a way. To make room, something would have to go. Who needs a kitchen table anyway?

The other item I bought was for Cara and a little more unique. A massage table. Last season, I purchased a few massages for her at a nearby masseuse. She loved them, but they were pricey. For the cost of three massages, I could just buy my own table.

The looks I got trying to transport a giant kid's playhouse and a massage table by hand to the train station and then back home were absolutely priceless. The expressions said it all. "I can't believe someone actually bought one of those." "Doesn't he have a car?" My T-shirt was drenched with sweat and it looked like I had just run ten miles in the Sahara desert.

I also stumbled upon an Ikea next to Costco. I went back a week later and really hit the jackpot. I found a rocking chair. Last year I looked high and low and only came across one antique rocking chair, which was over $300 and had no padding. This Ikea gem cost one-third of that, was comfortable, and would be perfect for reading stories to Hannah during bedtime.

When Cara and Hannah arrived in September, we enrolled Hannah in two play classes at a local health club. One class was like a gymnastics class and the other was a parent/child swimming class. Hannah had learned to float over the summer when she was just fourteen months old. She took an infant swim-and-rescue class in Florida, and we were anxious to keep her swim skills top-notch.

I loved taking Hannah to her swim-and-play classes on Tuesdays. It was just me and the mommies. All the other dads were working because they had normal jobs, while I generally had the mornings free. The giant white American with his little crazy blonde tornado and all the tiny Japanese moms and their perfectly behaved kids. We blended in like a homeless person at a black-tie event.

Have you been in a dressing room or locker room lately with others? Does the naked person stand right next to you, too? For some reason, of all the dozens of lockers around, Hannah and I always got the old Japanese naked guy next to us. And why did they seem so relaxed and free and comfortable in their bare skin with strangers next to them? Maybe it's just me.

I donned my Tommy Hilfiger swimsuit which, by the way, I was told that only gangstas and bad boys wore in Japan, thus proving my cool thuggish dangerous side. Hannah rocked her government-issued pink suit. No kids got wet without properly approved swimming attire in Japan. We brought some bathing suits for her from the United States but quickly learned that individuality was a no-no in our health club. Rules are rules.

Once we survived the locker room and went upstairs to the pool, I was forced to sport my sweet blue swim cap. Mandatory. I forgot it once and tried to jump in the pool. They came after me like I just dumped a barrel of oil in the water. "SWIM CAP SWIM CAP!" They freaked out. *Sorry. I thought that was why we put chlorine in the water.* You've got twenty babies peeing in it for an hour. I figured my receding, buzz-cut melon wouldn't kill any fish.

Sadly, my blue stretchy head-covering didn't make me look like Michael Phelps, as I'd thought it would. I glanced in the mirror one day as we were walking out the door, and I paused. *That's what I look like? Man, I look like an idiot.* But I guess when you're the only over-sized foreign dude among fifteen small Japanese women and their kids, what's a little more weirdness?

When the instructor told us to lift our little ones up and down while we stood in the water, all the mommies gave a nice little "wheeeee," barely raising their kids out of the water. I, on the other hand, threw Hannah as high as I could to see if she could touch the flag markers that hung crossways over the water. For the record, I never dropped her. I'm sure they were talking about us. But I'll never know.

The other kids allowed the instructor to hold them on the side of the pool before they jumped in to their mom, smiling the whole way. *Yay, water!* When it came Hannah's turn, she knew it all too well and screamed her face off. *Don't lay a hand on me, lady!* We meshed just perfectly with the crowd.

After swim class, the real fun began: gymnastics class. More like don't-get-run-over-or-step-on-a-tiny-person class.

In her first couple of classes, Hannah was not impressive. She couldn't climb over a shoe. Once she got acclimated, she dove head first down the soft slide, hurtled herself onto mats, and walked over to raise the volume on the stereo whenever she felt the urge to rock out.

The true highlight of the play class was bubbles. Hannah chased those bubbles down like a cheetah, plowing through any person or wall in her way. The other kids didn't find them as mesmerizing. *Yeah, yeah. You blow 'em. They pop. No biggie.* Hannah on the other hand was always thrilled. *Bubbles!!!* Her eyes got huge. When her tiny fingers touched it and the bubble burst, there was a split second when it caught her by surprise—*it disappeared again!*

Then came the big finale.

At the end of every class, they played a song and we danced a little jig. The song was in Japanese, and we all gathered in a circle to do the choreography. Few have been lucky enough to witness my stellar dancing prowess. You know you've reached a whole new personal comfort level when you can dance like a Disney character in front of fifteen moms who don't speak your language. Hannah danced like there was no tomorrow and hit every move right on beat, just like her incredible *Dancing with the Stars* mommy. As for daddy, let's just say it looked like he was hearing it for the first time, every time.

The best thing to come from the classes, by far, was a friend we made named Yoshimi (yo-SHEE-mee). Her son, Kensei (KEN-say), was a few months younger than Hannah. Meeting Yoshimi was truly an answer to our prayers. In our first year, we hadn't made any close Japanese friends outside of the team, and Cara really needed some social interaction.

We almost didn't meet Yoshimi. We first tried to join another athletic club that had baby classes, but we were denied entry because we didn't speak Japanese and the teachers were concerned about safety issues. So we landed at Central Sports, where Yoshimi and Kensei happened to sign up for the same time slot.

Yoshimi was very friendly and more outgoing than the other moms. She didn't speak great English, but enough for us to communicate. She invited us over for dinner at her house, and we were able to meet her husband, Takayuki (tah-ka-YOO-kee). When we arrived, there were sticky notes covering the walls in the kitchen and the living room. Yoshimi was practicing English every day and often stayed up late studying so she could communicate better with Cara and me. She was such a sweet woman, and she and Cara became fast friends.

* * *

Our Hitachi team was not quite as strong that season. We kept the same offense and defensive principles, and we were still a tough team to beat. We rarely turned the ball over, and we were steady. Most weekends we'd split two games, and we played .500 ball for the first half of the season. I was off to a better start than last year and had a few good games, but Lamar continued to play really well and received most of the playing time.

In January, we made it to the Finals of the All-Japan Tournament again. And of course we ran into Aisin again. We jumped out to a big lead early and played with much more confidence this time around. We played aggressively and held the lead going in to the fourth quarter. But once more, Aisin saved their best for last and they defended their All-Japan title. It was the third time in two years that we'd lost to them in a championship. We were like the Buffalo Bills of the '90s, who could make it to the Super Bowl but never win it.

* * *

Hannah enjoyed the games much more the second year because she was a little bit older. Sundy, our mascot, still freaked her out in person, but Hannah could positively identify every SunRockers player thanks to her new favorite book.

It wasn't just any book. She called it a "bookabook." That's one word, in case you didn't know. There weren't cartoons or fancy drawings in it, but there were plenty of animals and funny-looking characters. A *New York Times* bestseller for sure, if they ever discovered that it existed: the 2009-2010 JBL Media Guide, featuring Daddy and lots of Japanese people.

We read it every day. Hannah would plop down in my lap, open to a random page, and point.

An ad for Nike.

"Shoos," she said in her tiny cute voice.

"Good, Hannah," I said. "Those are shoes."

"Yeah," she smiled.

Next page.

"Sooosh," she said.

"That's right," I said. "That's the Nike Swoosh." Genius.

"Yeah."

She turned the page. Her eyes lit up. Her back straightened quickly. Her mouth opened wide with excitement, momentarily breathless, and her finger couldn't even make it to the page.

It's him!

"DAD-DY!!!"

"No, that's a Japanese man. On a different team."

"Yeah."

Next page.

It's a miracle!

"DAD-DY!!!"

"No, that's a black man with a beard, sweetheart."

"Yeah."

OK, not in the gifted program yet.

But it's like the lottery, right? Sooner or later, she'll point and it will be him.

We gave her books for counting and letters, and even baby Bibles. But who needs the three wise men when you've got the Panasonic Trians? It was the new Elmo. On our team's page in the media guide, I couldn't even read my own bio other than the words "Krispy Kreme," which they apparently don't have a Japanese translation for. Yet.

But the pictures are priceless to an almost-two-year-old. Shooos. B-balls. And Daddies! Lots of them. She knew more names in Japanese than English. Joji, Taiji, Yoko, and Oya. If nothing else, she'll make a great eyewitness in criminal lineups. Does that pay well, by the way?

* * *

The good news was that we'd finally found our rhythm after the All-Japan Tournament and were playing our best in the second half of the season. At one point we won four in a row. A few weeks later, we started another streak and won eight straight and made it as high as second place during the regular season. Lamar injured his ankle and was out for a couple of weeks. My playing time skyrocketed, and I was on the floor the entire game. I started scoring much more, and my confidence grew. I felt great, finally being given consistent minutes. Even if I made a couple of mistakes, I didn't have to force anything, because I knew I'd have another opportunity.

In the midst of our win streak, I got my first technical foul in Japan. I typically kept a pretty cool head when I played and tried not to get too high or too low. But one guy put me over the edge.

The short version was: he started it. I got in his face. The ref probably made the right call.

We were getting smoked by Hokkaido, a team up north that was perennially one of the weaker squads. Their point guard was trying to be tough with me when I set a screen on him. Admittedly, I was pushing him a little. But his response was more than I was willing to take.

He grabbed on to me with both of his arms and pulled me to the ground, igniting a small storm of fury within me. I jumped up and screamed in his face. He screamed back profanities in very broken English. Somehow I kept my arms at my side rather than heaving him over the bench. As angry as I was, I didn't want to give the refs an easy reason to throw me out of the game. His coach nearly ran onto the floor as he fiercely beckoned for me to come over and mess with him on the sidelines. Fortunately, I walked away before my ego tried to take on the entire stadium à la Tim Jones in Argentina.

After the smoke cleared, I had received a technical. But their team had received two techs. I got two free throws out of it and sank both. We also got the ball, when it had previously been their possession. We scored. The rage continued inside of me, and I played with more ferocity than I had all season, thanks to a fresh supply of adrenaline that I didn't know had been hiding inside. We erased a 15-point deficit and beat them on the road. Maybe I should get angry more often.

* * *

Unfortunately, we lost our momentum at the end of the season when our point guard, Toshi, tore his Achilles. I felt terrible for him. Toshi wreaked absolute havoc on the court with his play. I'd never seen someone cover as much ground as he did in such a sneaky way. He'd be guarding the ball at the top of the key and a split-second later he'd be down on the baseline stripping it out of the big man's hands. Toshi never lifted weights and had no muscle definition whatsoever, but it was impossible to back him down if he was guarding you on the block. His low center of gravity and balance were remarkable. He never taped his ankles and hardly stretched. Yet in two years he'd never twisted an ankle because he had the body control of a cat.

Toshi would often show up late to practice because he had to work longer at the office than other guys on our team. He'd just walk in and merge right into the drill as if he'd been there all along. Toshi was a fantastic three-point shooter and seemed to hit them most often at the end of the shot clock from four steps behind the three-point line. He didn't really put a ton of work into his shot. He just knew that he could do it and would show up and play well every day. He didn't get a lot of lift on his jumper, but he flung the ball with a quick release, and I'd give him the last shot to win the game any day of the week. In one game, Coach Ono did exactly that.

We were down by two with a few seconds left and Coach drew up a play for Toshi. For such a talented player, Toshi was really shy and nervous about taking the last shot. He waved coach off and told him to have someone else take it. Most guys would be dying to get a chance to win the game. But Toshi wanted no part of it. So Lamar got the ball at the top of the key and banked in a three for the win. Maybe Toshi knew what he was doing after all.

Losing Toshi to injury really hurt us because of everything he brought to the table, from defense, to big shots, to great passes. Without him, we dropped the final five games of the season. We slipped to fourth place, but thanks to our earlier hot stretch, we still made the playoffs. And since Aisin finished in first again, we matched up with them in the semifinals. Lucky us.

We led almost all of Game One. Aisin kept within two or three points in the fourth quarter and then tied it with two minutes left. We missed a couple of chances to take the lead, and with under a minute left, Aisin made a shot to go up by two. They held on to win, and it was a tough loss to swallow. J. R. had his typical big night with 23 points and eight rebounds.

But the most glaring difference was in free throws. Aisin shot 16-for-19. We shot zero, as in zero attempts. How in the world a team doesn't get to the free throw line in a playoff game is beyond me. I think the refs often assumed that Aisin would win and that they should be getting more calls because they were the better team. They may not have been deliberately calling it one way, but 19–0 is a pretty huge gap.

We responded with a great first half in Game Two. We were playing confidently, up seven. I got off to a great start, with 14 points and five rebounds by halftime. (Normally that would have been a good stat line for my whole game.) Again, the free throw disparity was evident, 10–1 in Aisin's favor. Nevertheless, we weren't going to go quietly. Aisin was beatable, and we knew it.

But something happened at halftime. Defensively we were still very stingy, but offensively we forgot how to put the ball in the basket. We made just two shots the rest of the game. Along with a few free throws, we totaled just five points in the third quarter and four points in the fourth. Throughout the season we had dry spells from time to time. We weren't a high-octane offense by any means. Unfortunately, we hit a drought at the worst possible time, shooting just 8 percent from the floor in the second half. We couldn't beat a team of grandmas with walkers shooting like that.

It was a heartbreaking way to finish the season. We'd lost our final seven games in a row, Toshi had gone down with an injury, and Aisin got the best of us in elimination games for the fourth time in the past two years. They were big and talented. And we couldn't seem to find an answer to them. I had played a good game, with 20 points and nine rebounds, but all I could taste was the disgusting loss that ended our season. Surprisingly, Lamar didn't play in the second half of our final game. I had no idea why, and I thought he could have given us a spark offensively. Once he came back from his ankle injury later in the year, he had played some great games.

But the 2009–10 season was all over for us at Hitachi. A return trip to the finals just wasn't meant to be.

Chapter 15

BUT THE ROOM KEPT SHAKING: JAPAN YEAR THREE

I liked Hitachi and wanted to go back there again. Within a month of returning home, we had agreed to another one-year deal. Again, it was less than what I had made my first year, which still didn't make much sense to me. But at least it was a small raise from last season instead of a twenty percent decrease. This would be my third year with Hitachi. During that stretch, we had gone to two All-Japan Tournament finals, one JBL playoff final, and one JBL playoffs semifinal. I played better in my second year with Hitachi than I had in my first, and I was eager to keep that trend going.

It definitely helped that we had a nicer place to live and Cara had become such good friends with Yoshimi and her family. Cara no longer felt alone on an island, literally. I took it as a good sign that when I agreed to a third season with Hitachi, she didn't shed tears this time.

Cara was always very supportive of the decisions I made about where we'd go as a family. I always discussed each offer with her and we would pray about it and get as much info as we could on what we were heading into. Packing up our lives and moving every year was not the easiest lifestyle. Throw in the fact that we didn't know which continent or hemisphere we'd be living in only a few months from any point in time and it was a perfect opportunity for anxiety and worry to set up shop in our brains. Everyone has something to stress about.

Cara and I did our best to rely on the Lord and find rest in the peace that He offered.

Our particular world didn't offer a lot of peace. The ups and downs of wins and losses, injuries, contract disputes, frustration with communicating in foreign languages—none of those things made us want to sing "Kumbaya" around the campfire and exhale, smiling, "Ah, finally some tranquility and harmony."

I know. You say, "Well, you're choosing to put yourself in that situation, so don't cry me a river about how it's hard."

Agreed. But the truth is that we make choices all of the time in our lives for good things, but they still come with their share of struggles and challenges. For example, kids are a blessing. But every parent knows that they cause plenty of inconveniences in life, like when they get sick and, instead of sleeping, you're doing laundry at 3 a.m. and Googling how to get vomit out of a mattress. Or when your house decides it doesn't want the toilet to function properly anymore. In either situation, you don't get rid of the kid or burn down the house. You chose them and you love them. So it becomes a question of, "How do we handle the adversity that comes our way?"

* * *

As far as my new Hitachi contract went, there were two parts of the agreement that I wasn't enthused about. The first was the date of re-entry.

We had to return to Japan on July 20. In case no one knew this, July is a baseball month. And the Japanese, of all people, should know this, given their love for baseball. It's not even a football month. So that means that it's definitely not time for hoops yet.

But they don't see it that way. The local players only got a couple of weeks off in April after playoffs. Then they were back to practicing. They never really had an offseason, which blew my mind. The body needs some downtime after a long season. It needs to be able to heal and recharge. While I admired their work ethic and discipline,

I thought that sometimes the Japanese needed to work smarter, not harder.

The second annoying part of the contract was the plane ticket situation. We now needed three tickets instead of two because Hannah was two years old and couldn't sit on our laps anymore as an extra carry-on. For the past two years we had been very fortunate to get two business-class seats from the team. This year the team wouldn't offer a third business-class ticket. I told them that they could give us four or five economy-class tickets instead, as that would still be far cheaper than two business-class tickets. The team would save money, we'd sit together, and even have a couple more tickets to fly over a personal chef and nanny in case we won Powerball.

The team refused. They insisted that I fly business class because it was a long trip and they wanted me to be comfortable.

"But you won't buy two more business tickets for my family," I told them, insinuating that this was a problem.

"They can fly economy," the team said.

Hang on; let me put wife on the phone so you can say this directly to her. I'm sure she'll be very understanding of your logic.

I'd be stretched out in business class sipping champagne and getting my neck rubbed while Cara got to entertain a two-year-old child who refused to sleep on planes for fourteen hours straight. Apparently no one within Hitachi basketball had ever flown anywhere on a plane with their family.

The team wouldn't budge on their narrow-minded airline ticket plan. So I had to get creative. I took their offer of one business and two economy tickets and made sure the economy tickets were upgradable. Then I used miles to upgrade their tickets so we could all get pedicures together in business class. It took about nine calls to United to get it done, but my toes looked fantastic by the time we landed.

* * *

On our second day there, it was as hot as Africa. I'm not sure who put Lucifer in charge of the temperature, but somebody needed to stop him. Blinking made me sweat. Chewing practically made me need to change my shirt. I walked to practice that day, and I might as well have walked through a downpour.

It was my first practice of the season and it lasted two hours and fifteen minutes, normally not a big deal. But it was like trying to play in an oven. You spoiled little air-conditioned office people just don't get it. You guys laying asphalt in July in Arizona—you get it.

I assumed practice was over. Then Coach Ono decided that we needed one last game. Never mind that at that point I was basically a jogging sponge that had just emerged from a pond. I had my own personal manager following me around with a mop. And the "one last game" put me over the edge. Throughout practice, I'd been drinking like a frat boy on the Friday after finals. Water, that is. But it wasn't enough.

Once the final game ended and we broke our huddle, I walked to the side of the gym and collapsed. I rolled onto my back and closed my eyes. I was on fire. My body had nothing left. I was basically just trying not to die. I sipped some water, but I had no idea who handed it to me.

I was lying there alone, as no one seemed to be paying attention. Exhausted, I planned on being there a while until my vital signs returned. I could hear some rustling around me and figured it was Coach Ono. He didn't speak English, but I happened to lie down next to where he kept his clipboard. He pointed the fan at me, which felt glorious.

All of the sudden, I felt an ice pack being placed on my sensitive man area. *Excuse me?*

I heard Nomo say to me, "Coach says if you're really hot, the best way to cool down is to put an ice pack there."

While that might be well and good, don't you think we should have talked before acting upon such impulses? I was too hot and exhausted to argue. Or agree.

Then I felt a second bag placed upon my region as well. *What the —? I* mean, seriously. Is your boss willing to do something like that? How close are you with your superiors? Because I'm pretty sure we just bonded.

Hey, this might actually be working. You tell that little old guy that whatever chi-type stuff he's into might be saving my life. I eventually cooled down enough to make it to the shower and limp home.

I made the mistake of lying on the couch without moving for about forty-five minutes. When I tried to get up, both of my legs seized up. I had no control over my quads, hamstrings, or calves and they were cramping relentlessly. I had never experienced that before, and it was awful. Cara stretched and massaged my legs, poured water down my throat, and eventually the spasms subsided. But man, you talk about scary. When your body begins doing something you definitely didn't tell it to do, it freaks you out a little.

* * *

I signed up for a regular cell phone plan during my first week in Japan. I then switched the Japanese SIM chip from my Japanese cell phone to my shiny new American iPhone and *voila!*—I was connected to the universe. iPhones were pretty much the coolest thing invented since the Model T. They can do everything. Mine found me an island in the Caribbean and then built a plane to fly me there.

I used the phone casually for the next few days, as we did not have Internet in our apartment yet. A few emails. A couple of calls. It made me dinner. Nothing too outrageous.

Then, I got "the call."

"Sir, you owe $4,000 for data charges. What have you been doing with your phone?"

Excuse me? What have I been doing? Apparently I've been calling collect to Baghdad Hot Date Lines for twenty-five hours every day and downloading The Lord of the Rings *trilogy in over 600 languages. I haven't done a thing! You must have the wrong number.*

I thought they would say, "Oh, OK, you silly American. We'll waive the charges because you're clearly a moron." Let's be real. How is it even possible to have $4,000 in charges in five days? Wouldn't that occur to them also? *Hey, how about you call me after I passed $1,000 in the first day? Oh, no. You were ready to take me to the bank and cash out my IRA.*

I should have known better. It was Japan and everything was by the book. It's one of those places where if the crosswalk was red and there wasn't a car within miles, people still waited for green to cross the street. I swear they didn't even need police there. The guilt washed over me when I jaywalked, ate a snack on a train, or talked on my phone on the bus—all big no-no's. It's a wonder they allowed me to remain in the country. I very easily could be writing this from a Japanese jail cell.

I ran to the Japanese cell phone store, sweating. It was Sunday night and I was praying about as hard as one could pray. *Are there any mobile phone passages in Psalms?* My mind was racing ... *All the things that you could buy for $4-grrr ... How many stupider ways can you just give away four thousand bucks?*

I didn't see this ending well.

My life was in the hands of our team's director of basketball operations, Masa, who had become a good friend. He happened to be with me at the time of the call and was probably the only one who could get me out of this. He pulled his baseball cap down low, focused in on the mobile phone company employee, and he went to work.

I really have no idea what was said or if Masa promised the guy vacations in Tahiti or my next born child. But the employee made a call and said something to Masa. Then he addressed me in English.

"You are not allowed to put the SIM chip in a US iPhone," said the cell phone rep.

Yeah, thanks. I got that much.

"Your cell plan has high data charges for this type of usage."

Hmmm, that would seem to be the case.

"Would it be okay if we waived the $4,000 bill and just charged you seventy dollars, but you can't use the iPhone anymore?"

Would it be OK??? I want to kiss you and invite you to family reunions.
Yes, it's okay.

And so it was. My bad country-western song just became a *Sesame Street* jingle as I danced for joy.

"Masa" just shot to the top of the list of names for any future Smith children.

* * *

We settled back into a nice routine in Kashiwa. Cara felt much more comfortable this year, knowing that we had activities lined up for Hannah and friends to hang out with. Hannah moved up to the next level of swim-and-play classes. She and Cara spent many days with Yoshimi and Kensei, going to parks and playing together. Yoshimi's English had improved so much, and she was teaching Kensei, too. Takayuki had even begun taking English classes for his work. His company wanted him to start selling their products and services in Europe and elsewhere, so he needed to be able to communicate in English. He was very nervous to take on such a big role, as he wasn't very confident in his English yet. But he was getting better.

* * *

Hitachi did not bring back Lamar for a third season. Instead, we signed Alfred Aboya. Alfred had played for Tochigi the previous year and helped them win the title, sweeping Aisin in three games. It was an impressive run, and things really came together in the second half of the season for Tochigi. Alfred was a 6-foot-7 warrior who had crazy strength. He didn't lift weights because he was just a natural freak athlete and didn't need to. He played terrific defense and was a great rebounder. He was relentless on the boards and made it a complete nightmare for me every day in practice, trying to box him out.

Alfred had come to the United States from Cameroon in high school. On his first day of school in the States, he didn't recognize any of the foods in the cafeteria during lunch. Then he spotted something familiar, bananas. Starving and needing to fill his stomach with something, Alfred ate fifteen bananas to quiet his hunger pains. He could still eat ridiculous amounts of food and claimed that he never actually filled up, he just stopped eating.

Alfred went to UCLA, where he played on three Final Four teams, including one that lost in the championship to Florida. He was a really hard worker and a great teammate, always singing and joking with everyone.

Coach Ono named me a co-captain, and I was getting more time on the floor, which helped me to find my groove. But even though I was playing better than in my first two years, we were terribly inconsistent and started the season 1–4. One weekend, we won the first game by 16 points on a Saturday and then lost by 16 on Sunday to the same team.

In October, we were playing Mitsubishi and it was back and forth all game. In the fourth quarter I missed shot after shot but we continued to hang around. Then, trailing by one point with eight seconds left, I grabbed an offensive rebound, made a move, and scored to put us up by one. Mitsubishi took one final shot and there was some contact, but no foul was called. We won, 72–71. I had not played well the entire game and had only four points until I hit that game-winner. Fortunately, I made the one that counted.

The next day we faced Mitsubishi again, and I was hot, making everything that I threw at the rim. But again it was close, and with 25 seconds left we were down by one point. I made another shot to put us up by one.

Mitsubishi's point guard then made a free throw to tie it, 68–68. He missed the second free throw with five seconds left and there was a brief moment of chaos, with everyone scrambling to get the ball. For some reason, I thought we were losing, and I fouled their point guard on purpose, sending him back to the free throw line. My whole team stared at me with their mouths open.

I looked at the scoreboard and suddenly realized what I had done. I had lost my head in the excitement and it cost us the game. He made one free throw and we lost. What had been my best game of the season so far turned into my worst. Despite 21 points and 12 rebounds, I made a crucial mental error in crunch time that never should have happened. *Those were the boneheaded plays that rookies make, not thirty-year-old veterans.* I was furious at myself.

We lost the next three out of four games, and things weren't looking good. Alfred limped into the hotel lobby one morning during a road trip. Something was wrong. He had been stretching with Nomo and, all of the sudden, something in his knee popped.

He tried to walk it off, but couldn't. Coach Ono took him to see his "chi-guy" as we called him, an alternative doctor in Tokyo who did all kinds of weird stuff. "Lick your lips, wiggle your toes, and talk like a chicken. All better!" The doctor did some quirky stuff to Alfred and after five minutes of this nonsense declared Alfred fixed and gave him the green light to practice again. But Alfred could barely walk.

He got an MRI, and it turned out that he'd torn his meniscus. Since the "chi" didn't take, Alfred had surgery and was told he'd be out at least six weeks.

* * *

Thanksgiving isn't celebrated in Japan. In fact, you could only find turkey at Subway, and it was pricey. I was walking to the grocery store alone on Turkey Day when I noticed a big commotion just outside the entrance. Police had barricaded off an area, and everyone was looking up at a newly constructed apartment building. I followed their gaze and saw something standing on a ledge fourteen floors up. It was a figure wearing a black robe with a hood. At first I couldn't tell if it was real or some sort of creepy decoration, because it wasn't moving. Whatever it was, it was about an inch from plummeting to the ground.

Then it moved. It was definitely a person who was about to jump.

My stomach dropped to my feet. I had never seen anything like that. This person was about to end his (or her) life in front of a few hundred people watching from the ground.

It was scary to see this person at the edge of the balcony and the edge of existence. What drove that person to this point? What was going through their mind right then?

I prayed. *Lord, I don't know what that person has been through, but please speak to his heart and soul right now. He doesn't need to do this. Help him see that there is hope in You and that no matter what he feels can't be fixed, it can get better.*

If God can take such an awful event as the murder of Jesus Christ and turn it into the greatest victory of all time, surely He's able to take our pains and sufferings and redeem those as well.

I watched for ten minutes as that person stood there on the edge, gripping the railing behind him. Why was I watching? Was my brain captivated by the raw reality of life and death right in front of me? Eventually, I walked inside the store. I didn't want to witness someone hurling himself off that building. I imagine that's something that I couldn't erase from my mind.

I bought my groceries and walked home. When I got back to my apartment, I looked back at the high-rise where the person had been teetering on the edge. He was still there. Something was keeping him on the ledge. But something was also keeping him from jumping. I said another prayer. At that point, it was between that person and God. With a shaky heart, I turned and walked inside.

The next day I returned to the grocery store and asked the vendor who sold snacks outside what happened. We had become friends, and I often bought delicious *yakitori* (chicken-on-a-stick) from him. He said that the person had not jumped. *Thank you, God.* I bought some chicken and he threw in a few extra freebies as he always did.

* * *

One of the wives of an American on the Toyota team mentioned to Cara that Hannah could try modeling in Tokyo. Many Japanese companies used American and European kids in their advertising. Cara was a bit skeptical, but I thought it might be an interesting opportunity to do something we normally wouldn't do. I had no desire to go the whole *Toddlers & Tiaras* route, where moms dressed their kids up to look like they were sixteen years old instead of sixteen months. That was straight-up disturbing. However, if it was something family-friendly that Hannah enjoyed, it might be fun to have some nice pictures taken and an interesting experience to look back on.

We signed Hannah up at a kids' modeling agency called Sugar and Spice. I tried to not let the goofy name bother me. She was selected to do a photo shoot for a kids' clothing line, and it went well. Hannah put on six different outfits, and it only lasted forty-five minutes. She was well behaved, and the photographer and producer seemed very pleased with the outcome. They paid Hannah a couple hundred dollars, and all of a sudden we had a new breadwinner in the family. She made more money than I did per hour. Too bad we didn't have a second kid because together they could have become the Olsen twins of Japan.

Hannah received more calls for auditions and jobs. She and Cara travelled into Tokyo for shoots with companies that sold mostly clothes and travel systems like strollers and car seats. Hannah loved eating snacks on the train and watching *Sesame Street* while they travelled. Occasionally there were long days but for the most part she enjoyed the uncommon activity. It was fun to see her picture in catalogs and magazines. We didn't always know where her picture would be used, but the agency always sent us a copy.

One day, Yoshimi, Takayuki, and Kensei took a vacation in Okinawa. When they got on the plane, two-year-old Kensei said, "Look, Hannah!"

Yoshimi thought he was confused and assured Kensei that Hannah was not on their flight.

"Yes! Hannah!" he insisted. He pointed at the seat in front of him.

Hannah's picture was on the back of the airline magazine in an advertisement. Maybe we could score some free plane tickets out of it.

* * *

Masa pulled me aside one day and told me that Champion, our team apparel sponsor, wanted an American face for their company in Japan. I thought Charles O'Bannon would make a perfect fit, as he was a terrific player who had been in Japan for about a decade and had a big name there. However, Masa said that they wanted to use me. Well then, use away. Who am I to get in the way of Champion's genius marketing plan? If you really think that the foreign guy with the fewest dunks in the league and who prefers a short-corner jump shot to a behind-the-back pass will sell more shirts, then I'm your guy.

Champion was going to send me a bunch of free gear—and here's the kicker—they were going to pay me to wear it. Listen, I'll wear most anything that's free. If you give me something that looks half-decent and doesn't give me a rash, I'll probably sport it. You don't have to pay me.

But they offered, and who am I to turn down cash in exchange for pulling on a sweatshirt? It wasn't like Nike or Adidas were knocking down my door. To top it off, the gear was really nice. They sent two huge boxes full of stuff and even a few items for Cara.

My only job requirement for Champion was a ninety-minute photo shoot one day before practice. I was stealing money. I did some dribbling, shooting, and general posing like the male model I was always destined to be. They asked me to dunk for some action shots. While physically it was possible for me to dunk, I wasn't all that warmed up, so I gave them my best finger roll and told them that somebody had better be a wizard on Photoshop. Just because I'm 6-foot-8 and play professional basketball doesn't mean that I am a dunking fool. Stereotypes are the worst.

* * *

In December, I made the All-Star Game. It may sound impressive, but it's not like there were hundreds of candidates to beat out. Each All-Star team was allotted two Americans, and there were only eight possible guys to choose from on each side, East and West. The fans voted, and since I had been in the league the past three years and hadn't stabbed anyone, I was selected.

I was even selected to participate in the three-point contest. We were all sitting on the bench waiting to take the floor and warm up, when, amidst the blabber over the loudspeaker, I heard my name. *Surely, we weren't starting now.* None of the players had so much as dribbled a ball.

I walked to the first rack of balls. They put one minute on the clock. *Are we really shooting now without a single warmup shot?* The buzzer sounded. And away we went.

I might as well have closed my eyes and shot them lefty on the first rack. But then I found my rhythm in the second rack and sank a few. I wasn't that great on the last three racks, but I did manage to make the money ball several times. I finished with a pathetic total of nine. Incredibly, I had the second-highest score until the last guy. If I beat him, I'd advance to the final round and have a chance to win $1,000. He didn't shoot well either, and he had to sink the money ball on his very last shot to beat me. He went on to win it in the finals.

The actual All-Star Game was like a bad pickup game where guys didn't try until the last three minutes. It was actually a bit awkward to play in, because I was better at competing than looking cool. And in this game, it was all about fancy dribbling and alley-oops, which I'm amazing at … on eight-foot hoops versus six-year-olds.

We ended up losing by three in the end. Normally I wouldn't care, but the winning team got a bonus. Oh well. I had already missed out on the three-point contest prize money. So what was one more?

* * *

In January 2011, the All-Japan Tournament started up again and we were still without Alfred. I was playing 40 minutes a game—half loving it and half wishing Alfred would get his butt back on the floor. It was great playing a lot of minutes and having a bigger impact on the game, but it was exhausting, too, when I had to play back-to-back nights.

We made it to the semifinals and ran into our friends from Aisin. Again we went up by about 15 points in the first half before they started coming back. In the fourth quarter we were down by two with three seconds left. Our shooting guard launched a three for the win and missed. But I snuck around a defender, grabbed the rebound in mid-air and put it back in just as the buzzer went off. We went to overtime.

This was it. We had them. We were playing tough and Aisin wasn't walking all over us. We were finally going to beat them in a big game.

I picked up my fourth foul on a very bad call by the ref. Then a minute later, I got whistled for my fifth when J. R. Sakuragi drew contact. I was done.

We didn't have the size to keep up, and we ended up losing once again to Aisin. It just added salt to the wound when your nemesis is nicknamed the Seahorses.

I was named to the All-Tourney team, which was quite an honor, as no American had been selected for many years—just trying to make Champion proud.

* * *

One week later, we started the JBL regular season again and good old Aisin was our first weekend matchup. I was guarding J. R. in the first game when he drove to the basket and kneed me in the groin. It was unintentional, I think, but it hurt like a son of a gun and I had to stop and focus on not crying out for mommy. The soreness and pain remained for the rest of the game.

I woke up the next morning with a serious problem. I apologize in advance for the sensitive material. I'll do my best to navigate this topic gently.

Instead of being normal size, one of my guys had swollen to the size of a baseball. It hurt to walk and coughing was definitely not a good idea.

I really wanted to play though and was forced to tell Nomo about it if I was going to have any chance at getting on the court. I didn't know if anything could be done, but it was my only option.

"Yeah, uh, Nomo," I said. "You know how I usually hurt my back or my feet... "

"Yes," he said.

"Well, I kind of hurt something else this time," I said. "Something more fragile."

"Your balls?" he asked.

"Indeed," I confirmed. Poor trainers. There are just parts to every job that stink.

He evaluated the situation. "Whoa!" he said.

"Yeah, I know."

"I can try and put tape over your Spandex to see if that will help," he said.

"Sure," I said. Why not? I had no better plan.

The tape provided some much needed stabilization and security. As long as I didn't get hit there again, I thought I could manage. If I took another shot like the day before, God help us all. *Oh Lord, if there was ever a prayer to be heard, let it be this one.*

The prayer was answered and I survived the game. We took a three-point shot to win it at the buzzer but missed. Was there any way we could just take Aisin off of our schedule?

The next day, Nomo took me to see the doctor, yet another awkward moment. It was bad enough showing Nomo. Now someone else would weigh in on my predicament. My "injury" had only worsened, and I'll spare you the details.

The doctor said that there was an internal tear and if he'd seen me earlier, he would have operated. If I'd seen *him* earlier, he would have had to wrestle me to the ground before he got me on an operating table. Rest and ice was all that could be done from here on out.

By Tuesday, word had gotten around about my sensitive situation. Usually it's polite to ask about a guy's injury. "Hey, how's your knee?"

"What's up with your ankle?" But how do you show concern for such a personal injury?

Masa knew my "situation."

"Hey Tyler," he said with a straight face when he saw me in the practice gym on Tuesday. "How is your big ball?"

Seriously, Masa? Did you really just ask me that? In his Japanese accent, I could only laugh. Not too hard though, because that was painful.

"I'll be alright, Masa," I said. "But Hannah might end up being an only child."

* * *

Nomo went the extra mile and bought me a cup. It was back to my high school baseball days. I'm pretty sure I was the first basketball player ever to wear one in competition. It felt very strange wearing one in a gym rather than on a baseball diamond. But it did the trick and allowed me to get back on the court the next weekend versus Toyota.

We were slipping away from playoff contention and needed some wins. In the first game of the weekend against Toyota, we beat them by six. Toyota was one of the top teams that year, and it was a big win for us.

The next day, I had my greatest finish to a game ever.

We were down by six with less than two minutes to play. Toyota had been in control for just about the entire game. We weren't playing with much energy and were having a very hard time getting buckets. Somehow I had only taken two shots the entire game, which was inexcusable, since I was playing all 40 minutes with Alfred still injured.

I drove to the basket and was fouled.

We can still win this game. I made both free throws. Down four.

Toyota came up empty on their next possession, and on offense I was fouled again. I might have traveled first, but we'll assume that the ref actually got the call correct this time.

Now is not the time to miss free throws. I didn't. Down two. One minute and twenty-three seconds left.

Toyota missed again. Then I got the ball at the other end, this time in the post. Rather than try to back down Jeff Gibbs, who should've been in the NFL instead of pro basketball, I stepped back and shot over him. *Swish.* Tie game. Forty-eight seconds left. Timeout Toyota.

They ran a play for their best shooter. He missed. Our ball.

We ran a pick and pop and I caught the ball two steps past the three-point line on the wing, just beyond my comfortable shooting range. Seventeen seconds left.

I had our two-guard open in the corner, and he'd already hit three threes that night. A Toyota defender was between us and he assumed I would make the extra pass to the open man. Normally, I would. It was the right pass to make. But I was feeling pretty good. I gave a hard pass-fake that made the defender jump toward my teammate and gave me just enough space to step into the three.

Swish.

The place exploded. Our bench was going crazy. Up by three.

Toyota scored on the next possession, but we hit our free throws when they fouled us and we won by three.

I had scored nine points in under two minutes. If I had kept up that video game pace throughout a full game, I would have scored over 180 points. I didn't miss a shot the entire game, which was a first for me. It must have been my lucky cup.

Alfred came back the next week, because he had some kind of African superhero power. There's just no other way to explain it. He was an anomaly. The guy had surgery less than four weeks ago on his knee when he could barely walk, and he was supposed to be out a minimum of six weeks. But he was bouncing around again in practice like nothing had happened, ready to make me look bad in rebounding drills.

With Alfred back, we won four out of our next six games and were closing ground on that fourth playoff spot. With only six games remaining, if we played well, we could still make it happen. Then … bonus time.

We had a weekend series with Aisin that was crucial, and the word on the street was that J. R. might not play because of an injury. My personal feeling was that he should get plenty of rest and let his body heal. I would even suggest that he take a three- or four-year sabbatical. You can't be too careful with your health.

On Friday, March 11, 2011, our game versus Aisin was scheduled for 7 p.m. At 2:46 p.m., I was reading in my hotel room in downtown Tokyo.

And then things went bad. Very bad.

The room started to tremble. I didn't think much of it, because earthquakes were pretty normal. I lay there and waited for it to stop.

But the room kept shaking. Harder. And harder.

Pieces of plaster from the ceiling started chipping away and dropping to the floor. *Getting a little concerned here.* The earthquake wasn't stopping.

My bathroom door slammed open and closed. Typically, an earthquake would last five to ten seconds. This one was already well past a half minute.

I pulled my shoes on quickly and ran to the door. I opened it up and looked down the hallway. Every player on Hitachi was bracing himself in his doorway to keep from falling over. We all looked at each other, wondering what to do. Clearly this was something that no one had experienced before.

Do we wait it out? Or do we make a run for it? I didn't know if it was safer to stay where we were or to get out of Dodge. We were eight stories up. It wasn't like we could just walk out of the building. I figured many of my teammates had been in way more of these than I had, so if they were going to head for the stairs, I'd be right behind them.

I don't know who took off first, but I was right on his tail heading for the stairs. We were flying down the stairwell, jumping almost half-stories at a time. Many guys didn't have shoes or socks on and were slipping and turning ankles as they went.

The building shook violently. The creaking and grinding of its structure screamed at us. The deep, loud rumble of the earthquake echoed fiercely through the stairwell. I couldn't believe the hotel was still standing. *Maybe the top stories had already begun to crumble and we were racing against gravity.*

As I descended toward the ground floor, visions of Haiti's destruction from its earthquake just one year before flashed through my head. People buried under rubble. The entire city demolished. It was like a war zone.

We kept flying down the stairs.

Lord, please don't let this building come down on me. Dang, this is gonna hurt.

We were getting closer. Third floor.

Please don't let it fall.

Second floor.

Please, God.

First floor.

Please.

We crashed through the doors into the sunlight.

We were out.

Thank you.

* * *

By the time we reached fresh air, the earth's shaking had slowed. But the buildings hadn't. I looked up at the skyscrapers all around us in downtown Tokyo. They were swaying back and forth like skinny trees in the wind.

This is not going to be good.

Surely, something was going to come crashing down.

I tried to call Cara, but no cell calls would go through. I tried nine or ten times, nothing. I started to get worried.

Lord, please protect them.

Cara and Hannah were at our apartment, one hour away in Kashiwa. I wondered if the earthquake was as bad there as it was in Tokyo. Maybe it was worse.

We didn't want to stand next to a massive building in case it decided to fall. So we ran to a nearby park that seemed far enough away from any towers that might collapse. I continued trying to reach Cara, but couldn't.

After twenty minutes, no buildings had collapsed and we hadn't felt any other earthquakes. We were told that it was safe to return to the hotel. When I got to my room, I looked in the bathroom and there was water all over the floor. I looked at the toilet and it was empty. The earthquake had shaken the hotel so violently that all of the water in my toilet had splashed out.

The Internet was somehow still working and I called Cara on Skype. She and Hannah were okay. They were scared out of their minds, but they were safe. Poor Hannah had been taking a nap and when the earthquake hit, the metal doors to her closet banged so loudly that they woke her up and scared her so much that she started screaming. Cara ran into Hannah's room, picked her up, and raced out of the apartment down seven flights of stairs, wondering if they would make it to the ground alive.

They returned to the apartment a short while later. And while we were talking on Skype, another earthquake hit. This one hit with the same force as the first one.

"It's shaking again!" Cara said.

"Just get out of there!" I said. "I love you!"

She ran down seven stories with Hannah and I ran down eight with the SunRockers once more.

We waited over an hour at the park this time. There were hundreds of people there, most of them business people who had escaped their downtown offices. One group of over fifty were wearing their usual business suits ... and white hard hats. *Man, these people are prepared for anything.* I could picture them sitting at their office desks on the phone when the earthquake hit. They probably instinctively grabbed their hard hat from their bottom drawer and ran out.

We returned to the hotel yet again but stayed in a conference room on the second floor this time. It was easier to escape from there than the eighth. Our games had been cancelled for the weekend, but we couldn't go home because the train system was shut down. We couldn't drive, either, because the highways were damaged and insanely crowded. We'd be staying the night in Tokyo. We were told to fill our bathtubs with water and have towels nearby in case there was a fire and the water stopped working. Also we should have everything packed before we went to bed that night. Sleeping in our shoes probably wasn't a bad idea, either. A bus was scheduled to take us home in the morning. I didn't know how the roads would be fixed and clear in less than a day, but I wouldn't put anything past the Japanese.

I walked to the convenience store to get some snacks, but it had already been cleaned out. There were empty shelves where all the goodies used to be. The Japanese didn't waste any time. If this was going to be the end of the world, they were going out with chips and cookie crumbs on their faces.

One of my teammates had been on a train when the earthquakes hit. He had stayed behind in Kashiwa because he wasn't going to play in our game since he was recovering from knee surgery. After doing his rehab in Kashiwa, he was on his way to Tokyo to watch us play. After the earthquake, the train stopped in the middle of its route and opened the doors.

He was able to get off the train safely, but he was miles from anywhere. So he started walking back towards Kashiwa. He tried to check into a few different hotels along the way for the night, but they were all booked. His phone didn't work. He was stranded. After walking for a couple hours, his injured knee hurt too much to keep going. So he found a kid's playground and slept on a slide.

Our team had been extremely fortunate. The next day, Saturday, we were supposed to be playing up in Sendai, where the most damage had been done by the earthquakes and the tsunami. If they had hit just twenty-four hours later, our team would have been in the heart of the destruction and I might not be here writing this book.

Another team from Sendai escaped disaster. They were in the other Japanese pro basketball league and luckily had an away trip that weekend.

They left Sendai on a bus just an hour before the earthquake and tsunami hit. Some of the players didn't have homes to go back to. Sendai had been completely demolished. Their possessions on the bus were all that they had. But it was more than the people who survived the disaster back home.

The next morning, we started our journey back to Kashiwa by bus. The usual hour-long ride took almost three hours as we navigated back roads and side streets since the highways were off-limits.

Someone had picked up a newspaper and showed me a picture of the Tokyo International Airport completely underwater. There were shots of the destruction up north in the Tohoku region. Boats were on top of buildings. Cars were flipped over and under water. The 9.0-magnitude earthquake was the most powerful earthquake Japan had ever seen and the fifth-largest in the world since recording began around 1900.

Its force was so powerful that it moved the entire island of Japan eight feet closer to the United States. According to scientists at NASA, it even shifted the earth on its axis by four inches, causing the earth to rotate faster and shorten the length of day. No one knew how many people had been killed or were missing, but it was likely in the tens of thousands.

* * *

Yoshimi and her family showed up at our door in the afternoon. They stood holding three grocery bags full of food and water.

"What's this for?" I asked. They were such a nice family, but they didn't need to be doing our grocery shopping for us.

"We wanted to bring you some food and water because everything will be sold out very soon," Yoshimi said. "And the water at your apartment might not work, too."

They were right about the food. Grocery stores were wiped out. We couldn't buy bread, eggs, milk, or water anywhere. Parks were empty. No one walked the streets. Kashiwa was like a ghost town.

Restaurants were closed—even McDonald's kept limited hours. You know it's bad when McDonald's wasn't open.

Then we found out that the nuclear reactors had been severely damaged and, as a result, we would be without any power. Announcements were made that electricity would be cut off from different regions of Japan in an attempt to conserve power. With the country having lost six nuclear reactors, the government tried to have scheduled blackouts.

Unfortunately, they never came at the times that were reported. A five-hour blackout scheduled for the evening would happen in the middle of the day. Traffic lights were down. Some police officers directed traffic, but there weren't enough police to go around and cars were left to navigate each intersection by themselves. As a rule, the general public was not capable of being responsible enough to take turns at large intersections. They need flashing lights to tell them what to do.

Not only were we without power, but a great deal of radiation was leaking from the nuclear plants, too. No one knew how bad it was at first and the Japanese government and media were downplaying everything. "It's not that bad . . . It will be fixed soon." But the American media was having a field day with it and Cara's mom called from the United States, worried out of her mind.

"It's not safe there. When will they let you come home?"

At first, I didn't realize how bad things were. I tried to assure her mom that we were fine and that things were not a big deal. After all, no one around us said that radiation was an issue.

Then, more information started coming out. Levels of radiation were twenty times higher than normal around Tokyo. People were told not to go outside unless absolutely necessary. It rained at one point and there was talk of acidic rain and the long-term effect it could have on your body. We kept Hannah inside for three straight days, not the easiest thing to do with a two-year-old in a small apartment.

* * *

Every day there were fifteen to twenty earthquakes. I turned on the TV to see the news anchors sitting at their desk in the studio giving the news and wearing hard hats. The earthquakes came every hour or so. Every time, Hannah's closet doors would rattle loudly and she would relive the fear of that first mega earthquake. We never knew if the next one would be as big as the original. Two of the aftershocks were over 7.0. Another two big ones lasted longer than I was comfortable with and I grabbed Hannah and ran to the door.

One time, Hannah was in the bath. I grabbed her wet, naked body and raced to the door. The earthquake stopped just before I could get outside. At night, we would wake up to our bed shaking beneath us and I'd jump up, ready to sprint to grab Hannah. Then, it would inevitably die down. We kept an emergency bag filled with food, water, and supplies at the entrance to our apartment. All of the concern about radiation, electricity shortage, food, water, and the next big earthquake hitting was nerve-wracking and we were ready to leave.

Our team scheduled a meeting at our practice gym on Tuesday to discuss the league situation. Japan's pro volleyball season had been cancelled. So had the women's pro basketball league despite being in the middle of the finals. American players in our league were announcing on Facebook that they were flying back to the States that week. Surely, our meeting was to confirm the obvious: our season was over.

"If something big happens again while I'm gone, let's meet at the park," I said.

"Ride fast," Cara said as I walked out the door to take my bike to practice. The concern over radiation was very real at that point. Maybe I could hold my breath the entire way.

When I arrived at the gym, everyone was just sitting around. Then, Nomo said, "Tape up."

"What? Why?" I asked as if he has requested that I put on giraffe suit.

"Coach said we're practicing," Nomo said.

"You're kidding," I said.

"Nope," he said.

"Does he realize that the season is over and players are going home?" I asked.

"He said that the JBL has not officially announced it yet, so we are practicing," he said.

I was dumbstruck. Everything had to be by the book. As wonderful a country as Japan was, sometimes it desperately needed a little common sense. Nuclear reactors were melting down an hour away and Coach wanted to practice. I had never been so unmotivated for a practice in my life. It wasn't a light shootaround, either. It was a full-contact two-hour practice. One of our guards injured his ankle. This was a whole new level of insanity.

After practice, Coach Ono called a meeting in the locker room.

"The season is over," he said.

You just had to get that one last practice in, didn't you?

We arranged a flight for Friday, exactly one week after the first earthquake hit. Business class was full so we flew economy and didn't get the extra baggage weight allowance as when we had arrived. We had over $1,000 in baggage fees. But good old Hitachi picked up the tab. *Arigato.*

* * *

I was so happy to be leaving before any other buildings tried to fall on us or I grew an extra couple toes from the radiation. However, I felt bad for our Japanese friends and teammates who didn't have anywhere to go. Japan was their home. Some ended up going to southern Japan temporarily where the radiation wasn't so high. Others, like Takayuki, Yoshimi's husband, never missed a day of work through the whole ordeal.

During the aftermath of Hurricane Katrina in New Orleans, there was violence, looting, and chaos. Following Japan's worst earthquake and tsunami in history, there wasn't even a hint of crime. Organization, discipline, and orderliness served the Japanese well during that traumatic time. If there were any people who could handle a crisis of that magnitude, it was the Japanese.

Chapter 16

RELOCATION, DISLOCATION, AND *THE PRICE IS RIGHT*

Hitachi offered me a $3,000 raise for another season with them. I preferred more, but knowing their track record, I wasn't holding my breath. And they still weren't throwing in a sixty-inch flat screen.

Tochigi, a different JBL team, then jumped into the mix. They offered a two-year deal for $35,000 more each year than Hitachi was offering. It looked like an easy decision.

I turned Hitachi down. They said it was the best they could do. Then they discovered that Tochigi was in the picture, too. All of the sudden, Hitachi's offer jumped $20,000. *Wait a second, I thought you didn't have it.*

Hitachi was the only home we knew in Japan and it was going to take a very good offer to get me to leave. But they would not offer me a two-year deal. They said it was against JBL rules. *Well, the rules are dumb. What kind of league prohibits a team from signing a player for multiple years?* Instead of building a long-term roster with a core of players and having fans connect more with a team that doesn't change players every year, the league forced teams into negotiating twelve new contracts every summer.

Tochigi was a professional team and none of its players worked another job like some of the Hitachi guys. Tochigi did things a little bit differently and were willing to offer me a deal that would give me and the team more consistency. Throw in their American coach and their four Japanese national team players, plus the fact that I didn't have to leave town for home games, and I was now a Tochigi Brex—whatever that was.

"Bre" was for "breakthrough" and "Rex" meant "King" in Latin. So we were the "Breakthrough Kings." Not sure how the whole Japanese and Latin thing really went together. The coffee must have been laced with something the day they picked the mascot.

My one worry was that Tochigi was actually closer to Fukushima's nuclear power plants. But what's a little radiation between friends? We were still a good 100 miles away. And the radiation levels were ironically lower there than in Kashiwa despite Tochigi being closer to the meltdown.

* * *

During our friendly five-hour layover in Washington, DC, the airlines (ANA, yes you) tried to pull a fast one on us. We were sitting at the gate, actually sprawled out on the floor because it's impossible for anyone to stretch out in those seats. The ANA staff rolled up to the gate in their prim and proper airline attire. And they broke out … a scale. Voilà!

What in the world were these people doing with a scale at the gate? The bags were checked and long gone. Were we all getting complimentary physicals? Were they kicking overweight people off the plane? I could already tell you that this would not go over well with any female on the planet if we had to start weighing in.

One female gate attendant approached my lifeless body on the floor. "Sir, we are going to need to weigh your carry-ons. They can only be twenty-two pounds."

This was going to be bad. They were at least double that. I put all kinds of heavy stuff in there—video camera, books, fire extinguishers. It's the way around the annoying "fifty-pound-checked-bag" rule. They never checked the weight or size of your carry-on. Until today.

Bag one. Thirty-seven pounds.

Her face looked like she had just witnessed a horrific assault on an elderly person. "Sir, this is too heavy."

Bag two. Twenty-nine pounds. A similar look of shock and dismay.

Thank goodness she didn't weigh my backpack. I had a piano inside. She wrongly estimated that it would fall within legal limits and left it alone. But I can promise you that bad boy was at least fifty strong by itself. I was a freakin' marine walking through those terminals with my gear.

In her nicest voice possible she said, "Sir, you will have to pay $150 per carry-on that is overweight. Since you have two overweight bags, you will have to pay $300."

For overweight carry-ons. Really. You have to be kidding. There was no way I was paying $300 to haul Disney Princess books and 100 packs of chocolate protein powder, no matter how delicious it was. I had just flown with these "overweight" carry-ons on United for the first leg. Now, ANA was telling me I had to pay for them on the second leg of my trip to Tokyo? I kindly said in my friendly-angry voice that it was ridiculous that I would have to start paying now.

"OK, maybe just $150," she whispered, as if she was cutting me a special deal that she didn't want the other passengers to know about.

Guess what: we were ALL about to know about this fiasco. *How about I tweet this to the masses?* "ANA sucks. Buy a ticket and find out why. #unhappypostplayer."

One-hundred and fifty dollars? How about no?

"OK, I will call my supervisor," she said.

Take your time. A lot of it, actually.

As much as I knew that this was the dumbest thing ever, I also realized that they were serious and would pin me down and take the money right out of my wallet if they had to. Miraculously, airlines get this very rare type of power. The rank in order is the Secret Service, the IRS, and the airlines. The CIA and telemarketers are remarkably only fourth and fifth in the power to invade and annoy your life.

One way or another I was getting those bags down to twenty-two pounds each. So I started shifting things. Fortunately, Hannah had her little backpack with maybe two lollipops in it. *Guess what, Hannah? You gotta start pulling your weight around here. Well I know it's heavy, sweetheart. You can tell it to the lady over there who doesn't want you to be happy.*

After I pulled on my winter coat, stuffed Hannah's car seat lining with protein packs, and put the video camera around Hannah's neck as her "accessory," we were down to twenty-two pounds. *Boo yah. How you like that, ANA?*

The gate agent weighed my first one—22.8 pounds. I gave her a look that said, "Don't even think about it." That 0.8 pounds was my little victory for the day. I knew it was there before she weighed it. But this was war. I wanted them to feel my triumph over their insanely moronic rules.

What happened to those extra pounds? Let's just say that my fifty-pound backpack became even heavier. And Hannah's pink and purple backpack was bursting at the seams.

I'm fairly sure my family and I have now been red-flagged and are on the no-fly list. Or at least the "Hey, yeah, that's the guy" list.

I'm taking a boat to Japan next time.

* * *

We arrived at our Tochigi apartment after twenty-six hours of door-to-door travel. We weren't tired or anything, since Hannah slept for a full two hours of that twenty-six. The child would not sleep anywhere but her bed. We walked into our newest mini Japanese apartment and there was a mattress on the floor for Cara and me. But no bed for Hannah.

"Why is that?" you say. "Were they being rude?" No, they were being practical. Number one, it's normal for Japanese to sleep on the floor on tiny futons. Number two, Japanese kids slept with their parents, often until they are six or seven years old. It's incredible that families ever ended up with more than one kid.

Hannah was only three. So why would we ever need another bed, right? While I appreciated their effort to help us assimilate into the culture, I preferred not to begin my day with my kid lying on top of me as I tried to pick myself up off the ground.

Thankfully, a couch folded down that became Hannah's temporary bed. It was about as comfy as sleeping on the street, but Hannah didn't seem to mind. We bought her a new bed within a week.

A rice cooker was waiting for us, just like at Hitachi. I wonder what the standard kitchen appliance would be if foreigners were coming to the United States and we were supplying furnished apartments for them? Something economical, practical, and easy-to-use. Yes, the George Foreman grill.

* * *

I never enjoyed going to practice so much in my entire life as I did at Tochigi. And it was all my head coach's fault.

Bruce Palmer was one of the funniest people I'd ever met. And I don't know if he even meant to be that way half of the time. It was just his makeup.

"Amino!" he said to our 6-foot-5, 190-pound Japanese forward during practice. "You need to be 6-8, 230 pounds by Thursday or it's a $100 fine."

He was an American that spent the last twenty years coaching in Australia. He called everyone "mate" which was awesome because he was saying it to a bunch of little Japanese guys. He liked his Skoal and asked me to smuggle over ten cans from the States. Well, me and two other guys, making it an even thirty cans, which theoretically would last him until Christmas.

As much as he liked his chewing tobacco, he loved golf even more. Bruce would walk into practice after our day off with a huge smile on his face. "Ask me how I played yesterday?"

"How'd you pl—?"

"Eighty-three!"

One day I asked him, "Coach, are you married?"

He smiled. "To the luckiest woman in the world."

* * *

Lamar Rice and I were reunited again on the Brex. We were rolling with laughter every day at Coach's quick wit. What made it even funnier was that he would say things so quickly and sarcastically that the translator couldn't keep up and relay the message. So Lamar and I would be pulling our shirts over our faces to muffle our laughs while the rest of the guys stared with blank looks, waiting for an explanation that never came.

One time, we went over the scouting report of an opponent before a preseason game. They had the heaviest guy in the league on their team. He was a house, and you couldn't move him with a bulldozer.

Bruce pointed him out on the video. "This guy warms up with a bowl of cereal in his hand and a spoon around his neck." I just about fell out of my chair.

A terrific coach, Bruce was nothing short of a basketball expert. He was very clear in his expectations of each player and was specific about details and preparation. Practices were short and intense.

Bruce held up a sheet of paper in the team huddle before practice one day. "I have one hour and seventeen minutes on this schedule." *Can I hug you?* "We won't go a minute over." And we never did.

Do you know what a head coach usually means when he announces the length of practice before the practice begins? Nothing.

Bruce wanted his guys to be tough, of course. Over the summer, he told me that I had better be in the best shape of my life when I arrived in Tochigi. On the other side of his demands though, he swore he'd never play a guy who was hurt. Bruce trusted his players and would never jeopardize our health. I was ready to go to war for him.

Sadly, my war was over faster than microwaving two bags of popcorn.

In the first game of the season, I scored five quick points and was feeling great. Then, just six minutes into the game, I reached high for a rebound and had my left arm yanked back. It ripped out of its shoulder socket before I hit the floor. I lay there screaming in pain, trying to grind my teeth through my mouth guard.

If my arm moved a quarter inch, the pain was excruciating. I couldn't hold it still enough for it to stop throbbing.

"Do you want me to put it back in place now?" the team doctor asked. "Or do you want to go to the hospital and get some pain medicine?"

You can tell a lot by the expression on someone's face and their tone of voice. To me, his look meant "Get to the hospital ASAP because I have no idea what I'm doing." I had zero confidence in him reattaching my arm. It was an easy choice.

Maybe he could have done it, but I probably would have punched him in the face from the pain, and we had seen enough violence for one day. While I wish I could have been more like Mel Gibson in *Lethal Weapon* and smashed my shoulder back in place, my toughness level at that point was more like *My Little Pony*.

So I got my first Japanese ambulance ride in the slowest emergency vehicle ever. We should have just ridden bikes without pedals. *Hey driver, you do have the lights and siren on. Feel free to live on the edge and go over the speed limit by two or three km/h.*

This guy was stopping at all the intersections, bowing to other drivers in apology. *We're not going to Grandma's, OK? Let's pick this up a little. Mucho pain-o back here.*

I don't remember everything because I was trying to take my mind to a happy place where all my appendages were connected. Maybe the driver stopped for a rice ball and snuck in a couple quick games of pachinko (a favorite Japanese casino game). All I know is it took forever.

We arrived at the hospital and I sat down in a waiting room with about five or six doctors/important medical people in full view about ten feet away. Finally, relief was closer. My left arm still hung low with my shoulder completely out of its socket.

Wrong. They were just chatting it up, glancing over now and then. Probably saying something like, "Ha-ha, we're so special with all of our medical know-how. Those people are probably in lots of pain. We'll get around to them after I finish telling you this pointless story about what I had for breakfast three weeks ago."

Where was *Grey's Anatomy* when you needed it? Throw me on a gurney and start yelling. "Blood pressure's dropping! I need an EKG and give me 500cc's stat!! Too late—we're going in! CLEAR!!!" (The extent of my medical knowledge at the time, neatly wrapped up for you.)

Instead of urgency, I got this look of disappointment from them: "Oh, just a shoulder. Looks like something might be wrong with it. Let's wait until a real emergency happens."

My arm was throbbing.

I glowered my I'll-kill-you-with-a-spoon stare back at them. *Nothing important is coming through those ER doors tonight. In case you hadn't noticed, there is no crime in this country. No guns. People don't drive fast. And everyone obeys every rule and then some. I'm the best you've got! I am the emergency. Now, take me out of my misery.*

One of the nurses approached. "Tyler, we need to take some X-rays," she said.

How about you put the shoulder back in first? Then we talk.

A no-go, of course. I suffered through X-rays as they attempted to put my still-dislocated shoulder in positions that it had no business being in. They acted curious as to why my arm wasn't working the way they thought it should.

I returned to the waiting area, sitting there in obvious discomfort with a very noticeable unnaturally-elongated arm. Twenty minutes passed by, feeling like twenty hours. Somebody please help.

The nurse came in again. "We need to take some more X-rays." *Oh sweet Jesus, I'm gonna shoot you.*

Another thirty minutes later they returned. It was time. They gave me an IV and knocked me out. I woke up feeling like a million bucks.

Where can I get my hands on some of that good stuff? My arm was back in place where God intended it to be. I was made whole again.

Overall, it had taken an hour and a half to return my arm to its normal position. Why they couldn't have solved this in a third of the time boggled my mind.

What I didn't get was this: it was an *emergency room*. When body parts were facing the wrong direction, didn't that kind of classify as an emergency, even a minor one? On the scale of emergencies, it's not a ten like a gunshot victim. I had no stab wounds or a tire iron sticking out of my leg. So I was more like a six. But give an American brother some love and put a shoulder back in place.

* * *

The Japanese doctors told me that I should immobilize my arm for two weeks and I would be cheering from the bench for at least three months. My American doctor and trainer said pretty much the opposite. Immobilizing my arm would only make things worse and that I could return in about six weeks. I chose to listen to my American doctors, who specialized in sports medicine, while the Brex management believed their doctors who specialized in the elderly and expected me to be out for a while.

Our team signed another American player to replace me for the short term, and Bruce fully supported me taking my time until I was healthy again. Unfortunately, two bad pieces of news came along with it.

First, the Brex decided to cut my salary by a third. Technically, they could do it because a clause in my contract said that if I missed a quarter of the season then I would forfeit some of my salary. The team assumed that I would miss that time and didn't waste any time amending the contract. I understood that they were enforcing what the contract said, but was it too much to ask to have a little optimism and hope that maybe I could come back sooner than expected?

Second, the JBL called the Brex and told them that if another player replaced me, even temporarily, then I could not return to the team at all that season. The Brex didn't know that the rule even existed. It was another piece of nonsense that was outdated but no one had bothered to fix. Since the team needed another American badly and couldn't afford to wait for me to return, I was out of a job.

Thankfully, the team honored the contract and would continue to pay me an abbreviated salary for the rest of the year. Most teams around the world would not do that. So I was very fortunate and I appreciated their professionalism.

On the other hand, I didn't want to sit out for eight months. I could probably be ready in one or two months, and I wanted to play and make up some of the lost salary. The Brex offered to let me play elsewhere, but if I made more money than what they took away, they wanted me to pay them anything over the difference. I politely declined and explained why that was the dumbest idea in the world. It didn't make any sense for me to play somewhere else and then pay them the money that I had earned in a different country.

Surprisingly, they understood and came back with a different proposal which was worse than the first. The team said I could play elsewhere and make as much as I wanted. But they would take a flat percentage of my new salary. Not only were they cutting out a huge chunk of my contracted salary with them, they were going to profit if I played somewhere else. Sitting at home, collecting a check, and watching *The Price Is Right* for the next eight months was beginning to sound like a pretty awesome idea.

* * *

We returned to Pennsylvania and I was back in rehab mode again with Saz at Penn State. The bright side was that we got to experience Christmas in our own home for the first time as a family. And there was other big news. Cara was pregnant with our second child.

We had been hoping for a couple of years to receive some good news, but it never came. Cara had undergone some tests, and they all came back looking fine. The doctors couldn't give us any medical explanation. Cara went on a medication that had a very high success rate in assisting a woman to get pregnant, but after five months, nothing. Frustrated, she threw the remaining pills in the trash. The following month—*Yahtzee!*

We were ecstatic. After years of constant praying, trying, and waiting, God had finally answered our prayer. He had waited until we were at the end of the rope. We weren't actively trying. We had given up on the medicine. Then, God showed up. Funny how He has a habit of doing that even when we think all hope is lost.

Chapter 17

X-FACTORS: SIX WEEKS IN URUGUAY

I got a call in December 2011 from good old Daniel Morales down in Uruguay again. A team in Montevideo needed a 4-man. It was Defensor—the team with the mini-court where I had torn my Achilles seven years earlier. Oh, how it all came full circle. This time I wasn't worried about their awful floors. My shoulder was the problem.

Although two months had passed since my shoulder injury, it still didn't feel right. It hurt to turn the steering wheel in the car. But I wanted to go. Uruguay was familiar, and the contract was only for about three months, which I liked because it was less time when I could reinjure my shoulder. Defensor needed an answer.

I decided to test it out and play some pick-up ball that night against some middle-aged out-of-shape guys who probably needed a break from their wives. It was my first "competitive" play since my shoulder came out of place in Japan back in October.

When a 5-foot-9 guard cut through the lane and I tried to check him with my weak left forearm, I pushed him with the strength of a three-year-old. It was all the force I could muster. I couldn't hold my ground in the post against anyone larger than a fifth-grader. I couldn't react quickly with my bad arm, and I was still very hesitant to go up for rebounds against the high-caliber office workers that they were. I wasn't ready.

Disappointed, I called Daniel and told him that I couldn't go. He reassured me that it was no problem and that he would keep looking.

A team from Japan called and made an offer. Their head coach was a friend of Bruce. My old teammate from Argentina, Nichy, was on the team, too. It was a nice situation in some regards, but the salary wasn't great and their season lasted until May. The length of the season concerned me a little because I didn't want to risk injuring my shoulder again and then lose out on the second year of the Tochigi contract. I turned them down, too, and continued with my rehab.

At the beginning of February, Daniel called again from Uruguay. Defensor was back in the picture. The player they had signed in December had not panned out the way they expected and they wanted to sign me again. My shoulder had finally gained back enough strength to where I felt confidence in it. It wasn't perfect, but it was much better than the last time I'd spoken to them.

I was on a plane for Montevideo two days later. Cara and Hannah stayed home because the team wouldn't throw in any extra plane tickets. Plus, I didn't know if the situation would be conducive for them.

I stayed in a hotel for the first week when I arrived because my apartment wasn't ready yet. There were no laundromats nearby, which was odd for Montevideo, since I remembered them being everywhere. I didn't want to have the hotel wash my clothes because usually they acted as if they owned the very last washing machine on earth and charged you practically the same price for a load of laundry as for the room. But after a few days of smelly basketball socks and shorts piling up, it was time to do a load. Otherwise, management would think I was hiding decomposing bodies in my suitcase.

I picked up a slip of paper that stated the hotel laundry prices and it was actually very reasonable. Shirts were eight pesos. Shorts were five. Socks were three. I dropped off my bag of laundry at the front desk.

Two days later I received the bill. Seventy-three dollars. What the—? I could buy a car in Uruguay for $73. Were they hand washed by a prince with bars of gold?

I looked at the breakdown of the bill. What I thought were pesos were actually dollars. How can you charge five dollars to wash one pair of shorts? I showed the bill to the person at the front desk assuming that there was some sort of mistake on their end. Either I was on crack or they had the highest salaried housekeepers in South America.

They assured me that the bill was correct. At least I wasn't on crack. *Gracias.*

* * *

Uruguay's pro league had finally instituted a rule that stated that teams were required to have wooden floors (which my new team Defensor did not) and be regulation size (which Defensor's *Saved by the Bell* gym was definitely not). So they shared a gym with another team in the league, Bohemios. It was awkward. We would finish practice and they would be waiting in the stands to use the floor. Thankfully, we weren't major rivals and our team had a much better history of success in the league, but it was still strange to walk into another team's facility every day and get eyeballed by their players.

Bohemios had a wooden floor, but it was light years from NBA quality. And I've already told you about the waist-high wooden railing surrounding the court that served no purpose other than to injure players attempting to save a ball heading out-of-bounds and the three-point line that almost touched the sideline in the corners. This was "regulation"?

Not to mention the filthy glass backboards and the leaky roof that canceled practices during hard rains.

On game days, we dressed in a public locker room along with men who were taking showers and getting ready for their cycling classes. During halftime, we met outside under the stars in white plastic chairs because it was too hot in the gym or the locker room.

What the gym lacked in modern value, it made up for in acoustics. With nothing but concrete stands and walls, a thousand loco Uruguayans packed in made it sound like the NBA Finals. Minus the eight dollar beers. No adult beverages were needed for a good time there.

In my first game with Defensor, I was playing well, with nine points and a few rebounds in the fourth quarter, and we were up by at least 15 points. I was dribbling in the open floor and made a move to go by a smaller defender. He wildly threw his hands up at me as I sprinted by him and one of his fingers sank deeply into my eye socket. Very deep. He may have touched my brain. I crumpled to the floor like a newborn calf, holding my eye and wailing in pain.

Here we go again. *Lord, please let me see when I take my hand away. Why can't I get past the first game wherever I go this season?*

I cautiously pulled my hand back. It was blurry, but I could see a little bit. *Great, only partial vision loss. So much for becoming a fighter pilot.*

Then, I remembered that the haziness could be a result of losing my contact lens. My head was throbbing, especially my eye socket.

The team president, Jorge (HOR-hey), took me to the hospital, which either didn't have an ER or just didn't really consider anything an emergency. At 1:30 a.m., sitting in a Uruguayan ER waiting room with my eye swollen shut, I wondered if Uruguay just hated me.

What is it about this place? The first time I came here I tore my Achilles. The next time, we didn't make it past the first half of the season. Now, I hadn't been here a week and couldn't get through a full game. I might be going home before I could barely begin.

If there was a plus side to the evening, it was that Jorge and I bonded while we waited two hours for an eye doctor to show up. Jorge was a young guy in his late thirties who had made over a million dollars, lost it all, then made it back.

"The first million is the hardest to make," he said. "After that, the next million is much easier."

Jorge travelled to China a lot for business. Once he bought 100,000 pairs of shoes there that he was going to sell back in South America. When he opened the huge container full of shoes, they were all left-footed shoes. The Chinese got him on a technicality. *Well, you didn't say you wanted half right and half left. You just said shoes.*

Jorge was furious, but he had already paid for it and couldn't change the order. So he bought another 100,000. This time for the right foot. The Chinese got that order correct.

Finally, the eye doctor arrived around 2 a.m. and examined my eye. No serious damage had been done and I was free to go. Fewer close calls would be much appreciated.

* * *

We had another game three days later. My eye was feeling better and I was excited to see if I could survive a full game. By then, I had moved out of the hotel that had air-conditioning and into a small apartment that did not. Temperatures were in the 90s or higher most every day.

The team ended up paying for my insane hotel laundry bill as I played the "dumb foreigner" card. It's not an excuse I like to use often, as I much prefer personal responsibility as a general rule. But being a dumb foreigner can come in handy when you don't pay attention to hotel laundry rates. Or Japanese iPhone rules.

As I walked out of my new apartment at 9:30 a.m. to head to our game day shootaround, I bent down to lock my door with my medieval dungeon keys. As I stooped over, my back gave out. Just like in Japan a few times before, it completely locked up and I could hardly move. I was so mad.

Why do these stupid locks have to be so low? Why do these keys suck? This is ridiculous. In less than a week, I almost got my eye gouged out and I throw out my back. Maybe I'm not meant to be here.

I told the team that I hurt my back that morning bending over and that I wouldn't be able to play that night. Showing up the morning of a game and announcing that you can't play is pretty embarrassing. I left out the part about my putting the key in the lock.

It turned out that the Uruguayan player who played in my place had the game of his life with 30 points, 12 rebounds, and a number of key plays. Since I wouldn't have played any better than him and most likely would have only made a fraction of the impact that he did on the game that night, I considered my back injury my own small personal contribution to the team. You're welcome. Too bad we still lost.

* * *

After a week of being there without Cara and Hannah, I was really missing them and didn't like the thought of two more months by myself.

Question: if you had to pack yourself and your child in ninety minutes to leave the country for an unspecified amount of time, could you do it?

Oh and you're six months pregnant.

My wife did. And she wasn't even running from the law. It was simply her husband calling to tell her that her plane was leaving that afternoon. For South America.

We had to use frequent flyer miles to get Cara and Hannah down there. Of course, United Airlines makes it more difficult to book a trip with miles than to swim through a pool of burning magma without melting.

So I did what we all love to do: call the airlines.

"I need two tickets to Montevideo."

"We don't fly there."

"Right. Why would you?"

"But we fly to Buenos Aires."

Yeah, but again, I'm in *Montevideo*.

"Were there seats available this week?"

"No."

"Next?"

"No."

"Any time ever? To any where?"

"Not that I can see, sir."

"OK," I said. "This is a dumb question. But do you have any flights available that are leaving *today*?"

"Actually, yes we do," said the United rep. "It leaves at 4 p.m."

OK, I thought. *How much does my wife really love me?*

It was my only chance. If the girls left the house at 3 p.m., they could make the flight. It was already 1:30 p.m.

Cara is a superstar. She can do it.

She was only six months pregnant. The hard stuff starts at seven months. Don't pregnant ladies love to fly long distances and have their legs swell, with three-year-olds next to them complaining about the food? I figured if Cara was really upset with me about it, she would have over thirty hours to cool down before I greeted her with a huge hug and flowers that I could find by the side of the road.

Did I mention they'd have to take five flights and pass through five countries first? State College to Philly to Toronto (yes the one in Canada) to Brazil to Argentina to Uruguay. *Maybe I'll leave that itinerary part out when I tell her.*

I reserved the ticket and called Cara.

"The flight is *when?*" Cara said.

"Um, in like a couple hours," I said casually.

"What? Today? I just got out of the shower," she said. "Hannah is in the bath."

"Perfect. You'll both be fresh and clean for the trip," I teased.

"This is insane," she said. She paused. I heard her take a deep breath. "OK, I'll see what I can do." We hung up.

I was impressed with her poise. It was a crazy position to put her in, and she was awesome. She left Hannah to play in the bath for over an hour while she raced around the house throwing things in a suitcase.

I called Cara back.

"One quick thing," I said nonchalantly. "Throw in Hannah's inflatable bed and ours, too."

"Why? Don't we have beds?" she asked.

"Uh, yeah, kind of," I said. "Just in case though."

"Great," she said unenthusiastically.

The trip was the best day Hannah had had in a while. Movies and snacks all day long. "Why don't we do this every day, Mommy?" Put

Daddy in charge and this may not be the last time it happens. Lucky for you, Hannah. Cara, not so much.

Big props to the ladies. They did it. Champs. High fives all around. And not a single bitter word or any attitude given whatsoever.* Truly.

I love my wife.

* * *

The humidity was through the roof and people told me it was the hottest summer in Uruguay in forty years. When we were in Japan the previous year they said *that* was the hottest summer in Japan in 100 years. I couldn't figure out why hell kept following us around.

The difference in Japan was that we had air-conditioning. In Uruguay, we had a fan. Oh joy. The hot air can just reach us faster now. The team said they would install air-conditioning. But the team was only renting the apartment, and of course the owners of the place didn't want an AC unit installed for no good reason.

Two weeks went by of sleeping in our own sweat. Hannah had a heat rash. Preggo mommy was none too comfortable. And I was ready to start sleeping in the shower with freezing water dripping on me all night.

In order not to lose our minds, we soaked wet towels with chilled water and draped them over our skin as we fell asleep while we cranked the fans full blast on our faces. We had one bed that barely fit me, so I gave Cara the bed and put Hannah on her air mattress, which she actually loved. I rearranged the living room furniture every night to make room for the big air mattress I slept on. We were baking, but happy to be together.

The team found us a different apartment, and we visited it one day. It was much nicer and had an oven and a washing machine. Air-conditioning would be installed and everything would be brand new.

---

*Note to husbands worldwide: Results may vary. Outcome not typical. Do not attempt. Professional drivers were used on a closed course.

It felt like a Hollywood mansion to us after living in our tiny sweatbox. Hannah was the only one who could sit normally on the toilet, as there was no legroom and we were forced to sit sideways. Other than that, we felt like we were about to be upgraded to heaven.

We packed our bags from our old place, as the team told us to be ready to move into our new apartment on Friday at 1 p.m. It was brutally hot again, and we were ready to say goodbye to the torture chamber.

At 5 p.m. there was no sign of the team. The paperwork wasn't ready yet for the new place. Bad news: the apartment wouldn't be ready until Wednesday—we would have to spend another five days in our sauna.

"Then put us in a hotel," I said to Jorge exasperated. I was tired of all the running around.

"I tried to get you a hotel room," Jorge said, "but it's the biggest holiday weekend of the year. Every single hotel is completely booked in the city until Wednesday."

I mean, who do you get mad at? The air? I was mad at the air. *Quit being so hot, air.*

The hottest summer of the past half-century plus zero AC plus zero hotel rooms equaled I might start kicking puppies.

We unpacked and waited out the perfect Uruguay summer heat storm for five more days.

* * *

On Wednesday we moved into our new place. The AC wasn't ready yet and some lights still didn't work. But it was already cooler and about four times the size of the tiny one-bedroom furnace we had been living in. We fell asleep for the first time with smiles on our faces and a sense of hope in our new place.

At 7 a.m. the next morning I woke with a jolt. Someone was trying to drill through our bedroom wall. Someone else was hammering in our kitchen. Why was a table saw in the bathroom? And there might as well have been a bulldozer in Hannah's room.

I looked out a window and saw that the entire building next to us was under construction. I think the workers had bonuses in their contracts for how loudly they could smash something into a wall. It continued for five straight hours until their lunch break. After snack time, it was World War III all over again. The building project was nowhere near being completed which meant there was no end to the banging in sight.

Cara and I just looked at each other. It was the angriest I'd been in a long time. Hannah? She slept through it all.

We packed up again and I took us right back to our old sweaty apartment. Someone else could live with the demolition crew inside their bedroom.

During the heat-filled days we would hang out at the mall to stay cool. Hannah's favorite place was the kiddie arcade, where all suckers, I mean great parents, take their kids. She hopped on one ride and I popped a coin in the slot and it began to gently rock back and forth. She had the time of her life. It was moments like those when I felt like the best father in the world, watching her beam with joy.

I briefly stepped back from my "proud father" haze and looked a little closer at the ride. It was a donkey carrying a massive barrel of tequila on its back. How did I know it was tequila inside? Because it said in huge bold black letters TEQUIIA on both sides of the barrel. And there's my three-year-old blondie smiling away sitting just in front of the liquor drum. Wheeeee.

She jumped on the next ride. This one was even better. It was a pickup truck with two mega beer steins in the back overflowing with lager, resting comfortably on top of two kegs. The word OKTOBERFEST was proudly displayed in tie-dye coloring on the rear door. The kids rode shotgun. Nice to see the product's positive message of drinking responsibly.

Which drunken German and Mexican kiddie-ride designer thought it would be funny to create, sell, and then ship some second-hand thrill rides to Uruguay's playland?

I was laughing and disturbed all at once. I wish I could make this stuff up. If you don't believe me, I'll show you the pictures.

* * *

The contrast between Japan and Uruguay was pretty extreme. Japan was on-time or early. Uruguay was two hours behind. The Japanese planned things to the second and every penny was accounted for. Uruguay didn't know the game schedule two weeks ahead of time. The Japanese cheered for the opponents, while I had seen Uruguayans storm the court in fury.

My friend J. P. had driven me to my first game. When I asked him later how he liked the game, he told me that he only saw the first quarter. He had been thrown out for verbally abusing the ref. You can get away with a lot in Uruguay, so he must have behaved pretty badly to get thrown out. Oddly enough, J. P. is one of the nicest guys you'll ever meet. You just don't want him cheering against you in a public setting.

Later, we played a closed-door exhibition game against Bohemios. Within the first four minutes of the game there was an argument between one of Bohemios's staff and the referee. Both threatened to leave and cancel the game. The staff guy was eventually thrown out of a scrimmage played in front of no one and meant absolutely nothing.

* * *

My team had some nice young talent and a beast of a center, an American named Chris Jackson. Our guards were quick, but the games were often out of control. We played way too fast. But that was the way these guys were used to playing, and it usually worked.

Defensor gave me the jersey number 23, surely because of my game's resemblance to Michael Jordan's. I did grow up in the Chicago suburbs watching him bring home six NBA titles, so maybe my team thought it rubbed off on me. When I was a kid, I tried to go trick-or-treating at MJ's house once with my friends, but he wasn't there. Our relationship was pretty one-sided.

My body was falling apart with some sort of new ailment each week. My Achilles was yelling at me, and since we didn't have a training room, I took a taxi to our trainer Eduardo's house every day.

Eduardo was a great guy who spoke excellent English and had a terrific sense of humor. He was also very resourceful and nicknamed himself "MacGyver" because he could fix just about anything. The team paid him a few hundred dollars in salary per month, but they didn't give him a budget for rehab items that would help the players. He did his job because he loved basketball and the Defensor players.

He couldn't afford one of the most basic rehab tools for athletes, an electro-stimulation ("stim") machine, so he built one. It looked like the first stim machine ever made back in the 1960s, encased in a worn-out briefcase. I swear he used old bike parts and there might have been portions of a Lego set in there somewhere. But it worked. The guy was remarkable. He kept me on the court despite my fragile state.

I was playing pretty well, but I wasn't as dominating as the last time I'd been in Uruguay when I had averaged over 20 points per game. Nevertheless, we won a few games in a row and qualified for playoffs.

Every game started at 9:30 p.m. Inevitably, after taking into account the usual fan or coaching interference during the game, we wouldn't get out of there until almost one in the morning. As a result, Cara and I had to make a choice about what to do with Hannah's bedtime—miss every game or stay up wicked late.

Typically, Hannah went to bed around 8 p.m. in the United States, but if we went that route, they would have flown all the way to Montevideo never to see a single game. We decided to keep late hours for the short time we'd be there. Hannah went to bed at about midnight most nights and Cara and I would crash around 2 a.m. We'd all sleep until 11 a.m. or noon most days. With the three-hour time difference with the United States, we were almost keeping the same hours as back home.

* * *

We ate out at restaurants for lunch and dinner every day because I received meal money as part of my contract, a major perk. One night, we went to an outdoor restaurant that I had seen on a flyer. The steaks looked delicious. We had never been there, but I wanted to try it because we had been eating at the same two restaurants for about a month.

The new place was on a street corner and the tables were outside on the sidewalk. Our table was about ten yards from a pair of dumpsters. Apparently, the cockroaches had seen the flyer as well, because they scurried about under our feet while we ate. Throughout the meal, four people came by and dug through the dumpsters looking for recyclables and other valuables.

Cara and I looked at each other with guilty hearts. It was very sad to see people sifting through trash to make their living. Every day, dumpster-diving was a very normal scene throughout the city. Once, I even helped a guy after the Coke bottle he'd used to prop it open slipped out and the massive door slammed shut, locking him in darkness. I opened the lid and he smiled back at me in appreciation.

At the restaurant, when we saw people rummaging through waste on the very same corner where we were enjoying a meal, the emotion of the moment was even more powerful.

Instead of turning to crime, these people were making ends meet, even if it meant digging through things other people thought of as worthless junk. What led them to this point? Maybe they didn't have opportunities for a decent education. Maybe their parents couldn't give them the means for a better future. Maybe jobs were just hard to come by these days.

I'll never know exactly what caused those people to decide to jump into a container full of nauseating trash over and over again. But I do know that they should never be looked down upon. We are all given different opportunities in life and born into different situations. Frankly, some people have an easier upbringing: they don't have to worry about abuse at home or where their next meal is coming from.

Those without these serious worries should be humbled and thankful. And we should remember Jesus's words, "To whom much is given, of him much is expected."

* * *

"Cara, you've *got* to watch this!"

It was an email to Cara from Morgan Gomez, the wife of my old teammate, Nichy, from our days in Argentina.

Cara clicked on the link and it was a video of *The X-Factor*, the TV show where contestants displayed their particular talent and were voted to stay or go by a panel of judges.

But this wasn't just any *X-Factor*. It was *X-Factor Chile*. As in the country.

And this wasn't just any contestant.

It was Tim Jones—the flashy American guard I played against in Argentina who was loaded with incredible athleticism, ability ... and a love for the crowd.

Maybe for his talent he'd try to beat someone up in the audience.

Cara and I started laughing in amazement. I was shocked and yet not surprised. Tim unquestionably loved the spotlight. And the lights didn't get any brighter than on one of the most popular shows on television. Fittingly, he was wearing his sunglasses.

What was he going to do?

"*¿Cómo estás, Tim?*" asked the first judge.

"*Super bien,*" said Tim with a cool smooth smile. The perfect Tim response.

Then I heard some back and forth between the judges and Tim, "spanishspanishspanish ... Marvin Gaye."

The music was queued and Tim broke right into "Let's Get It On."

Now, you can often tell if someone can sing or not within the first few notes.

Well, Tim could *sing*.

Maybe I was biased because I knew him, but he sounded as good as Marvin Gaye—maybe better. I don't know what I was expecting, but he completely nailed it. The audience freaked out. The judges loved him. And he moved on to the next round.

I don't know how far he went in the competition, but he had some great vocals and he definitely knew how to perform. Who knows where he'll reappear next?

* * *

I received a very disappointing email while in Uruguay, too. Tochigi fired coach Bruce Palmer. The team had been struggling and they lost two in a row one weekend, ending their playoff chances. Right after the second loss, management fired Bruce and escorted him off the premises. They didn't even let him say goodbye to the team in the locker room.

I felt terrible for Bruce, because he was a great coach who knew the game very well and was doing everything possible to help the Brex win. He had been dealt a very bad hand with injuries, players underperforming, egos, and player changes all year long. It was the perfect storm of disaster, but Bruce had continued to fight through adversity every week things got worse. I felt there were things beyond his control and he should have been given more time. He was the fourth coach in four years, and it's very difficult to win without continuity on the bench.

Bruce was a big reason why I went to Tochigi. He believed in me, and I liked his style. Plus, he was one of the funniest human beings I had ever met. I was pissed that I wasn't going to be able to play for him next season.

* * *

My Defensor team qualified for playoffs and faced Welcome in the first round. They were led by none other than my former Salto teammate, the Uruguayan legend himself, Bicho.

He played his typical wild game throughout the series—pulling jerseys, diving into the stands, and working the refs over to win calls down the stretch. At one crucial point, he pulled his signature move and shoved me from behind into his own teammate who was shooting the ball. The ref whistled me for the foul. I was pissed and gave Bicho some choice words. I knew what he would do, but we couldn't stop him. It's very hard to kill a tick.

We won the first game and were in control of the second, but we gave it away. We lost in overtime in the third and were down, 2–1, in a best-of-five series.

We had the more talented team, but they played a very physical, blue-collar style, with Bicho leading the way, wreaking havoc all over the floor. Our center, Chris, was unstoppable, but he got into foul trouble a couple of times and we couldn't keep him on the floor. The refs made some terrible calls, as usual, and without Chris to anchor the paint for us, we weren't able to play our best basketball.

We ended up losing in four games and going out on a disappointing note. We should have won the series, but Welcome came up with some big plays and outworked us. I had a couple of good games but went scoreless in one of the games, which was inexcusable. I just couldn't get a shot to go in. I felt terrible that we had lost in the first round because I felt like we had the talent and coaching to make it to the finals. Whether or not it was true, I felt responsible for not having had a bigger impact and helping us advance.

Throughout my six-week stint with the team, Defensor and Jorge were always great about paying me on time. I'd walk fifteen minutes to the team office any time I felt like getting paid, and the team secretary would hand me cash on the spot in American dollars. There were no "Come back tomorrow" or "We don't have enough" excuses ever. I gave them a lot of credit for honoring their side of the agreement.

I shouldn't have to applaud them for paying me, any more than they should stand up and cheer for me showing up on time to practice. That was the contract we all agreed to. But after too many payment problems over the years, I was extremely thankful to have a team pay what it promised.

* * *

Through the first ten years of playing and living overseas, I learned quite a bit.

I learned that I really only had control over two things: my attitude and my work ethic. I couldn't allow outside influences such as people and situations to determine my life. If I did, then my mind and emotions would be all over the place, I'd be stressed, and I would miss out on an incredible journey.

Of course, I wanted more influence over things such as my job placement, my health, and an endless number of things. We all do. But the reality is that there is more to life than just being comfortable.

Perhaps the biggest secret learned through it all was figuring out how to just appreciate where I was and who I was with at any given month. My adventure was taking me to places I never thought I'd go, to do things I never thought I'd do, and to meet people I never knew existed. It was opening my eyes to not just different cultures, but different ways to handle life's maddening curveballs. Remember the injuries, being cut by teams, and lack of toilet paper? (And we're not done yet.)

Through it all, I was a normal oversized guy trying to make his way in a fairly rough and tumble, show-me-the-money, what-have-you-done-for-me-lately world. To keep my sanity, I stepped back often to laugh at how unreal much of this all seemed. I tried to remember what was really important in life because in this physical world where you can be made to feel like a piece of meat, I welcomed the peace, the serenity, and the life of the spirit I knew I could always find in the love of my family and the sanctity of the church pew.

Chapter 18

NO TO THE DUNK CONTEST, YES TO THE PEE CUP: JAPAN YEAR FIVE

Alexandra Rose Smith arrived on June 4, 2012, back in State College, Pennsylvania. Cara braved her second C-section and we took another precious little girl home from the hospital. Plus, some pretty amazing and semi-disturbing film footage of the big event that will probably never be declassified. I like to record stuff because you never know what will be usable come editing time.

Lexi, her nickname from the hood, was actually decided upon over dinner at an Italian restaurant in Montevideo a few months before. Once she was born, we didn't waste any time in sending away for her passport because Tochigi was talking some crazy nonsense about coming back to Japan early.

When you hear the phrase "basketball in July," you envision the NBA summer league, or outdoor rec, perhaps.

In Japan, they call it preseason.

"Tyler, we need you to come by July 25," the GM told me by phone.

"Why? Our first game isn't until October," I said.

"Well, we have a fan event. We want you to be there," he said.

I want my own fighter plane and my mortgage paid off.

"Do we have a head coach yet?" I asked.

"No."

"Have we signed another American player?" I asked.

"No."

"So why am I coming if we have no head coach, no other American, and our first game isn't for two and a half months?" I asked as calmly as possible.

"Because we have a fan event," he said.

Got it.

Despite the fact that we'd have ample opportunities to see fans for the next nine months, my reasoning didn't really click with management. In their defense, the Japanese guys had been working out since May yet again. They had a couple weeks off from the end of last season and then it was back to work to prep for the new one. But to me, that didn't mean I should fly across the globe for a fan event in July.

But I did, because I was under contract and I didn't want them pulling any funny business. When they're writing the checks, you gotta go. With Lexi less than eight weeks old, our family of now four made the journey one more time to Japan.

* * *

I laced up my smelly sneakers, put a smile on my face, and went to my first Tochigi Brex practice of the season with no coach, no second American, and our first game a full decade away.

But there were fans there. And they even seemed happy to see me, which was better than, "Oh great, we signed *that* guy again."

And get this. I think I had my first groupie. I looked up and what was hanging over a railing in the stands for the whole world to see? A number 35 Tochigi Brex game jersey. And no, it did not say "Durant." Very funny. In four years of college and ten years pro, I was fairly certain this was the only poor fellow who owned one of my replica jerseys. They weren't exactly jumping off the racks.

There is one other jersey story worth sharing, however. One full year after I had been released from the Utah Jazz, my friend Jim emailed me an eBay link. "Check this out!"

Someone was selling a number 30 "Smith" jersey from my time with the Jazz. And there were bids on it! The seller was probably some team manager trying to make a little extra cash off the players' jerseys buried in the back storage room—guys who never made the team. *Who would ever buy that thing?*

Then I saw another jersey up for sale. This one was from a Jazz player who actually played decent minutes. Crazy enough, my jersey sold. Somebody even paid $120 for it—*more* than the real Jazz player who was still under contract with the team.

I was feeling pretty big-time until Jim reminded me that Smith was a fairly common name and some other "Smith" out there probably just thought it would be a cool thing to have. Thanks, Jim.

* * *

After we finished our first practice, we had some player-fan interaction. About 200 fans lined up to shoot baskets, and we rebounded for them. Then there was a small competition, and every fan took a single shot from the free throw line. Out of 200 fans, only six made it.

The final round was over within a minute, as only one of the remaining six fans made his shot and was crowned king of the open practice fan club. He got a wristband and some high fives.

And this was where things really got interesting.

It was paper airplane contest time. I'm dead serious. Marketing was doing one stellar job. Five Japanese players and I would face off making paper airplanes and sending them flying from the free throw line: one piece of paper, one flight per player.

Our team's leading scorer, Taku, was the emcee and had the mic.

"Tyler, when was the last time you made a paper airplane?" he asked.

In my head, I remembered about two weeks ago I had made one for Hannah and she thought it was amazing. "Wow, Daddy! That was a really good airplane!" I tell you, it is great being able to fascinate your kids when they are young. I can't wait until they're sixteen and

I'm like, "Hey, want to make paper airplanes and play hide-and-seek?"
"Yeah, Dad. You go hide. In another state."

My answer to Taku's question about my most recent paper airplane design blurted out of my mouth and into the microphone. "When I was seven," I said. *Why am I lying about the last time I made a paper airplane to a bunch of strangers in a hot gym in Japan?*

The crowd thought it was funny, though. Whatever.

Japan is the homeland of origami. Or at least I think it is. All of the Japanese guys could whip a pterodactyl out of their receipt from a convenience store in under a minute. I've seen it. They probably learned it before they could tie their shoes. So my expectations of bringing home the folded paper title were pretty low at that point.

The fans lined up in sections according to which player they thought would win. Only a few jumped on my bandwagon. Haters.

The Japanese guys tossed their airplanes. A few barely made it a body length. One or two wowed the crowd and made it to half-court. Then, the 6-foot-8 foreigner stepped up. *Here goes nothing.* I let it fly.

That bad boy shot like a rocket past midcourt, past the opposite three-point line, and glided to a sweet sliding landing, stopping at the opposite free throw line.

Kaboom. The place erupted.

A couple more silly games took place that the fans ate up and I thought we were all done.

Then they brought out the shot clocks.

They propped two portable scoreboards up on a table and covered up the numbers in the back of the shot clock on the mini keyboard pad area where the scoreboard operator would normally see the seconds tick down and control the score.

Two players would start the shot clocks with the time covered up so they couldn't see it ticking. When a player thought twenty-four seconds had passed, he would hit STOP. The idea was to come as close as possible to guessing exactly twenty-four seconds. Exhilarating, I know. That was what I showed up in July for. *Was I getting paid for this?* Oddly, yes.

NBC might need to pick this up for prime time.

Six Japanese players went and got 22, 23, and 26 seconds. Then they called my name. As if my dominance with paper airplanes wasn't enough.

Start.

One Mississippi, two Mississippi. My eyes were closed. I was drowning out the restless crowd. *13. 14. Is this too fast? Too slow? What am I counting to again? 22, 23 … I don't know … I'm probably way off …*

STOP.

23.94.

A new world record and 2012's best time-guesser from a different country. Put it in the Guinness book. We have witnesses.

The crowd was amazed again at my newfound ability of time-guessing. I hope I'd be able to get their same reaction during an actual game.

* * *

We raided Costco within about seventy-two hours of arriving in Japan. It's probably for the best that it's two and a half hours round-trip and costs over fifty dollars in tolls. In theory, I wouldn't be able to spend my entire paycheck there, as it was too far to go every day.

The one thing I don't get is that they yelled at you if your kid rode in the "wrong" part of the shopping cart. Children weren't allowed in the big part. They had to be in the specific kid-assigned seat on the cart next to the push handle. Apparently, not a single Costco employee had a child. When a kid sees a giant cart, where do you think he or she wants to sit? In the awesome big fortress cage. Duh. C'mon, Costco.

* * *

The other bad news besides Bruce not returning was that Pizza Hut left Japan. More accurately, they left our city of Utsunomiya. My streak of buy-one-get-one-free Wednesday nights finally came to an end after three seasons (my only record in Japan).

Sure, the pizzas were regularly priced in the twenty-five to forty-five dollar range. Sure, it was a bit of a drive to get there. But there were weekly promos, and I was willing to wait in traffic for wings.

Looking back, though, I blame myself. Had I not gotten hurt in the first game the previous year, I could have poured every last yen I had into that beautiful place and kept it alive.

The news came as a shock when I called Pizza Hut one night only to get "Doo Doo DOO ... I'm sorry, but this number has been disconnected. Maybe you should have bought more pizza." (Or whatever the Japanese recording said.)

Devastating.

But I got up off the floor, threw the tissues away, and did what any respectable man would have done.

I called Domino's.

There is a God. And He does show grace.

Technically, I had a Japanese friend call. Because if I was in prison for life and the only way out was to get a pizza order correct in Japan by telephone, I might as well start making friends with the guards and making sure Big Tony had enough cigarettes to keep him happy, because I'd be there for a while.

It's hard to understand the joy of a familiar pizza in a foreign country unless you've been there. But when you drive down the street and every restaurant you pass is a complete mystery and you can't read the menu—or even the name of the restaurant—a recognizable franchise becomes a beautiful thing. Oh that friendly red, blue, and white signage ... can you hear it? Angels.

All of a sudden, forty-five dollars seems like a fair price for eight slices.

* * *

Only seven days into Japan-life and a kid went down. Hannah practically blew up the thermometer at 103 degrees. It was on a Saturday morning when many hospitals and clinics were closed and I was supposed to be leaving for training camp in a couple of hours. *Here, honey, this one's screaming and won't sleep, and the other one is basically on fire. Good luck with that. See you next week.*

I called my go-to guy, Yuma, who was Mr. Everything for the Brex. His title was team manager, but one of his main jobs was point man for the Americans—not an easy task.

It turned out that there was a health clinic about 200 yards away from our house, yet somehow no one told us this beforehand. Hello? I never found out the reason why things just don't get out in the open in Japan sometimes.

We met Yuma at the clinic. As we walked in, the place was packed with nothing but old people waiting with their shoes off. Shoes were left at the door. No dirt got into any building in Japan.

The doctor finally came to meet us and said, "I'm sorry, this not kids' hospital. No help kids."

Hannah's not a golden retriever. She's the same make and model as the old folks out there, just a smaller version. *Do you think you can do something?* Her ear was killing her, and she was burning up. One of the most helpless feelings in the world is when your child is sick or in pain.

The doctor spoke slowly in English.

"Yes, she has fever and maybe infection. So she need chemotherapy."

Whoa, wait a minute. Cara and I looked at each other. The parents look of "What in the world is this guy thinking?"

I'm no doctor and I only went to public school, but don't you think you should take her temperature first before we go all anti-cancer drugs on her? How about that for a starting point? Hey Yuma, back me up here.

But Yuma was just nodding his head like, "*Yeah, yeah, chemotherapy.*"

Then I realized he meant "antibiotics" and Cara's and my blood pressure dropped a few hundred points. Antibiotics. Chemo. Neti pot. It's all the same. *Yuma, where were you on that one, man?*

Long story short, Yuma stepped up and found a "kids" hospital in the nick of time before it closed for a week. The doctor checked

Hannah and even let her listen to her own heartbeat through the stethoscope—a big highlight. They prescribed her quite possibly the most awful-tasting powder formula known to man to help fight the ear infection. *Thanks for making Mom and Dad's job even easier, Doctor-san.* Thankfully Cara recalled the magic bullet for downing nasty medicine: mix it with ice cream.

The conclusions are blurry as to what actually healed Hannah: Strawberry Häagen-Dazs or Cookies & Cream Häagen-Dazs.

* * *

After training camp was complete, a head coach finally showed up for our squad, Antanas Sireika (ahn-TAHN-ahs ser-AY-ka) from Lithuania. I didn't know a lot about Lithuania, but I did know they had very good basketball there. I also knew that some eastern European coaches had the reputation of being … fairly intense, shall we say? Running in the woods at 5 a.m. Two-a-days for nine months straight. That kind of thing. It would be accurate to say I was a bit nervous.

Coach Sireika was a big guy, a muscular 6-foot-5 and in good shape with a deep voice. He was half Arnold Schwarzenegger, half Tom Hanks from the movie *The Terminal*.

"You shooting. No vay. No vay! What you do? We like strong fist. Like team. Together. Faster play, moving, passing and ... OPA!" It was awesome. We'd get a solid five to ten "OPAs!" each practice. Best part of my day.

All that said, I really did like the guy. He did know the game quite well, and I thought he could really help our team. He had been successful in Europe, but whether that would translate to Japan remained to be seen.

He wanted us to play with freedom and to work hard. And I needed to cut him some slack because he was coaching in a second language that was unfamiliar. If I were asked to coach in Japanese, you'd get a lot of "Thank you," "What's your name?" and "Do you like basketball?" I'm pretty sure we'd win the championship.

Now, all we needed was a translator who met four key criteria: spoke fluent Japanese, English, and Lithuanian—and knew basketball inside and out. Let me just hop on Craigslist Tokyo and see what winners we can find.

Leave it to the Brex, though. They found one. Where? I have no clue. Maybe the United Nations. Yira (YEER-uh) was a very nice young woman born and raised in Lithuania, spoke great English, and had already spent a year in Japan and had a firm grasp on her third language, Japanese. Remarkable.

"Have you played much basketball?" I asked Yira.

She smiled nervously. "Only maybe in gym class," she said.

Maybe in gym class.

Three out of four ain't bad.

Welcome to the circus.

* * *

I think team management assumed that Coach Sireika would coach in Lithuanian and Yira would then relay the message in Japanese to the assistant coaches and Japanese players and then have the Japanese coaches translate it to English for the two Americans. I couldn't imagine a practice ending in less than six hours with that setup.

But Coach insisted on speaking English. He walked into his first practice wearing jean shorts and a European man-purse around his shoulder. He addressed the team at half-court and what would have taken a native English speaker about two minutes must have taken him twenty. I speak English and at times even I had a hard time following him. But I gave him a lot of credit for the effort, as I know it had to be difficult to explain himself and his philosophy in another language.

I saw this going one of two ways. It would somehow turn out to be a genius move by the front office and someone would make a movie out of it. Or it would be a train wreck.

I hoped and prayed for the former.

* * *

Coach Sireika was completely different from any coach the Japanese guys had ever played for. His repertoire was full of quirks. He made us shoot left-handed free throws every day in practice, claiming it would help. He refused to let the assistant coaches and managers rebound and pass for players before and after practice because players "need to work on their own passing." His favorite pass was the no-look dish, and we did drills emphasizing Harlem Globetrotter-type passing.

His philosophy on pick-and-rolls and spacing were opposite what many of the Japanese players had been taught, and some guys resisted him big-time. Having played in Europe for a few years, I understood what he was trying to do. Unfortunately, others just weren't buying in.

Some of it was just a communication barrier. Players would become furious because they couldn't understand what he was trying to explain. Then Coach would raise his voice because no one was doing what he had asked ... and the players would just get angrier.

The other big issue was that the Japanese players had never played his style before, and they just didn't believe in it. They thought it was ineffective and they wouldn't buy into the system. Some guys tried to run it the way he wanted, and others just refused to cooperate. So as anyone who has ever played a team sport can tell you, no unity equals no wins.

* * *

In our fifth preseason game, we were facing Panasonic. They had one of the best teams in the league and it would be a great early test for us.

We walked off the bus and into the locker room, where a table of food awaited as usual before the game. Mostly snacks like bananas, small sandwiches, and the Japanese staple, rice balls.

I dropped my bag on the ground and was the first to the table. I picked up a sandwich and started to open the wrapper when Coach Sireika erupted.

"Ty, close! *Close!*" he yelled, looking right at me.

The place went silent.

I was taken completely off-guard. Close what?

"No eat before game!"

"Coach, I –"

"You eat lunch at the hotel?" he asked.

"Yes, I ate lunch," I said. "But that was about two hours ago."

"Close!"

I just stood there in the middle of the room with my half-opened sandwich in hand, and the entire team watching in silence. What now? I was hungry. The game was ninety minutes away and my stomach was raging. It wasn't like I was pounding a Big Mac in the huddle before tipoff.

Clearly, he was wrong. Everybody in the room knew it. Had he not seen everyone eating from the table full of food in the middle of the locker room during the previous four games? I was furious because who was he to tell me when I could and couldn't eat? I had known Coach Sireika only a few weeks. Plus, I was a thirty-two-year-old grown man who just so happened was not in prison.

I had to make a decision. Should I rebel? Shove the sandwich in my face, yell "Haha!" and throw my fists above my head in triumph? Or should I take the opportunity to defer to the man in charge and set an example? I didn't particularly want to. But other guys needed to see that we all had to be willing to do things that were different and really buy in, no matter how ridiculous it seemed, so that we could give ourselves a chance at being successful.

With a disgusted look, I set the sandwich down. *You don't want me to eat? Fine. We'll see how well that turns out.*

I got dressed and left the locker and went up to the gym. Naomi, our manager, came up to me.

"Ty, are you hungry?" she whispered.

"Yes, I'm hungry," I complained. "But apparently I'm supposed to starve myself in order to play well."

Naomi revealed a granola bar she had hidden in her pocket. It was like a back-alley drug deal.

"Take this," she said. Naomi was the sweetest person you'd ever meet. She loved her job and worked extremely hard to make sure that everything was set up perfectly for games and practices, down to the finest detail, like the flavor of gum that the players liked best.

"Thanks, Naomi," I said. "But I'm good. I'm OK." I turned it into some sort of personal protest against Coach. As stupid as it sounded, I thought that my anger and hunger combined would fuel me against the idiocracy of the moment.

Naomi could tell that I was upset and she wanted to help. She cared deeply for every player on the team, and she taught me quite a bit about what it means to serve others.

Once, I asked her what she would like to do down the road in her career.

She looked at me puzzled. "This," she replied with a smile. As in *Why would I do anything else?* "I love my job. This is what I want to do." When you can say that with sincerity and a part of your job includes walking twenty minutes in the snow to do laundry for a dozen guys at 1 a.m. on a Saturday night, you've found your calling. Naomi was a very bright young woman who performed her job extremely well and just so happened to throw the best passes for shooting drills of anyone on the team—when Coach wasn't looking.

With eight minutes to go before game time, I was still fuming. My stomach had only become emptier, which made me hostile. I couldn't let it go.

I grabbed a ball and launched a three-point shot. I felt a twinge in my back and knew instantly what happened. My back had locked up again. It went into spasms and pain seized my lower back.

There are fewer things more embarrassing to an athlete on any level than having to tell your head coach that you can't play because you injured yourself in warmups with no one around you.

I felt angry, embarrassed, hungry, and a bit justified.

Maybe next time he'd let me eat a snack.

* * *

Hannah was now four years old and had loved going to preschool in the States for the brief time we would be home. She thrived in a classroom environment, and we wanted to find her a school in Japan. But locating a school wasn't easy because most international schools could cost between $20,000 and $30,000 a year.

The other option was to send her to an all-Japanese school, which wasn't ideal for her. I knew that she was capable of understanding and learning so much in school. But Cara and I didn't like the idea of her not understanding her classmates or teachers. Hannah was a sensitive little girl, not a toughie, and it seemed like too much to force her into that situation if we didn't have to.

Fortunately, we found Sunnyside International, which was a blend of Japanese and English and didn't break the bank like many private schools. It turned out that Hannah was the only non-Japanese kid enrolled. So, technically, she made it "International."

There were two teachers in each classroom. One was Japanese and the other was a native English speaker. It was a school geared for children ages three to six to learn English. The first month was a challenge for Hannah, as she didn't speak any Japanese, and the other kids only knew "hello," "thank you," and "toilet."

But before long, our little blondie was making all kinds of friends. She came home from school early on and I asked her who some of the friends in her class were.

"Mo-mo-a, Ko-ko-na, and Ma-ya," she said.

"No, no, sweetie. I don't understand those Japanese words. What are your friends' *names*?" I repeated.

"That's their names, Daddy," she insisted. "Mo-mo-a, Ko-ko-na, and Ma-ya are my friends."

"OK, then," I said, unsure of whether she wasn't remembering correctly or if these really were her new school friends.

"But Maya sometimes is mean to me," she said.

Hannah hugs everyone. So who was giving my cute little sweetie a hard time?

"Why? What makes you think she is mean?" I asked. None of those kids could put a full sentence together in English, so it didn't make sense that kids would be saying rude things that Hannah could actually understand.

"She didn't smile at me," Hannah said.

"She didn't smile at you?" I asked.

"No. I smiled at her, but she didn't smile at me," Hannah explained.

Of course. Hannah and her classmates couldn't communicate with words. So facial expressions and body language were what Hannah understood. By not returning a smile, Maya initially came across as the meanest kid in school. Thankfully, Maya softened up, and she and Hannah became best friends.

Pretty soon, Hannah was speaking better Japanese than I was. One day we were at the pool and I left Hannah to go get a couple of kickboards. I could still see her at the other end of the pool, but to others she appeared to be abandoned. A lifeguard walked up to her and they had a brief conversation. None of the lifeguards spoke English, so I was curious what happened.

"Hannah, what did that lifeguard say to you?" I asked.

"She asked me where my mommy or daddy was?" she answered.

"Did she speak English?" I asked.

"No, only Japanese," she said.

"And you understood her?" I asked.

"Of course, Daddy," she said.

"What did you say back to her?" I asked.

"I said that I was with my Daddy and he is right over there," she said as she pointed across the pool.

Duh. It's *just* Japanese. I'd been there five seasons and this little peanut knew more than I did after having been in school for only a couple of months. Kids are amazing.

* * *

The other American who started with our team in preseason was Sylvester Morgan. He was a 6-foot-10 rebounding and shot-blocking machine. Sly ran the floor very hard, had a nice touch around the basket, and caused all kinds of problems for opponents with his defense and length in the paint.

On his first day of practice, Coach Sireika introduced him to the team.

"This Sivesta Morgun," Coach said in his deep-voiced broken English. "Very good player." Coach looked at Sylvester. "You have nickname?"

"Sylvester" was a mouthful for the Lithuanians and Japanese in the crowd.

"'Junior.' My friends call me 'Junior,'" Sylvester said.

Coach looked confused and even a little annoyed.

"You have another nickname?" Coach didn't like Choice A.

"Another nickname?" Sylvester asked. Now Sly was confused. When someone asks you what your nickname was, you usually get to decide. "Umm, or you can call me 'Sly.'"

Coach smiled. "Sly, OK," he said, clearly happier with Choice B.

Unfortunately, Sly hurt his foot before the season started and left the team. We brought in another player who was a good rebounder, but not a big, strong body. After just six weeks, he was cut.

We were losing games left and right and our All-Star point guard, Yuta Tabuse (YOO-tuh TA-boo-say) hadn't stepped on the court yet. He was recovering from a foot injury and had barely begun to practice. Yuta was our missing link. He was the only Japanese player to ever make the NBA (with the Phoenix Suns in 2004) and was the most recognized player in Japan. He was a great floor leader and knew how to set up his teammates for easy looks. Without him, we were trying to drive a motorcycle with the front wheel missing.

By December, we were on our third import player, Olumide Oyedeji (o-LOO-mih-day o-yay-DAY-jee). Olu was originally from Nigeria and played on their national team in the Olympics the previous summer in London. He was a big guy with a big personality. At 6-foot-9, 280 pounds, there was no way to move him. Olu could rebound with the best of them and was a very good passer out of the post. He joked around a lot with the guys on the team and was always the biggest voice in the gym.

The import curse continued with the Brex, though. In Olu's second game, he broke his shooting hand and had to have surgery the next day. Olu was so strong, I have no idea how anyone could break a bone in his body.

Olu's home was in Orlando and he planned to go back for five weeks of rehab there. But before he left, he wanted to make sure he gave everyone on the team their Christmas presents.

Christmas presents? He's only been here a week.

He handed out brand new Coach backpacks to every player and manager on the team.

I brought something, too—T-shirts. Not just any T-shirts; Penn State T-shirts. *Aren't I a giver? Thanks a lot, Olu. How about you let me go first next time?*

Olu and I lived in two different financial worlds. He had played in the NBA for a few seasons and then made more big bucks in South Korea and China. He was very generous with his earnings and did lots of charity work through a foundation that helped kids in Nigeria to choose a better way of life. He sponsored young boys and paid for a number of them to attend college in the United States, right out of his own pocket. Olu ran basketball camps and clinics nationwide in Nigeria, encouraging kids with the foundation's slogan, "Pick a book, not a knife. Shoot the ball, not a gun."

With Olu out because of his broken hand, Sly returned. His foot was feeling better and we picked up a couple of wins before the Christmas break with his help in the paint. But even with Sly's big minutes for us, we had an awful first half of the season.

We were 6–18 and had lost to everybody. The teams we should have swept in a weekend series, we split with. One weekend we lost the first game on Saturday to Mitsubishi, a team in the bottom half of the league. On Sunday, before the game, Coach Sireika promised to take the team out for sushi if we won. We did. He probably should have played that sushi card more often.

In another weekend doubleheader we smoked Hokkaido by 38 in the first game. The next day we lost by three, pretty stellar consistency. I suffered two cracked ribs in the first game. The only redeeming value was that I did draw a charge on the play. Not much redeeming value considering I couldn't breathe pain-free for the next four weeks.

Despite our dismal record, I had plenty to be thankful for. First, I still had a job. I played decently so far, but I could have shot the ball better on certain nights.

Second, I won a trip to the All-Star Game over Christmas break. The one in Japan, not the NBA All-Star Game. And it wasn't like a vacation package that I won from a Coke bottle top. I actually got to *play* in the game as a "Star." More of a faint off-in-the-distance "maybe-it's-a-plane-or-a-satellite" kind of star, but technically a "Star" nonetheless. So I'll capitalize the "S"—it's my story. And hey, if you can't be a real NBA star, a Japanese Star is a close second.

Of the four Americans playing in the game, three were selected to participate in the dunk contest. Can you guess which one wasn't? Hmmm. His name starts with a T, ends with an R, and in the middle is "Slow and White." You'll get it later. Anyway, my feelings weren't exactly hurt since I had zero dunks on the year and just one dunk in the past five seasons.

But when I showed up to the All-Star Game, a league official said that a bunch of players had injuries and couldn't do it. They needed guys to participate in the dunk contest. After all, the fans paid big money for us to put on a show.

"Do you want to do it?" the All-Star director asked me with a straight face.

I laughed. But he was serious.

The winner did get $1,000. It was tempting and it sounded like all the really good dunkers weren't going to be in it.

I quickly reviewed the two dunks I had in my arsenal.

1. Coming from the left side, praying to God not to let gravity pull so hard on me, going up off of my left leg, and hoping the ball cleared the front of the rim.
2. The same dunk from the right side. With even stronger prayer.

"Ahh, not this time," I said. As if I'd be ready next year or something.

The dunk contest arrived. We walked out of the locker room, and they said, "OK, first up"—no one even had a chance to warm up. It was insane. Nobody had touched a ball, stretched, or even tied their shoes. For as organized a country as Japan was, they needed some help with their sporting events at times.

Of course, two guys miraculously overcame their ailments in time to amaze the crowd with some ridiculous dunks—all without a single stretch. Oh, what it must be like to be a freak athlete. I clearly made the right decision by just sitting on the bench and clapping.

The three-point contest was more of the same. They announced the first shooter, handed him a ball, put one minute on the clock, and said, "Shoot!" Not even a layup or dribble was allowed for a warmup. The contest lasted only one round. Unreal. Taku, my teammate from Tochigi who could shoot the lights out, needed no warmup and burned up the nets.

Our coach, an American named Don Beck, was from the defending champion team, Toyota. He called a timeout in the first quarter and put me in the game for the first time. He proceeded to draw up an alley-oop play for me on the next possession. *Clear out and throw it up to the sky. I'm sure the slow meandering Caucasian who wasn't even in the dunk contest will throw it down with ease.*

I mean, I really appreciated the vote of confidence. But I don't even draw up alley-oop plays for myself during summer camps versus nine-year-olds.

I looked around at the rest of the guys in the huddle. And the Japanese guys, they're just good soldiers. They nodded and focused their eyes on the coach's drawing board as if all of it made perfect sense.

None of it made sense. There were four other guys we should have drawn that play up for.

I had to speak up. I did not see this ending well.

"Coach, I don't know if you know my game all that well," I joked. But he insisted that we run the play.

I looked at my Japanese point guard as we walked out onto the floor. "Maybe make it kind of a lower pass," I said motioning with my hands because he didn't speak much English.

We ran the play. But it turned into more of a Princeton backdoor cut and I laid it in, with my hand almost touching the bottom of the backboard. That was as flashy as I could get. *Hey, it was their fault for inviting me to this thing.*

The actual All-Star Game was kind of a joke because no one played hard for three quarters. Lunchtime pick-up ball with the Geek Squad from Best Buy would be as exciting. The whole All-Star Game setup didn't exactly fit my game, as I don't really have a cool slow-motion I-make-it-look-easy type of playing style. Then, in the fourth quarter, everyone played hard because there was a $300 bonus per player for the winning team.

I ended up dropping in some other buckets and finished with 17 points to make my appearance respectable. We won the game in over-time, and I brought home the cash. It made up for the $125 fine that I incurred for being late to practice earlier in the year because I got lost on my way. It all evened out.

* * *

After the Christmas break, we lost in the first round of the All-Japan Tournament to our good pals, the Aisin Seahorses. When we returned to regular season play, I set a new personal record of 0-for-8 from the three-point line against Mitsubishi. Oddly, we won that one.

The following weekend, I was drug-tested after our game on the road against Panasonic. After a loss, the last thing anyone wants to do is pee in a cup in front of a stranger. As I walked off the floor, some officials with yellow arm bands and fancy ID tags jumped me before I could even get past the watercooler behind our bench. It was the Japanese anti-doping mafia.

"Mr. Smith, we are from the Japan Anti-Doping Agency," the one guy said as he flashed his JADA badge. *We're here to watch you urinate. Come with us and don't make a scene if you ever want to see your family again. Now get in the trunk.*

My trainer spoke up, "Have you ever done doping test?"

He looked nervous for me, like he thought something really bad was going to happen.

"Mizuno, don't worry. I've peed in front of lots of guys," I reassured.

For the past fifteen years, dating back to college, I'd been taking drug tests. Lance Lie-Strong and I do have one thing in common: we've both passed 100 percent of our tests. I just happened to do mine legally. The anti-doping people always had the worst timing. They showed up right after you've just lost fourteen pounds of sweat during a game. *How in the world do you expect me to pee now? And you're just going to stand there and stare? I hope you don't have a date tonight because we're going to be here a while.* Sometimes it took me two or three hours to pee after a game because the tank was completely dry.

And they're so particular with everything. They told me to choose a cup wrapped in plastic. So I chose a cup. And I started to open it.

"No no no," he said. He gave me another cup.

"What's the matter?" I asked.

"You must open right way," he said.

What right way? It's a two-cent plastic cup wrapped in clear plastic. You've got a hundred of them sitting here. What does it matter how I tear the plastic? What is this— special Christmas wrapping paper that my mom wants to re-use? (Note to reader: she doesn't do this anymore. Our family is all very proud of the positive steps she has taken to let that go many years ago.)

My pee official and I visited the men's room, and we were successful. Turns out his name was "Kawai" which means "cute" in Japanese. If you're into balding with glasses, then I guess his name was fitting.

When was the last time you had to pee in a cup at the doctor's office? Maybe it's routine for the anti-doping officials because they get a good forty samples of urine a day. But it's still a weird feeling carrying your warm pee in a cup and handing it over to a stranger to inspect. Should I be proud of my sample? Disgusted? Or slightly embarrassed? How about all three?

So there I was—at a table opposite two Japanese anti-doping officials with a cup full of my pee as the topic of conversation. I smelled. I had just played a game and they hadn't given me time to take a shower. I tried to convince myself that it was someone else. But I couldn't lie to myself anymore. It was me. And I hate to smell.

My rather large cup of urine sat between us, making the whole thing uncomfortable. They were acting like it was no big deal, so I had to fake it, too. As if we were all just sitting around eating rice balls and sipping green tea, watching the Super Bowl together with my pee in a cup next to the nachos. Perfectly normal.

Then they told me to pour some of it in one separate bottle. I did. Then they said to pour the rest of it in another bottle.

Man, this is weird. Lord, please don't let my hand slip and spill this refreshment all over these nice men's suits. They're just trying to do their job.

I finished pouring. Perfection.

They read me my Miranda rights, I secured the two new bottles of fresh liquid in a box, and I was finished.

How did someone even become an anti-doping official? Does it just hit them one day? "I really feel so strongly about people playing by the rules that I am willing to watch people pee in cups and then fill out forms for years to come. Think of the thrill when we catch someone!"

How do they even hear about the job? *"Hey, ya know, my cousin Donny just put in his application for the whole anti-weed-testing job. Got good benefits. Said somethin' about you might gotta watch people pee, though. Either way, you might wanna check it out."*

Was it a full-time gig? There were maybe eight guys running around testing all the players. But we only played on weekends, so there wasn't that much testing going on. I'm not sure if they worked part-time at the Mitsubishi factory and it was just supplemental income or what. If they were volunteers, that might be even weirder.

* * *

Our point guard, Yuta, returned from injury and big Olu's hand healed, so we had both of them back on the floor. We won four of six games, but that was the best streak we could put together. Some players were too frustrated with the communication barrier with Coach Sireika. Even though Coach's English had improved a lot over the season, a few key players resisted his coaching style more than they embraced it. Coach was firm on the way he wanted to do things, and despite several open displays of defiance from some guys, he never kicked anyone out of practice or penalized their playing time. He continued to initiate a relationship with players and make multiple efforts to bring guys together. Unfortunately, our team was beyond repair.

It was disappointing because on paper we easily had as much talent as the top teams in the league. But our lack of chemistry and communication, combined with injuries and poor attitudes, made for a pretty disastrous season. We finished in sixth place at 14–28, miles from a playoff spot.

I still had much to be thankful for. I completed the season injury-free. Hannah loved her school and made numerous Japanese friends. Our family became close with some of those families, and they welcomed us into their homes for meals and we did many activities together. Plus, we even met some great American friends who were doing missionary work in Utsunomiya.

And it didn't hurt that none of my checks from the team bounced.

But one looming question remained after my eleventh season of pro basketball. I thought about it every single day.

What am I going to do when basketball is over?

Chapter 19

NO ONE STORMED THE FLOOR, BUT I MADE MY LAST SHOT: THAILAND

I headed into another offseason of uncertainty. My body felt good, and I was thirty-three years old. I felt like I could play for another year or two. But there were no guarantees that I could get a job playing, which led to the question that had haunted me every day for years: "What am I going to do after basketball?"

I had no clue. My answers were feeble at best. Depending on the day, I was going to be a basketball agent, wedding videographer, referee, Italian restaurant owner, or run a bounce house play place for kids. Maybe all of them at once.

I came out of the womb wanting to play sports—tennis, soccer, basketball, football. Baseball was my first love as a kid and I dreamed of playing for the Chicago Cubs. While that never materialized, being a Cubs fan did play a part in molding my character. I learned to deal with disappointment at an early age.

As I grew to 6-foot-8 and my fastball topped out at 80 mph, my dream switched to pro basketball. And here I was realizing my goals and getting paid to play a game I'd been having fun with since my dad put a hoop in our driveway. I'd always had something to strive for over the last eleven years—a quicker shot release, a better team, a bigger contract.

Now, my dream could be ending. And I had no clue what dream to start next.

* * *

While I had played pretty well and had gotten along with everyone at Tochigi, who knew what would happen next? The league was about to undergo some significant changes.

The Japan Basketball League (JBL) was being revamped as the National Basketball League (NBL) with four teams being added, for a total of twelve. Teams now had a salary cap of $1.5 million, whereas in the past there was no limit to what a team could spend.

But the biggest change that affected me was the foreigner rule. For the past five years, only one import was allowed to play on the court at a time. Now, the new rule said two imports could play in the first and third quarters, and one import in the second and fourth quarters. The league was saying, "We want another import player on the floor, just not all the time." It became a game within a game and was a strange way to incorporate foreign players, but nothing really surprised me anymore.

As a result of the new rule, some teams changed the types of players they wanted. They needed more than just large post players. Tochigi wanted a big center and a wing player. I was neither.

Playing for Hitachi would have been a possibility, but they fired Coach Ono, whom I'd played for. The new coach was a great guy from England, and I spoke with him during the summer, but he signed two different players.

My old assistant coach from my NBA D-League days was hired as the head coach of one of the new NBL teams in Japan. Despite some interest from them, nothing materialized.

My stock in Europe had dried up because I'd been over in Asia for the past five years. Now it seemed that I'd worn out my welcome in Japan, too.

I received a call from Mike Taylor, who was the head coach of an NBA D-League team. He asked if I was interested in being the assistant coach of his team in Maine, which was the Boston Celtics affiliate. It sounded like a tremendous opportunity. A few days later, we spoke again and the job had been filled by someone whom Brad Stevens, the new Celtics head coach, had appointed.

It was now August and we were in need of an income. Japan and Europe were out. South America wasn't as family-friendly as I was looking for. Maybe my time had run out.

I was at a crossroads and knew it. Were my basketball days over? I felt things were beyond my control. Doors were closing and I wasn't sure others would open. One day I lay flat on my back on the locker room floor after a workout and thought about everything at once. "God," I said out loud, "I could use some guidance with this stuff."

I went home and considered all my playing options. The one place I hadn't explored was the Middle East. Many teams there paid well. Who doesn't love oil money? They didn't know anything about me, which was good, because a legit agent could sell me as a mysterious and versatile white assassin. I knew just whom to call.

Thursday night, 11 p.m., mid-August 2013.

My phone rings. It was an agent. (Insert a female's middle-eastern accent. Yes, agents can be women. Don't discriminate.)

"I have job for you. You ready to leave?"

It was Hend. She was originally from Jordan but now lived in California. I met her at one of the pro exposure camps that I had run in Los Angeles a couple of years before. She was nice. But she was tough and all business. In a male-dominated industry full of testosterone and egos, she had to be.

Was I ready to leave? That depends.

"A team in Thailand. They need player now. Maybe you leave tomorrow. Don't go to sleep. I call you back."

And that's where the story began.

It was a short-term job as I would be replacing an injured player. There were only six weeks remaining in the season and they were going to pay me pretty well for the time I'd be there.

Thankfully, I did not have to jump on a 6 a.m. flight the next morning. But I did end up leaving thirty-six hours later, on Saturday, which was more than enough time to pack. Took me forty-five minutes to make sure I had enough socks and Skittles to get me through six weeks in Thailand.

I made the trip solo because it was a short stay and the team wasn't going to pay for extra plane tickets for Cara and the girls.

Hend claimed that she was very close with the GM and the team and that she sent players there every year. I trusted her, but there were a few red flags that caught my attention before I even got on the plane.

First, the team sent the plane ticket before they sent the contract. It was completely backwards. Why would they purchase a ticket for a player when neither of us had signed anything? I didn't receive the contract until I was at the airport checking in for my flight.

Second, the contract amount was wrong. I had agreed to one amount with Hend. The contract said something different, meaning less. She assured me everything was okay, but it wasn't her word I was worried about.

Third, the team didn't even have a website. Eurobasket.com is the king of overseas basketball coverage and even teams like the Mozambique U-16 team had a presence there. My Thai team was a mystery.

I thought Japan was far. Thailand was another seven-hour plane ride after arriving in Tokyo.

I landed in Bangkok at midnight, and the team dropped me off at my dorm-style residence at 1 a.m. I had no sheets, pillows, towels, or ... toilet paper. With the last concern being the most imminent threat to comfort, I found a 7-Eleven two blocks away at 2 a.m. and secured a six-pack of happiness—as in six rolls of double-ultra-soft, not Budweiser. I could improvise on pillows and sheets. Toilet paper, not so much.

If you like Thai food in the United States, you'd love it in its homeland. As long as you don't get too worked up about health code violations, you could enjoy dish after dish for a fraction of what it would cost you in the States. Most plates of food were two or three dollars. Granted, it usually took three plates to fill me, but when my 6-foot-10 American teammate, Justin Howard, and I could max out our appetites with a combined eight-dollar tab, it was a beautiful thing.

The food there was a whole new level of spicy. Cereal was spicy. Ice cream was spicy. A typical rice and chicken dish could engulf my mouth in flames. I asked Justin how well he could speak Thai. He said, "I can say 'left,' 'right,' 'straight,' and 'not spicy.'"

* * *

Just fourteen hours into my stay in Thailand, our team translator/ assistant named Patty picked me up for my first practice—on her motorcycle. Before you envision a Harley-Davidson, tone it back to a scooter/motorbike model and then throw a 6-foot-8 guy on the back. I was as giddy as a schoolgirl with cotton candy. Patty took notice.

"You've never ridden on a motorbike before?" she asked, clearly surprised at my enthusiasm over a two-wheeler.

No, Patty. I hadn't ridden on a motorbike in years—as evidenced by my whoops and man-giggles.

We snaked our way through traffic, avoiding pink taxis and other bikers. Congestion there could be outrageous and my knees brushed against another vehicle or two along the way. Who needed a helmet? My sunglasses were more than enough protection.

* * *

After my first practice, the assistant coach asked me what jersey number I wanted.

"How about thirty-five?" I asked.

"No, no. We have thirty-five," he said, meaning another player was already wearing it.

Didn't know I was a trendsetter.

"I'll take eight, then," I said.

"No eight," he replied.

Hmm. I was running out of my good numbers that felt best on my chest.

"I give you thirty-three," he said.

Thirty-three?

"Yes, I already ordered," he said.

You already ordered it? So why were we having this conversation again?

Thirty-three actually worked well on many levels for me. Scottie Pippen, Larry Bird, Titus Ivory. Seeing as my team in Uruguay gave me MJ's number, 23, the last time I was down there, I could now complete the Chicago duo and wear Scottie's 33. After all, Pippen and I have plenty in common. We both have a hard time finding clothes that fit in regular stores.

"What name you want on jersey?" coach asked.

"What *name*?" I clarified.

"Yes, you choose," he said.

You're telling me I can have any name on the back of my jersey?

Now this was going to take some brainstorming. *I might have to get back to you. "Smith" is way overdone and "Tyler" seems too easy. I'm thinking my high school Spanish class name "Roberto" is feeling pretty legit right now. Can you fit "Below D. Rim"?*

He needed an answer. It was too much pressure. I went with "Smith." Wasted opportunity.

I approached the team owner, Mr. Surasek, after a practice during my first week and asked him about my contract. The figures were wrong on the copy they had sent me and I needed him to make the necessary changes and then sign it. He assured me that everything was fine and he had a copy at his office. I gave him the benefit of the doubt since I had just arrived in Thailand and I didn't want to be a jerk about it during my first week. But somewhere deep down inside, a familiar and uncomfortable feeling began to bubble.

* * *

Thailand reminded me of Uruguay. The practice gym was located at a university and was old and run down with holes in the floor in various places, thankfully not in the lane. The baskets were not regulation size or height. There was no air-conditioning and it was as hot and humid as any gym I'd ever played in. I sweated through four pairs of shorts every practice and drank an average of one gallon of water throughout the two hours in the gym.

The level of play in Thailand was not as strong as other countries I'd been. They played a chaotic, undisciplined style that at times made Uruguay look like the Princeton offense. Players would turn the ball over from stepping out-of-bounds at least three times per practice, which meant it inevitably happened in the games, too. Little things like that drove me nuts, because guys just didn't recognize where they were on the floor.

Practice started at 6 p.m. every day with the national anthem blasting over the loudspeakers of the university's campus. Everyone and everything came to a standstill exactly like it would during "The Star Spangled Banner" at an American sporting event. There was no dribbling, shooting, or joking around. Just a brief two minutes of calm while we froze in place, listening to their national tune.

There were days when 6:45 p.m. rolled around and only five players had shown up for practice. It was even worse when it rained, because many streets flooded easily, causing the terrible Bangkok traffic to become even worse.

I had never practiced in such a laid-back environment. Stretch if you feel like it. Or don't. Maybe some three-man weave drill to loosen up. But not always. We often just jumped directly into five-on-five. Games to twenty-five. After three or four games, we'd call it a night. At thirty-three years young, I was happy to have practices that were fun. But part of me knew that we desperately needed to do more breakdown work on offense and defense if we wanted to make the playoffs.

Different players showed up for practice each day. It took me some time to figure out who was who. One particular teammate was quiet, but when he opened up, I discovered that he spoke very good English and his nickname was "First." I asked a few guys where he got the nickname, but in classic male behavior, no one on the team knew or had ever bothered to ask.

"Why does everyone call you 'First'?" I asked him one day.

"My mom called me that growing up because I was the first son," he explained.

"Oh, OK," I said. "So do you have brothers or sisters?"

"No," he said. "I'm the only one."

"Well, that still makes you first then, doesn't it?" I laughed.

The back of another player's game jersey said "Big Freedom." I wondered if he participated in demonstrations and protests. It turned out that his nickname was "Big." I never did find out what the whole "Freedom" thing was about, nor did I learn his actual Thai name. Big was 6-foot-2 and maybe 150 pounds, so there really wasn't much big about him. But he did have the highest vertical leap on the team in addition to being the heaviest smoker. Maybe Marlboros were what I'd been missing all these years.

* * *

Our first game, we played the Mad Goats. Not sure why they were upset, maybe they hadn't been milked lately.

With three minutes left, the score was tied, 60–60. After an impressively horrible thirty-seven minutes of officiating, the refs missed a shot clock violation (surprise, surprise) by the "MGOATS" (their scoreboard name), and the Goats grabbed an offensive rebound and then scored an "and one."

The refs stopped the game to discuss the matter. It was a simple fix. Either take away the basket and give us the ball, or count the basket and a Goat shoots a free throw.

After fifteen minutes of the refs arguing with each other and the coaches, our coach ordered us to grab our bags and leave. Game over. We walked out.

Apparently, our bluff worked. The refs did not count the Goat basket and they gave us the ball, the game still tied at 60–60. Sadly, we went down on offense and turned the ball over for one of our 25 TOs of the game. After playing hardly at all the entire game, I was thrown in at the end to try to tie the game with a corner three-point shot. I missed, and the Goats walked out with the victory.

* * *

The next game was the following day versus Pathum Konga, which likely means "We're terrible." They were the last-place team, and you know you have budget issues when your team's shorts don't match. Even better, both teams walked out onto the floor wearing purple jerseys.

The game was at a neutral site as many of the league games were. Maybe because it was a decent gym by Thailand's standards, glass backboards and minimal air-conditioning. Still, no wooden floor.

I didn't expect either team to have their other uniform color with them. I voted for shirts-skins. A few minutes later, I looked over and the Pathum Konga players were pulling on *our* yellow P.E.A. jerseys from practice. Seriously? Luckily, someone from our club had our smelly practice jerseys in the trunk.

But rather than our team wear *our own* P.E.A. practice jerseys and have them wear *their* team's purple game jerseys, we made them wear our stuff. It was P.E.A. Yellow (them) vs. P.E.A. Purple (us). Can you imagine having to wear the jersey of your opponent *while* you play them? And then get smashed by 24 points? You get no love when you're in last.

What we learned that weekend:

1. The Mad Goats may possibly be the greatest mascot name of all-time.

2. I still didn't know our own team's mascot nor what P.E.A. stood for.

3. If you want to field a team in a pro league that's not the NBA and money is tight, just tell the players to bring their own shorts.

4. Don't bother Googling our team or league website. Unless you were one of the seventy-five people at our game, we didn't exist.

After the game, we stopped to eat at a restaurant. I use the term "restaurant" loosely, as it was more of an open-air shelter. There were no walls or doors, just some poles holding up a roof, old tables, and cracked plastic chairs, which were probably five for a dollar.

As I was being cultural and eating whatever was placed in front of me, including bony chicken feet, an elephant stuck his head inside the eatery. I about knocked over our table as I jumped up and whipped out my phone to take a picture. Justin and I were the first ones to walk over and start snapping photos. The elephant was with two trainers, and we bought some sugarcane from them so we could feed him.

I glanced back to see if anyone else wanted to join in for a chance to rub its trunk. No one moved. The entire restaurant seemed very unimpressed.

Hello! Do you people not see the elephant standing next to your table? They were more fascinated by the fact that a couple of overgrown American tourists were actually amused by the giant creature. *Listen, folks, elephants don't just cruise around in public in the United States, much less walk into restaurants.* But to the locals it was, "Ah, there goes Babar again."

* * *

I loved Coach Seng. He was our Thai head coach in his late forties who coached in flip-flops and smoked cigarettes during water breaks. Nothing made him happier than being in the gym with his team. Coaching was more than a job to him as he genuinely cared about his players and wanted guys to improve. Every day he would grab a guy who was sitting around before practice and work one-on-one with him even if he was the worst player on the team.

He walked into the gym one day in his typical cheerful way, wearing a T-shirt with some sort of crazy red and black tie-dyed design that could only be described with one word: loud. It surprised everyone because Coach didn't come across as a particularly edgy or flamboyant person.

"Coach, I like your shirt," I said.

"Yes!" he exclaimed. "You like?"

"Yeah, it's great," I smiled.

Coach Seng pulled it right off of his back and handed it to me.

"For you!" he said.

OK, now you're half naked. And this is awkward.

"No, coach. You don't have to do that," I protested. I was just trying to give him a compliment and some recognition of his hip style.

"Yes, of course!" he insisted. He whipped out another T-shirt and pulled it on.

Three days later he did the same thing. Only this time it was unprovoked.

"You like?" he asked, smiling and pointing to his shirt as he walked up to me before practice. It was black and made for someone twice his size. "Too big, too big," he said with an ugly look on his face. "You take." He took it off.

"Coach, you don't have to—"

"Yes, you take!" he smiled as he held it out to me.

I looked at Justin, who was sitting next to me. What could I do? I couldn't turn it down.

Justin and I laughed as Coach Seng handed me his shirt for the second time that week.

"Hey, Coach," Justin said with a smile. "I like your car."

* * *

After practice, the general manager, who always had a Bluetooth earpiece attached, addressed the team in Thai. My teammate, Sal, interpreted for Justin and me. He didn't do it word for word, but we got the big idea. Players weren't getting paid, but Bluetooth assured everyone that the money was on its way. The team was several months behind on player salaries, and the players weren't amused. It wasn't like they were owed millions, either. The Thai players only made a few hundred dollars per month. I wasn't due to be paid for a few more weeks, but it made me a little nervous.

I had another money issue. My ATM card wasn't working. I tried five different machines and none would show me the money. When I called my bank in the United States, they told me that Thailand was red-flagged as a high risk for identity theft, and my card wouldn't work there. How convenient. I needed cash because many places didn't accept credit cards. Fortunately, Justin and Chris loaned me some money until I could figure something out.

* * *

There were only two games left in the season, and we had to win them both to make the playoffs. Our next game on Sunday was up north in a city called Chiang Mai (Chang My). You might think that with such an urgency to win, we would prepare thoroughly and arrive early in order to be well-rested. Neither happened.

We didn't practice Saturday, and rather than traveling to the game the day before, we woke up at 5:30 a.m. on Sunday (game day) to catch a plane up to Chiang Mai for our 2 p.m. tipoff. When we landed, we drove to a Buddhist temple, where an orange-robed monk said some sort of prayer over us and sprinkled us with water.

A courtyard surrounded the temple and the inside had the formal yet peaceful feel of an old traditional church in Europe. People meditated while standing or sitting on the ground in front of a large statue of Buddha. I'd envisioned monks as being silent and expressionless, but the monks we saw offered smiles and one even took pictures with us.

My teammates Sal and Big had each become monks a few years before. But rather than spend the rest of their lives sporting the orange cloth, they left the quiet monk lifestyle after a few months and returned to normal life.

"Why did you leave?" I asked Sal.

"My mom came and got me," he said.

We hopped in the team van and went to eat lunch at another health code violator's bistro. The soup and noodles weren't my favorite, but they filled me enough to keep my stomach from grumbling. The game was set to start in less than two hours and I figured we would head to the gym. Nope.

We drove to one more temple, where I watched my teammates burn incense and lay flowers at a shrine. They were focused on relaxing the mind and body while I was more concerned about having enough warm-up time.

For most of our games, we were only given about eight minutes total to warm up on the court. With fifteen players and two balls, there weren't many shots to go around during pregame. On one particular night, after only getting up four shots before tipoff, I ended up shooting more shots in the game than during warmups.

We arrived at the gym about one hour before taking on a team with my newest favorite mascot: The Flying Mammoth. Not a team of them, just one mammoth.

We played our best game to date and won, eliminating the Flying Mammoth's chances of making the postseason while coming one game closer to securing our own playoff spot. More importantly, we had discovered the secret to playing winning basketball: less sleep, less practice, and more travel.

A few days later, Bluetooth pulled the team aside after practice for another meeting. The message was the same as the week before: "The money's coming. Don't worry. It will be here. Just keep playing." I felt bad for my teammates. They worked very hard every day and management was robbing them of their paychecks. Justin had said that the

Americans were paid by a different person which reassured me enough to hold off on a protest.

Our final regular-season game was against a team in the bottom half of the league. We needed to win in order to secure the final playoff spot. We led by 10 to 15 points the entire game and walked off with a win.

After the game, we gathered on the floor for a team picture. Who was organizing the picture? None other than Bluetooth himself. He stood next to us in the picture and handed an oversized sign to one of the players to hold up. It was a giant check made out for 1,000,000 Thai *baht*, which equaled roughly $33,000 US dollars. He had some nerve presenting the check when none of the players were getting paid. That piece of cardboard had about as much value as his weekly promise of paying salaries.

* * *

The team owner, Mr. Surasek, picked me up from my apartment in his Porsche Cayenne SUV, the nicest car in Thailand, the night after our most recent victory. He had promised to get me some spending money, as I had been in desperate need of cash from the day I arrived.

He was on the phone when I got in the car and greeted me with a small wave. I had no idea where we would go to dinner. He was the kind of guy who liked to choose the restaurant and then order for you. He wasn't snobby about it, but it was more his way of trying to show you a good time. He'd ask you if you liked the food about seven times throughout the meal. Mr. Surasek was proud of his country and enjoyed sharing it with foreigners.

My guess was that we would drive down the street to one of the dozens of restaurants available nearby. It was dark and raining outside. After twenty-five minutes, we were still driving and he was still on the phone, speaking in Thai, and we hadn't said a word to each other since I sat down in the passenger seat. At one point, he was holding the phone to his ear when he let go of the wheel with his other hand. His free hand fished a second phone out of his pocket and he began dialing another number. Now neither hand was on the wheel and the car continued straight down the road in the pouring rain. I was poised to grab the wheel as time seemed to slow down. *Would you please pay attention?*

Eventually, he grabbed the wheel again and I resumed breathing normally. He finally hung up the phone and said, "Seng no more coach."

Mr. Surasek had fired the head coach mid-drive with me sitting right next to him.

"Joe is coach now," he said, referring to Joe Bryant, Kobe's dad.

Let me get this straight. We just made the playoffs with the semifinals starting in a few days and you fired the coach on the phone while I was sitting here next to you? Does that mean you are taking me to the airport to send me home on a plane, too?

Mr. Surasek had known Joe Bryant for a few years, as he had coached his teams in the past. I knew Joe from Japan, where he had coached a different team in our JBL league. When I first met him, he was extremely down-to-earth and treated me like we had known each other for years. He was friendly and very outgoing. Players loved playing for him because, having played a number of years professionally, he understood players as well as anyone.

After an hour in the car with Mr. Surasek, we arrived at a country club.

"This is a nice place," I said. "Do you belong here?"

"This my club," he said.

"It's very nice," I repeated.

He's pretty wealthy. Of course he would belong to a golf club.

"I own. I own club," he said.

Oh.

"You *own* the club?" I clarified.

"Yes, yes. I own," he confirmed.

Sure enough, just after he said that, he pulled right up to the front door where no one else would park unless you had built the place. Two valets opened our doors on cue and we walked inside the clubhouse restaurant.

True to form, he ordered my food for me. After dinner, he handed me an envelope with 10,000 Thai *baht*, roughly $300 US. It was enough to pay my debts and have enough left over to eat for another week. I probably should have asked for more.

I asked him about my contract and he insisted everything was okay. Maybe he thought it was okay, but I still didn't have anything signed from anybody. As far as I knew, I was playing pro bono.

Mr. Surasek loved basketball and was spending a lot of his own money to get it going again in Thailand. The Thailand Basketball League (TBL) was only in its second year and Mr. Surasek was instrumental in getting it off the ground. He also started the Thailand Open, which was a different one-week tournament that brought in teams from all over the world. This year, there were teams from China, Libya, Kuwait, the United States, and Australia. Two Thai teams would compete as well.

There was just one tiny issue. Our TBL league playoffs were scheduled during the same dates as the Thailand Open tournament. And the two guys in charge of each tournament were archenemies. Mr. Surasek was in charge of the Thailand Open and a different big-timer headed up the TBL. So, like middle school girls planning a weekend party, they scheduled their events on top of each other in some sort of power struggle.

* * *

I stepped back to review my situation. No contract. Teammates weren't being paid. Coaches were changed. Ramshackle league. Far from home.

Living the dream, baby.

What am I doing here? How long can I keep doing this?

I was about one month in and if I left abruptly, I'd definitely be going home with empty pockets. My only chance was to hold out until the end and hope that some cash showed up in our owner's wallet that he wanted to share. I loved playing basketball, but I couldn't afford to play for free with a family back home to take care of.

What if I couldn't get another basketball gig after I left Thailand? And even if I did, would it be a place that I could bring my family? My body hurt. Even with as little as we practiced and played, it hurt. I was starting to sense that this could be my last call. Better enjoy it now. I still had no backup plan for a real job.

So I made the decision to stick it out until the end. I'd play as hard as I could and as long as I could and see how the rest played out. I had to at least give it a shot.

* * *

The day after my cash-filled dinner with Mr. Surasek, we practiced at a new gym. I quickly discovered that I was the only one who was aware of the coaching change. Joe Bryant was there, but he was under the impression that he was simply helping out. Coach Seng was nowhere to be found.

It wasn't my news to break to the team or Coach Joe. No one had informed Joe that he was now officially the head coach of P.E.A. I just watched and waited. Players were standing around and casually shooting, waiting for someone to speak up. Eventually, Bluetooth walked in and pulled Joe aside. The team now belonged to Joe Bryant and practice started.

Coach Joe jumped in the mix when we played five-on-five. I was guarding him at one point, but was hesitant at first how hard to play. At fifty-eight years old, he moved well, but he wasn't twenty-seven, and I didn't want to go so hard that I could possibly hurt him. He was still very strong and in good shape, but it didn't feel normal going 100 percent against someone twenty-five years older than me.

Just as I had made up my mind to play steady against Joe but not super intense, he caught the ball in the post.

"Too late," he said, and he put up a shot quickly before I could get a hand in his face to contest.

Swish.

This guy can really still play. All I could do was smile. He smiled, too, and gave me a high five as my team got the ball and headed down court.

* * *

W e played the number-one team in the league, Hi Tech, in the semi-finals, a best-of-three series. In Game One, their big guy fouled out in the fourth period, and we hung on to win by four points.

The next day, Sunday, we couldn't capitalize on opportunities and had way too many turnovers. We lost, and the series was tied, 1–1. The deciding Game Three would be played on Wednesday.

But first, on Monday, the Thailand Open started. Our P.E.A. team was split into two teams for the Thailand Open. I was supposed to play with the best players from our P.E.A. team in the evening game. I made the mistake of showing up early to watch our number-two team from P.E.A. play in their afternoon game.

The TBL director issued an ultimatum that if any Thai player played in Mr. Surasek's Thailand Open, the player would be banned from playing in the TBL playoffs this year and the TBL League the following year. The Thai players were caught in the middle of a ridiculous power play by two stubborn old guys.

The Thai guys couldn't risk being kicked out of the TBL, so they walked out of the Thailand Open. Our number-two P.E.A. team suddenly had more coaches than players. We were playing the team from the United States, and Coach Joe convinced three of their American players to join our team.

Then he walked up to me.

"Do you want to play?" he asked me.

"I'm playing with the first team at 7 p.m.," I said.

"C'mon and walk with me," he said.

We went to the locker room and he told me that he was going to play. If Joe was playing, then how could I refuse to play?

We suited up and walked out to the floor to warm up. Joe was really excited.

"These boys don't know I can still play," he said with a huge smile on his face.

My agent, Hend, was coaching the American team, which was made up of the players she represented. She walked over to me with a scowl on her face.

"This is a joke. We are leaving. Bye," she said and stormed out of the gym. She was furious that she had brought her team all the way around the world to play against an opponent with one player pushing sixty years old. She ordered her team off the court and back to the locker room.

I kept stretching. I'd been in Thailand long enough to know that anything could happen. I understood her frustration. Our team consisted of three of her players, me, and a head-coach-turned-player. But Joe was trying to help everybody out by being our fifth man and filling in so that the game could be played. Without him, we'd have to forfeit the game completely.

Sure enough, ten minutes later, Hend returned to the court with her team. Joe had visited her in the locker room and had a "conversation" with her, as he put it.

The American team destroyed us. But not before Joe finished with 12 points and six assists, including two between-the-legs scoop passes, and one buzzer beater over a seven-footer from the top of the key. It wasn't hard to see where Kobe's talent and love of the game came from.

My stat line was less impressive as I finished with two and one. Two points, and one "got-dunked-on." When a fifty-eight year old outscores you, it may be time to move on to something else.

I went to the locker room and switched jerseys, because I wanted to play with our top P.E.A. team next. Our team manager, Patty, came over to me and said I wasn't allowed to play for two teams.

"Oh, so now they want to start having rules for this whole deba-cle," I said. I was annoyed. I didn't mind helping out and filling in the last game, but I wanted to play with the guys I knew because I thought we had a chance to win it all. I wore the jersey, but never played.

* * *

On Tuesday, I played another game in the Thailand Open, this time without Kobe's dad, because his knees were sore from his 40 minutes the day before. We picked up a couple of young Thai players who crossed the picket line and didn't care about being banned from the TBL. They weren't very good, but they were bodies and we would have taken some guys from the stands if we had to.

We lost again and were now 0–2 in Mr. Surasek's Thailand Open. I played better, though, and made some shots, but Libya got the best of us. That made four games played in four consecutive days for me. And there was more to come.

* * *

On Wednesday, we returned to our TBL playoff series, which was tied, 1–1, against Hi Tech. It was do-or-die in Game Three. I don't know if our guys were tired or if we just had an off night, but Hi Tech beat us pretty badly and they advanced to the Finals. I was disappointed, as I had some open shots that wouldn't fall. Defensively, I played a very good game, with three charges and a couple of big blocks, but Hi Tech proved to be too deep and talented.

Thursday and Friday had us back playing in the Thailand Open. We lost to a team from Kuwait on Thursday that we could have beaten. On Friday, we avoided finishing in last place by beating a junior team from China. We needed overtime to pull out the victory, but at least we went out on a winning note.

I had just finished playing seven games in seven consecutive days. My legs were done. But there was one final game to be played.

* * *

On Sunday, our P.E.A. squad had to play for third place in the TBL playoffs. It seemed unnecessary, but it was just a single game rather than another whole series. However, the Thailand Open was scheduled at the exact same time as our TBL third-place game. Mr. Surasek wanted all of P.E.A.'s best players, including Justin and Coach Joe, at the Thailand Open game because it was his tournament. The bottom half of the talent on our team would play in the TBL third-place game with me. I was instructed to take our benchwarmers and lead our team to victory over a team that we'd never beaten in the regular season. Thanks.

Before our third-place game, word got out that there was a cash prize for the winning team. The Thai guys got together and agreed that instead of splitting the $5,000 US reward evenly among the coaches, staff, and players, I should receive $1,000. I told them that was ridiculous, but they were adamant that I get the biggest portion. This was coming from the guys who hadn't been paid in months. I appreciated their generosity, but there was no way I could accept that. What was the chance of any of us seeing a penny of that money anyway?

"We want you to try really hard to win," one teammate said.

"I'll try to win anyway, guys. I promise," I assured them.

It was true. This could be my last game. My body didn't recover like it used to. I didn't move like I used to. I didn't feel like I was playing as well as I had in the past and maybe it was a sign that it was time to move on. But before I left my playing days behind, I wanted to go out with a win.

We jumped out to an early lead, and I hit some shots to get us going. I was feeling good and playing the way I knew I was capable of. Since arriving in Thailand, there were only a handful of times when I really felt comfortable and in-the-flow offensively during games. Now, I was getting a lot of touches and making shot after shot.

At the end of the third quarter, I dribbled in front of our bench during a broken play. I launched a shot just before time expired and it swished through at the buzzer. We were up six heading into the fourth quarter.

We held them off until the final minute, but they were putting a run together, threatening to take the lead for the first time. With under a minute to play, we were up by two and they had the ball. One of their guards threw a risky pass on the baseline and I stole it. We came down on offense and missed a shot. There was a loose ball, and I charged after it, knocking my own teammate out of the way and ripping it from his hands. I didn't trust anyone else with the ball at that moment. The defense chased me, and they had to foul me before we ran out the clock. I went to the free throw line with eight seconds left and up by two points.

Two makes would win it. One would likely give us the win. Missing both would be a problem.

Who knew how many tens of thousands of free throws I had shot in my lifetime? You'd think by now I wouldn't be nervous. But I was.

I missed the first one.

C'mon.

You can't miss this next one, too.

I took a deep breath.

I took my four dribbles.

It didn't feel that great coming off of my hand. But it went in. We were up three.

After a timeout, the ball was advanced to their side of the court just like at the end of the game in the NBA. They took the ball out-of-bounds across from their bench and lined up. I was guarding their American named X, who was their best player. He had introduced himself as "X," so I'm pretty sure it was short for Xavier, not Malcolm.

He had already hit a couple of threes from two steps behind the NBA three-point line. I didn't want him to get the last shot, but he did. He launched a deep three before time expired that could send us to overtime.

Don't even think about going in, ball.

It bounced off of the side of the rim. Game over.

I looked around. I didn't know anyone in the stands. Aside from about a dozen excited P.E.A. fans, the crowd was pretty mild. No one stormed the floor. No confetti fell from the ceiling.

I may have just played my last game. And I was okay with that.

I scored 23 points and grabbed 10 rebounds. I made my last shot. And I won my final game.

I felt great.

We shook hands with the other team. As after every win, I kept a straight face, but it was a lie. Inside, I was smiling and jumping around having a party, acting like I was seven years old again. It's not often that you are able to end your season with a win. So the win tasted that much sweeter.

I shook X's hand and gave him a hug.

"Great game, X," I said. "Where are you headed next?"

"Iraq," he said.

Hope you get paid.

The adventure never ends.

Postgame

My last two weeks in Thailand, I called Mr. Surasek every single day.

"I haven't gotten paid yet."

"Oh no? It should be there."

"It's not."

"Bring me your bank account information."

"You have it. I've given it to you twice."

"Really?"

On the day before I was scheduled to leave Thailand for good, I called Mr. Surasek again. For the fourteenth straight day. No answer.

Great. Before, he was at least taking my call.

I dialed again. And again. And again.

On the tenth try he picked up. "Hello?"

"Hi Mr. Surasek. This is Tyler —"

Click.

Redial.

"Hello?"

"Mr. Surasek, it's Ty—"

Click.

You've got to be kidding me.

I called the man eighteen times that day. Finally, I wore him down and was able to keep him on the line.

"Mr. Surasek, I leave Thailand tomorrow and I have not been paid," I said sternly. "We need to make this happen now."

"Yes, yes," he assured. "What time is your flight? I will meet you at the airport."

Yeah, right. There was no way I was going to bank on him magically appearing at the check-in counter with my salary.

"My flight's early," I lied. It left late in the evening. "We need to settle my salary in the morning immediately."

"OK, I pay you tomorrow."

"Mr. Sura—"

Click.

Tomorrow, huh? Where? What time? This guy was killing me.

I called him at 8 a.m. He was in his golf cart, but promised he was on his way to my place.

Two hours later I called again. He was en route. So he claimed.

I waited in the lobby of my apartment building. *Lord, please let this guy show up and pay me what we agreed to. Or, at this point, something close to it. Amen.*

Mr. Surasek pulled up and walked in carrying a thick envelope.

"This my family's money," he said before even saying hello. "The other guy is terrible man and I don't work with him anymore."

Sure enough, the other GM fellow was not only ripping off the players, but taking advantage of Mr. Surasek, too.

Mr. Surasek handed me the heavy envelope. He was paying me out of his own pocket. Granted, his pockets were deeper than most. But still, it was a kind gesture since this was not supposed to be where the money was coming from. It was supposed to paid by the sponsors and Mr. Big Fancy Check guy, Bluetooth.

I appreciated him covering the debt owed, but I needed to make sure it was all there. I opened the envelope and saw thousands of Thai *baht* all wrapped neatly together. Every last penny was there.

Thank you, Lord.

* * *

Cara joined me for my final week in Thailand and we toured a bit. We went underwater seawalking, which is basically scuba-diving for dummies who don't know how to scuba. It was awesome. We hiked a waterfall, rode an elephant, and went parasailing on the most illegal life-threatening ride you can find for fifteen dollars.

I returned home to the United States to the best greeting a dad could ever ask for from his girls. Being away is never fun. But coming home is incredible. Hannah and Lexi clung to me like leeches, and I couldn't have been happier to see them.

It was October 2013 and no teams were calling. It looked like the end of the road. I'd fooled plenty of people into paying me to play basketball for over eleven years. It was longer than anyone would have guessed. But it was time to move on. The market for slow 6-foot-8 white guys in their mid-thirties was dwindling. Who knew?

I began the search for my next career. And don't let the national employment numbers fool you. There are *plenty* of jobs out there. Just hop on Craigslist.

Webcam model. *Hmm.* Dog-sitter. *Been there.*

Cow-milker—adding, subtracting, and English required. *Save under "possibles."*

Gestational Carrier Surrogate. *Under-qualified.*

It turns out that taking charges and setting screens don't translate so well to other occupations.

I called a guy, Justin Kurpeikis, who was a former pro football player I remembered from our time at Penn State. "How did you make the transition? What do you do?"

Blah blah blah medical ... something something hospitals ... *"Tyler, want to shadow me for a day and see what it's like?"*

"Sure!"

"Have you ever seen a surgery?"

"My wife had two C-sections. Does that count?"

"See you tomorrow at 7 a.m."

Long story short, he and his business partner, Mike Lukac, ended up offering me a job. Right before I was about to say yes, Hitachi called. They offered me a deal for the rest of the season. *Where were you guys this past summer when I needed a job and was ready to play?*

Now, I had started to move on to my next life. My body was happy again. We were home. Hannah was loving kindergarten where everyone spoke English and she was allowed to eat chips at lunch. And I had a nice job offer working with some great guys in an interesting new field.

If I took the Hitachi job, in five months I would miss out on this new job opportunity and be right back where I was now, unemployed and unsure of what to do.

"If you make the contract for two years, I'll really think about it," I told the team.

They made it two years.

Oh boy. Now what?

It was a good offer. I would play until I was thirty-five and it would be my last contract, most likely. But the money wasn't life-changing. Had I received the deal during the summer or immediately after Thailand, I'd have gone without a second thought. But it seemed like it might now be a good time to make the transition to the real world.

Cara was great. She was willing to go and support me once more and make the move back to Japan. But it was getting harder for me to justify uprooting the four of us and packing everything up for another two seasons overseas.

I think the best advice I received was from my friend and college teammate, Joe Crispin. "Take your time and just know that you can make your choice in freedom. See what's best for you and your family now and pray about it. You'll be fine either way."

Thankfully, Joe's words sank in and helped me have peace with my decision. I knew things would be okay no matter the outcome. As had happened so often in my life when I had big decisions to make, I knew that I wasn't alone.

After much thought and prayer, I decided it was time to hang 'em up. You may have missed my press conference announcing "El Decision"—my retirement from basketball. It got pretty big ratings in Uruguay, the Netherlands, and Tokyo.

I started a new job with a medical device company by the name of Biomet (now Zimmer Biomet). They make all types of implants (think knees and hips, not Hollywood implants) and products used during surgery. If you know anyone who has had a knee replaced or has broken an arm, our company might have made the plates and screws and hardware the doctor used during the surgery. A medical sales rep assists the surgeon in the operating room during surgery, as the reps are the experts on their particular devices.

"Wait, you're in the operating room?!" you say.

Yes.

"Isn't that gross to watch?"

On my first day, I did have to step outside "for a drink of water." But I did not pass out and pee on myself as another young rep did on their first day. I'd say I'm ahead already.

Don't worry, I don't touch anything. I'm not allowed to touch anything. We're all safer in general if I don't touch anything. Just point and talk.

I watched *Doogie Howser, M.D.* growing up and I'm twice as old as he is now. A few episodes of *Grey's Anatomy* can prep most anyone.

* * *

I'm very grateful for the opportunity to play basketball and earn a living from it for a time. I feel so blessed to have played professionally in seven different countries on four different continents. Unfortunately, I wasn't able to get to Australia or Africa. Next time.

Looking back, it is remarkable to me how things had worked out along the journey. One job led to the next team and meeting one person often directed me toward a new experience. I worked as hard as I could and I accomplished most of my goals—signing in Italy, making six figures, and playing with an NBA team. OK, practicing with an NBA team. It counts in my book.

Of all of the time, energy, and money that I invested in my career, none of it happened just because of me. I didn't make myself 6-foot-8. I didn't give myself natural hand-eye coordination. I didn't offer myself contracts. Or the ability to sky. I guess nobody did. Well, you can't have everything. But I had a lot.

I had great parents, good opportunities, lots of strong coaching and guidance, helpful genes, a wonderful wife and kids, and certainly some divine help throughout the journey. I am humbled and thankful for the doors God opened and even closed at times.

I'm sure there'll be perfect wooden basketball floors waiting for us in heaven someday. And players who never miss a shot. Even refs who never miss a call. Well…

And maybe, just maybe, I'll rise above the rim.

Looking back, I never thought I'd say this. But I'm thankful I was called for traveling.

Acknowledgments

There are countless people to thank of course as with any life story. Over eleven years, I made so many great friendships that I will cherish as it was such a special time in my life and I appreciate so many of you. You all were a tremendous part of my experience. I'll do my best to recognize you here and apologize that I can't name every single person by name.

Cara, what a journey it's been! Thank you for the numerous laughs along the way. I love you! Hannah, Lexi, and Tori—you girlies are the best! Mom and Dad, I can't begin to thank you enough for all of your love and support from the time I could run the bases at Artesian Park to letting me play every sport possible simultaneously (even football, Mom!). Alli—I'll always remember being inspired early and often by you, especially watching you dominate at Savannah Country Day School on the middle school team! John, Elizabeth, and William—I love you so much! Margaret VanFossan, for your love and support even when I was a homeless and jobless son-in-law. Oh, and for raising one amazing daughter.

Tom Breit and family, Jon Breit and family, Roz Daniels and family, and Edmond Smith and family. Nothing but smiles when I think of you all.

Coaches Munda and Donlon at LFHS. Coaches Dunn, Swenson, Appleman, Boyd, and Callahan at PSU.

My miracle workers (agents) that helped me so much along the way. Lord knows your jobs are NOT easy—Patrick King, Max Raseni, Daniel Morales, Nino Burgan, Dave "Gaz!" Gasman, Lee Cohen, and Hend Abu Farie.

My pro coaches that gave me an opportunity—Herman van den Belt, Rod Griffin, Javier Espindola, Alvaro Tito, Fabio Demti, Jerry Sloan, Larry Smith, Reggie Geary, Mike Schuurs, Shuji Ono, Bruce Palmer, Gerardo Jauri, Antanas Sireika, Coach Seng, and Joe Bryant.

My trainers and doctors that kept me alive and kicking—John "Smitty" Smith, Jon "Saz" Salazer, Anneke, Gianluca, Mike Gay, Dr. Sebastianelli, Dr. Putukian, Dr. Bechler, Dr. Raymond, Drayer PT, Ron Baum, Tim Mazer, Craig Sechler, Brian Zettler, Gary Briggs, Courtney Watson, "Nomo" Koide Atsuya, Mario, Pablo, Mizuno, and Nozomi.

Rob Oshinskie and Victory Sports for taking my strength, speed, and power to the next level.

Every single teammate at LBMS, LFHS, PSU, Landstede, Imola, Salto, Malvin, Central Entrerriano, Utah Jazz, Anaheim Arsenal, Matrixx Magixx, Hitachi SunRockers, Tochigi Brex, and PEA.

Some unique individuals that went above and beyond—Rick Barry, Todo, Masa, Sassa, Paul Glaap and family, the Ueki family, Yuma, Thijs and Chantal, Mark van Schutterhoef, Kazuto Aono, Patty, the Suzuki family, the Rabetoy family, Diego Cervieri and family, JP, Jill Bruder, and Dave Hawkins.

My many awesome Lake Bluff and Lake Forest friends—you guys rock!

Loren Crispell, Joe Crispin, and Jim Watt, three amazing friends.

Pete Lisicky, for your hilarious emails about your pro basketball journeys. It got me started. Can't wait to read your book someday.

Pastor Danielson, Pastor Gazzola, Pastor Mitch, and Rebie Smith, and Pastor Dan Nold—I've learned so much from you. Thank you for being incredible leaders and strong men and women of God.

Jennifer Smith, for your wonderful help and great advice.

Peter Ferry, for showing me and thousands of other young students that writing can be really fun and intriguing. Your input and editing skills on this book were invaluable.

Noah Liberman, your guidance and editing were crucial.

Sandy Weissent, thank you for your friendship and believing in this book so much to share it. It doesn't come to print without you.

Rick Wolff, thank you for enjoying this and sharing it with Sky-horse. You played a key role in making this happen.

Skyhorse, Emmie Twombly, and the entire team—THANK YOU! You made this dream become a reality.

Ken Samelson, for tackling this project and believing in it all the way.

Justin Kurpeikis and Mike Lukac, for the opportunity to start a new career and season of life. And for endless humor with you guys.

Jesus, for being my Rock. This incredible journey starts and ends with you. Dank u wel. Grazie. Gracias. Arigato gozaimasu. Kob khun krup. Thank you!

ABOUT THE AUTHOR

Tyler Smith is a 2002 Penn State University graduate (Telecommunications) where he was a three-year starter on the men's basketball team and was an Academic All-American. He played a key role during Penn State's 2001 NCAA Sweet 16 March Madness run, when they knocked off North Carolina en route to PSU's best season in almost fifty years. Following his graduation from Penn State, Smith played professional basketball for 11 years in the United States and overseas, from third world countries to the NBA. His travels took him to seven countries (Holland, Italy, Uruguay, Argentina, USA, Japan, Thailand) on four continents as he played for 12 different teams. Tyler now lives in State College, Pennsylvania, and owns a company called CryoZone that offers Whole Body Cryotherapy. He also works for Zimmer Biomet, a medical device company. He is blessed to be surrounded by ladies at home with Cara (wife), Hannah (nine), Lexi (five), and Tori (two). He hopes his girls look more like mom each day.

"I have come that they may have life, and have it to the full."
John 10:10